PEOPLE AND SPACES

People and Spaces: Experience, Ethics, and Intent examines the dynamic relationship between built environments and human behavior in today's rapidly evolving world. Co-edited by a designer and a psychologist, this interdisciplinary collection reveals how the spaces we inhabit shape and reflect our self-expression, social structures, and cultural values. Drawing on diverse perspectives, case studies, and innovative research, *People and Spaces* equips readers from any discipline with practical human-centric knowledge to enhance environments in meaningful ways. This blend of essays and expert insights demonstrates the value of intentional approaches to design and research and offers actionable guidance for creating supportive and sustainable environments.

This book is relevant to a broad audience, including scholars, professionals, and students in architecture, interior design, psychology, and related fields, as well as industry practitioners interested in the intersection of built environments and human experience. It is an essential resource for those seeking to understand and influence the relationship between people and space.

PEOPLE AND SPACES

Experience, Ethics, and Intent

Edited by
Tamie Glass and Lindsay T. Graham

Routledge
Taylor & Francis Group
NEW YORK AND LONDON

Designed cover image: April30 via Getty Images

First published 2025
by Routledge
605 Third Avenue, New York, NY 10158

and by Routledge
4 Park Square, Milton Park, Abingdon, Oxon, OX14 4RN

Routledge is an imprint of the Taylor & Francis Group, an informa business

ISBN: 9780367436179 (hbk)
ISBN: 9780367436162 (pbk)
ISBN: 9781003004622 (ebk)

DOI: 10.4324/9781003004622

Typeset in Galliard
by codeMantra

CONTENTS

Editor Biographies *x*
Contributor Biographies *xiii*
Preface *xxiii*

PART 1
Introducing People and Spaces **1**

Introducing People and Spaces 3

PART 2
Shaping Experiences **13**

Framing Experiences 15

Connecting 1 17

1 Re-examining Taste in Design: Integrating Pragmatics, Symbols, and Aesthetics 18
Galen Cranz and Chelsea Rushton

Connecting 2 37

2 From the Sublime to the Vertiginous: The Psychology of Awe-chitecture 39
Hanna Negami and Colin Ellard

Connecting 3 49

3 Designing Meaningful Environments Post-Darwin: How Spaces Affect Perceptions & Behaviors 51
Kerry L. Marsh, Benjamin R. Meagher and Cassidy J. Burt

Connecting 4 64

4 Exploring Place Potential: Understanding Purpose, Perception and Activation 65
Susan Sung Eun Chung

Connecting 5 74

5 Spatial Politics 76
Kevin Nute

Connecting 6 90

6 Architecture as Platformed Places and Mediators of Data Exchange 92
Leah Scolere

Reflecting on Experiences 112

PART 3
Considering Ethics **115**

Framing Ethics 117

Connecting 7 119

7 BYOE – Bring Your Own Ethics 120
An interview with George Aye
By Tamie Glass and Lindsay T. Graham

Connecting 8 128

8 Design is Service to the People 129
Kia Weatherspoon

Connecting 9 137

9 Social Justice through Inclusive Design in the Built Environment 138
Ileana Rodriguez

Connecting 10 149

10 Big Data, Big Insights: Data-Driven Design for Desired Outcomes 150
David Euscher

Connecting 11 166

11 #WeCantUnknowThis: Design and Climate Change 167
Janice Barnes

Connecting 12 178

12 The Urgency of Biophilia as an Integrated Approach in the Face of Climate Change 179
Judith Heerwagen

Reflecting on Ethics 186

PART 4
Crafting Intent 189

Framing Intent 191

Connecting 13 193

13 Getting to Know *Clo* 195
Kit Elsworth, Billie Faircloth, Ryan Welch and Roderick Bates

Connecting 14 205

14 Person and Condition Centered Design 206
Dak Kopec

Connecting 15 221

15 Creating Optimal Learning Environments: A Case Study of Alexandria Country Day School's Classroom Renovation 222
Ellen Fisher and Scott Baytosh

Connecting 16 234

16 Designing a Value-Based (Health) Care Experience 236
Diana Siebenaler

Connecting 17 251

17 Design R[e]volution: Rethinking People and the Built Environment 253
Susan Sung Eun Chung, Whitney Austin Gray and So-Yeon Yoon

Connecting 18 264

18 When Sparks Fly: The Challenges and Rewards of Working across Disciplines 265
An interview with Richard Corsi
By Tamie Glass and Lindsay T. Graham

Reflecting on Intent 271

PART 5
Reflecting Forward **273**

Reflecting Forward 275

Index *289*

EDITOR BIOGRAPHIES

Tamie Glass is an award-winning designer, author, and educator with over two decades of experience studying the intersection of people and spaces. Her work focuses on psychosocial design interventions that enrich the human condition within complex systems and built environments. Her first book, *Prompt: Socially Engaging Objects and Environments*, received the 2020 Interior Design Educators Council's Book of the Year Award.

That same year, Tamie joined The University of Texas at Austin School of Design and Creative Technologies as an Associate Professor and the inaugural Faculty Director for the Master of Arts in Design focused on Health Program. Previously, she served as the Interior Design Program Director in the School of Architecture, where she taught Designing for Human Behavior and received the Regents Teaching Award. Thriving in spaces where theory meets practice, Tamie has also held visiting director positions at the Dell Medical School's Design Institute for Health and the Blanton Museum of Art.

Tamie's intercontinental design career began in Germany with Daimler, leading corporate identity projects for Mercedes-Benz, followed by practice in London with top firms Virgile and Stone and Conran and Partners. Her practice spans high-end hospitality and retail environments throughout the EU and Asia to wellness, healthcare, corporate, and residential spaces in the US. She is NCIDQ (National Council for Interior Design Qualification) certified in North America and maintains a design consultancy in Austin, Texas.

A champion for human-centered design and an inventor of spaces well-attuned to people, Tamie draws on her expertise to lead design thinking and collaboration workshops, bringing creative solutions to a range of professional contexts. She holds a Master's in Interior Architecture from the University of Oregon and a Bachelor of Environmental Design from Texas A&M University. Tamie is also a recipient of the Luminary Award from the American Society of Interior Designers, recognizing her outstanding contributions to the interior design profession through education, advocacy, and research. More about Tamie's work and projects can be found at www.tamieglass.com.

Lindsay T. Graham is a personality and social psychologist who specializes in the ways people form relationships with, craft, manipulate, and select their daily environments to best fit their lives. Lindsay's work spans the fields of psychology, architecture, interior design, engineering, and human-computer mediated interactions. She is an expert in the measurement of people within virtual and physical spaces and post-occupancy evaluation methods.

Lindsay uses her research and knowledge to promote academic inquiry and to consult with industry leaders and practitioners on how to leverage design to create spaces that support the people who use them. She strongly values interdisciplinary research and believes dialogue across disciplines is essential for true scientific progression. She advocates for the need for science to not only address "real world" problems, but to also provide relevant, actionable solutions.

Lindsay received her BA and PhD from The University of Texas at Austin. While there, she was recipient of a National Science Foundation IGERT traineeship focused on the interdisciplinary study of the indoor environment. After Texas, Lindsay went on to found and lead a research program focused on the Psychology of Space at the University of California, Berkeley's Center for the Built Environment. Currently she conducts research for Google's Real Estate and Workplace Services group to support the creation of work environments that promote wellbeing and productivity.

In 2015 she was a research scientist at CADRE (HKS, Inc.'s non-profit research consortium), and in 2017 she was a research fellow at Perkins+Will's Human Experience Lab. She also has experience in transforming and bringing scientific findings into the marketplace and was a recipient of the United States Department of Energy's Catalyst Business Innovation grant in 2016. Her work has also found its way into many popular media sources including the New York Times, the Wall Street Journal, the Washington Post, Kinfolk Magazine, Vogue, Bustle, and others. To learn more about Lindsay and her work visit www.SpaceOfBestFit.com

CONTRIBUTOR BIOGRAPHIES

George Aye co-founded Greater Good Studio in 2011 to use design to heal, be just, and be restorative. He serves as Co-Executive Director at the studio. Previously, he spent seven years at a global innovation firm before being hired as the first human-centered designer at the Chicago Transit Authority. Since founding Greater Good, he has guided clients and teams through complex projects that honor reality, create ownership, and build power. He speaks frequently across the US and internationally. George is an adjunct lecturer at Northwestern University. Previously, he was a Full Professor (Adj) at The School of the Art Institute of Chicago.

Janice Barnes is Founder of Climate Adaptation Partners, an NYC- and Asheville-based WBE, focused on planning, advocacy, and partnership-building for climate adaptation. With technical training in architecture and organizational behavior, she helps clients to critically evaluate their risk tolerances and possible adaptation pathways given current and expected hazard exposures and link these to appropriate design and financing or funding options. Working from the intersection of climate change and public health, Janice advances resilience principles and connects climate knowledge across communities. Janice co-chaired NYSERDA's Climate Impact Assessment Health and Safety Group and oversaw the New York City Panel on Climate Change 4th Assessment. Janice also teaches Public Health, Climate Change, and Cities at the University of Pennsylvania with Perelman School of Medicine and Weitzman School of Design. Janice previously led global resilience for Perkins+Will, working with 24 offices across multiple countries to advance resilience in concert with in-country initiatives and co-chaired the American Institute of Architects National Resilience Working Group. Janice has a PhD and Master of Science in Architecture (University of Michigan), Master of Architecture (Tulane University), Bachelor of Architecture (University of Tennessee), and certificates in Municipal Finance (University of Chicago) and GIS (UC Davis).

Roderick Bates has made a career out of seeking and developing solutions to complex design challenges. As the Director of Corporate Development at Chaos, he is responsible for tracking the industry and market trends shaping the way Chaos customers work, both today and in the future. He collaborates with technology partners, customers, and Chaos product and R&D leaders to assess new product opportunities that will shape the future design. Previously, as a Principal at KieranTimberlake, he led the efforts to develop and commercialize software and hardware tools used by the greater AEC community to improve the environmental and operational performance of buildings.

Scott Baytosh has served since 2012 as the Head of Alexandria Country Day School, an independent, K-8, coed, nonsectarian school in Alexandria, VA. During his tenure, Scott has overseen an overhaul of the school's academic program, the renovation of interior classroom spaces, including the installation of sit/stand desks in every middle school classroom, and the creation of the school's first substantial endowment. Prior to joining the ACDS community, Scott was the Head of Buckingham Friends School in Pennsylvania, the Director of Studies at Friends Academy in New York, the Dean of Students and Academic Dean at Alexander Dawson School in Colorado, and the Director of Technology at Sandy Spring Friends School in Maryland. Scott currently serves on the Board of the Virginia Association of Independent Schools. Scott earned his BA in Theater from Wesleyan University, his Masters of Arts Management (MAM) from Carnegie Mellon University, and his MEd from Johns Hopkins University.

Cassidy J. Burt received her PhD in social psychology from the University of Connecticut. Her primary research focused on how the use of public space and investment in the physical environment of a city can benefit the health of its communities. She previously worked with the US Forest Service and the University of Michigan Youth Violence Prevention Center to research the effects of community-involved vacant lot greening on city residents' mental health and fear of crime. She is currently an Evaluation Specialist at the NYC Department of Health and Mental Hygiene, researching effective implementation strategies for community-based HIV care programs throughout the city.

Susan Sung Eun Chung is the Associate Director of Enterprise Research at HKS, a global architecture firm, where she leads programs for deep-dive research and development, translates research into applicable design implications, and strives to enhance the synergies between research and design through communication and outreach. Her experience in comprehensive workplace research studies in living laboratory settings speaks to her commitment toward longitudinal evidence-based and outcome-driven design practices. She previously worked as the Vice President of Research & Knowledge at the American Society of Interior Designers (ASID) leading impactful research to advance the built environment industry. Her scholarly research is focused on creative performance and its relationship with physical and social environmental conditions and she received her doctorate in Human Behavior and Design from Cornell University.

Richard L. Corsi earned his BS in environmental resources engineering from Humboldt State University and his MS and PhD in civil engineering from UC Davis. He was instrumental in establishing the environmental engineering program at the University of Guelph before joining the University of Texas at Austin (UT Austin). At UT Austin, Dr. Corsi spent 24 years teaching and researching indoor and outdoor air pollution, with funding from federal, industry, and non-profit organizations. He directed a National Science Foundation training program on indoor environmental science and engineering and co-directed the Center for Sustainable Development in the UT School of Architecture. Dr. Corsi then served as Dean of the Maseeh College of Engineering and Computer Science at Portland State University and, since September 2021, as Dean of the College of Engineering at UC Davis. Early in the COVID-19 pandemic, he developed the Corsi-Rosenthal Box, an effective and widely recognized DIY air cleaner. Dr. Corsi has published nearly 270 peer-reviewed papers, supervised over 120 students, and is a licensed professional engineer in Texas.

Galen Cranz is Professor Emerita of Architecture at the University of California at Berkeley. She holds a doctorate in Sociology from the University of Chicago and is a certified Alexander Technique teacher. Dr. Cranz emphasizes ethnography in her research, offering insights from both users and creators of built environments, published as *Ethnography for Designers*. She incorporates diverse cultural perspectives in her teaching, meeting Berkeley's American Cultures requirement. In 2011, she received the Career Award from the Environmental Design Research Association (EDRA). Her research spans urban parks, sustainability, body-conscious design, housing for the elderly, and the sociology of taste. Notable works include *The Politics of Park Design* and *The Chair: Rethinking Culture, Body, and Design*, which won EDRA's 2004 Achievement Award. She has lectured internationally, served as a juror for park design competitions, and co-investigated a study on hospital lighting funded by the Latrobe Fellowship. Dr. Cranz holds two US patents for innovative bathtub and chair designs.

Colin Ellard is a Neuroscientist, Author, Professor, and Design Consultant. He holds a BSc from the University of Toronto and a PhD from the University of Western Ontario. His research focuses on how the organization and appearance of natural and built spaces influence movement, wayfinding, emotion, and physiology. Dr. Ellard takes a multidisciplinary approach, collaborating with architects, artists, planners, and health professionals. His current studies explore the psychology of residential design, urban wayfinding, and the restorative effects of natural settings. Dr. Ellard utilizes both field investigations and immersive virtual environments to study human behavior. In his book *Places of the Heart: The Psychogeography of Everyday Life*, he examines the relationship between emotion and place and how technology is changing this interaction.

Kit Elsworth is an Associate and Building Performance Specialist at KieranTimberlake. As a member of the firm's transdisciplinary research group, Kit performs proactive and project-specific research in the topics of occupant comfort, passive building systems, energy and carbon analysis, and post-occupancy building performance. A key aspect of this role is to interpret research and analysis to both generate actionable design decisions for firm projects and elevate the performance goals of the architecture industry. Kit also works closely with architectural design teams and clients to support the advancement of holistic sustainability initiatives on all projects. Kit serves on several industry advisory committees, such as the AIA Committee on the Environment (COTE) 2030 Working Group and the International Living Future Institute (ILFI) Energy and Carbon Technical Advisory Group (TAG). Before working at KieranTimberlake, Kit received his Master of Science from the University of California, Berkeley, where he researched human thermal comfort and conducted independent research on evaporative downdraft cooling towers. Kit was also an instructor at the University of Pennsylvania's for the Master of Environmental Building Design program.

David Euscher, for more than 30 years, has designed and led award-winning commercial interiors projects for corporate, multi-family, academic, retail, hospitality, and healthcare clients. David brings a passionate curiosity to his work, fascinated by the interrelationship between culture, technology, and design. He has shared his insights into these topics in speaking engagements at conferences and universities. He approaches each project with a desire to create spaces for belonging and improve the wellbeing of the people served by the space. David holds a Bachelor of Science degree in Interior Design from the University of Texas at Austin, and a Master of Architecture degree from The Ohio State University. He served on the ASID National Board of Directors beginning in 2020 and will serve as Chair in 2025. David leads the interiors studio for the Houston office of Corgan, a global leader in architecture and interior design.

Billie Faircloth, FAIA, is a Design Leader, Educator, and Transdisciplinarian who has transformed practice-based research and earned a national and international reputation for demonstrating its value, methods, and outcomes. As former partner and research director at the Philadelphia-based architectural practice KieranTimberlake from 2008 to 2024, Faircloth led the firm's research group, a team recognized for integrating knowledge from fields as diverse as urban and industrial ecology, anthropology, comfort science, and sculpture. Her central message: inquiry is a new-found form of professional agency and a driver for practice transformation. *Architectural Record* celebrated her relentless pioneering of integrated, transdisciplinary research in practice when it selected her as its 2017 Women in Architecture Innovator Award winner. Currently an Adjunct Professor of Architecture at the Weitzman School of Design, University of Pennsylvania, Faircloth will join Cornell University in 2025 as an associate professor in the Department of Architecture and a Senior Faculty Fellow at the Cornell Atkinson Center for Sustainability. Faircloth's current work focuses on existing buildings, their value, and representation in public consciousness, global sustainability practice, and policy.

Ellen Fisher, PhD, is the Dean and VP for Academic Affairs of New York School Interior Design, leading the college through more than a decade of growth and increased recognition for excellence in design education. As a scholar, her areas of inquiry include evidence-based design, design and literacy, and distance learning. Ellen Fisher has been named four times by DesignIntelligence as a "Most Admired Design Educator." Under her leadership, NYSID established an Archive of Interior Design to collect and preserve the history of the profession. A certified interior designer and Fellow of both the American Society of Interior Designers and the Interior Design Educators Council (IDEC), Dr. Fisher was awarded a 2022 Steelcase Social Innovation Fellowship. The Fellowship grant was used to actively recruit students with financial need or from marginalized communities to NYSID's existing Pre-College program with the goal of increasing diversity in the design profession. She is the author of "HOME: The Foundations of Enduring Spaces." Dr. Fisher serves on the New York State Department of Education Interior Design Board, and is past-president of NY11+, a non-profit organization dedicated to promoting the value of interior design education.

Whitney Austin Gray is the Senior Vice President at the International WELL Building Institute (IWBI), where she leads research that supports best practices in building design and operations that contribute to improved healthy places for everyone, everywhere. She led the development of the first WELL AP exam, the WELL Faculty Program, and the first case studies focused on the efficacy of the WELL Building Standard, helping to launch more than 100 educational sessions related to WELL in 100+ countries. Prior to joining

IWBI, Dr. Gray served as the health research and innovation director for Cannon Design and led building science research at the MedStar Institute for Innovation. She holds dual appointments as an adjunct assistant professor at the Georgetown School of Nursing & Health Studies and the Department of Urban and Regional Planning. She is the co-founder of the National Institutes of Health-Health in Buildings Roundtable and serves on the GSA's Green Building Advisory Committee. She graduated from Johns Hopkins University with a BA and the Johns Hopkins Bloomberg School of Public Health with a PhD in Health Policy.

Judith Heerwagen is an Environmental Psychologist whose work focuses on evidence-based design and the impact of the built environment on occupant health, wellbeing, and performance. She was a research psychologist with the US General Services Administration from 2009 to 2024. Prior to joining GSA in 2009, she had her own research and consulting firm, where she worked with clients to integrate social science research into design projects. Her clients included both the public and private sector organizations. She was a senior scientist at the Pacific Northwest National Laboratory and a research faculty member at the University of Washington, College of Built Environments, where she is currently an affiliate faculty member in Architecture. She is co-editor of *Biophilic Design: The Theory, Science and Practice of Bringing Buildings to Life*, which won the 2009 Publishers Award in architecture and urban planning. She received the 2014 Design for Humanity Award from the American Society of Interior Designers.

Dak Kopec is an Architectural Psychologist and Professor at the University of Nevada, Las Vegas in the School of Architecture. He is the author of several influential books, including *Environmental Psychology for Design* (4th Edition) and *Person-Centered Health Care Design*, as well as the novels *Broken Boys Beyond Friendships* and *Logan's Legacy Beyond Blood*. Dak has been honored with numerous awards, including two Polsky Prizes, IDEC's Community Service Award, the Fielding Medal, and an honorary Fellowship to ASID (HFASID). Dak has held various prestigious positions, including a visiting professorship at the University of Hawaii with joint appointments in the Schools of Architecture and Medicine. He was also recognized as a Fulbright Specialist and has served two terms as a Fulbright Reviewer. More recently, he provided expert testimony on accessible design to the governments of the Baltic states. Currently, Dak is researching the impact of storytelling in the design process and the role of refined empathy in meeting human needs throughout the built environment.

Kerry L. Marsh is Professor of Psychological Sciences at the University of Connecticut. From 2014 to 2016, she served as Program Director for the Social Psychology Program at the National Science Foundation. She teaches courses in social psychology, experimental research methods and analysis, and environmental psychology. Her research background includes expertise in motivated social cognition and attitude functions and a broad expertise in social perceiving and acting from an ecological perspective. Her current research in this latter area focuses on interpersonal synchrony and embodied cooperation (e.g., joint action); research methods include embodied and environmentally embedded approaches, using immersive virtual reality methods and nonlinear dynamical analyses. Recent applied areas of research focus on human-human-environment interaction, including social influence processes during emergency evacuation of virtual buildings and the consequences of self-driving cars for how pedestrians and human drivers communicate and behave aided or hindered by such technologies. Other research examines how individuals respond to different environments based on manipulations of solo and social affordances and examines the impact of key features of environments on immersive interpersonal interactions in virtual reality.

Benjamin R. Meagher, PhD, is an Associate Professor of Psychology at Hope College (Holland, MI), where he teaches courses in social, personality, and environmental psychology. His primary research focus is in the area of ecological social psychology, investigating the relationship between physical environments, social environments, and individual differences in personality. Recent projects have focused on the home as a source of psychological wellbeing, interpersonal hospitality, and the design and perception of sacred spaces. His research has been published in a number of peer-reviewed journals, including *Personality and Social Psychology Review*, *Journal of Experimental Social Psychology*, *Journal of Environmental Psychology*, and *Environment & Behavior*.

Hanna Negami, PhD, is a Data Strategist with the architecture firm Perkins Eastman's Design Strategy team. She completed her doctoral work in cognitive neuroscience at the University of Waterloo with Dr. Colin Ellard in his Urban Realities Lab. Her research focuses on how the aesthetics of our immediate environment shape our cognition and behavior. In addition to researching awe as an affective response to built environments, she also explores, from a cognitive perspective, how people perceive and interact with public and private spaces, as well as how the built environment can facilitate creative thought. At Perkins Eastman, she leverages her expertise in the emotional impact of built space to support human-centered design strategy decisions.

Kevin Nute is a British/American architectural theorist and Professor of Architecture at the University of Hawai'i, Mānoa. He trained at the universities of Nottingham and Cambridge, worked in architectural practices in Nottingham, London, Hong Kong and Singapore, and spent much of his early career in Japan, initially as a research scholar based at the University of Tokyo and subsequently as an associate professor of architecture at Muroran Institute of Technology. His work examines how built environments can be designed to reflect the parameters of existence; the human/nature interface; and the transfer of ideas between cultures. He is the author of *Embodied Time* (2024), *The Constructed Other* (2021), *This Here Now* (2020), *Naturally Animated Architecture* (2018), *Place, Time and Being in Japanese Architecture* (2004), and *Frank Lloyd Wright and Japan* (1993/2000/2025).

Ileana Rodriguez is the Principal at I Design Access, LLC, and an international architectural design consultant specializing in inclusive design. She is a Texas Registered Accessibility Specialist (RAS) and has worked on projects for the International Paralympic Committee, national sports organizations, and various architecture firms. Her projects range from Olympic/Paralympic stadiums and airports to smaller sports facilities, hotels, and medical facilities across the US, Europe, Asia, and the Americas. Ileana is a Paralympic swimmer and former member of the USA Team for the London 2012 Games. She served as Chef de Mission for the Refugee Paralympic Team at the Tokyo 2020 Paralympic Games and was a governing board member of the Americas Paralympic Committee from 2015 to 2023. She has also served as a Commissioner for the Houston Planning and Houston Airport Commissions and is a sought-after keynote speaker on inclusion and architecture.

Chelsea Rushton holds a BFA with distinction in Creative Writing from the University of Victoria and an MFA in Visual Art from the University of Calgary, and 500 hour certification as a yoga teacher. She developed *Art of the Soul: Creative Process as Spiritual Practice*, an undergraduate lecture, seminar, and studio course that profiles 20th-century modern and contemporary artists who engage in art-making as a method of spiritual inquiry and practice. Her independent research has been supported by the British Columbia Arts Council, the Alberta Foundation for the Arts, the University of Calgary's Centre for Research in the Fine Arts, and Calgary Arts Development. She has been working with Galen Cranz as her research Assistant since 2019.

Leah Scolere, PhD, Cornell University, is the Director of the Connected and Mediated Environments Design Research Lab and an Associate Professor of Interior Architecture and Design in the Department of Design and Merchandising at Colorado State University. Dr. Scolere's approach is informed by her prior design industry practice at Gensler and her advanced degrees in both interior design & new media communication. As an NCIDQ-certified designer and media communication researcher, her interdisciplinary focus exists at the intersection of connective technologies, designed environments, and wellbeing. Her research expertise includes designing for mediated experiences of place across connected environments using a range of communication technologies including augmented reality (AR), space utilization sensors,

3D capture scanning/digital twin technology, eye-tracking and VR technology. Drawing on her communication background, a second stream of research focuses on the design of information and how various populations interpret design communication. Using eye-tracking and VR technology, she has examined design communication and messaging across environments including on the scale of a label (health messaging) to the scale of environmental graphics and messaging in interior environments (branding and wayfinding).

Diana Siebenaler is currently the Sr. Director of Experiential Design at Oak Street Health. In her role at Oak Street she works with patients, providers, and care teams to create human-centered experiences with an emphasis on rebuilding healthcare as it should be. Previously, Diana's career has spanned interior design, business, customer experience, marketing, and product strategy. Prior to joining Oak Street she was the Director of Partnerships and Network Strategy at the Design Institute for Health, where she worked with international innovators on upstream interventions to positively impact the social determinants of health. She also spent 6 years at Steelcase Health where she engaged with leading healthcare clients in designing experiences to leverage space as a tool for healing (of both patients and their providers). Diana holds an MBA from York University in Toronto with a Diploma in Health Industry Management and a Bachelor of Science degree in Interior Design from the University of Texas at Austin. She is an NCIDQ-certified interior designer and a certified Forest Therapy guide. She has a relentless passion for creating experiences that can heal.

Kia Weatherspoon is the most decorated interior designer of a generation. Kia Weatherspoon, NCIDQ, ASID, DFA (h.c) has spent the last 15 years defying every design stereotype. The most damaging—interior design is a luxury reserved for a few. Her voice, advocacy, and firm's Design Equity ® services, have shifted the narrative, making interior design a standard for all. Kia is challenging the lack of these standards in economically challenged communities. Her voice, presence, and leadership have created ripples, prompting housing developers, agencies, and industry partners in economically challenged communities to not just take notice of her work—but to do better. She is the design voice of impact and change. A design industry advocate and educator in business leadership, equity, and diversity. Kia has been recognized as an ICFF Designer of the Year, awarded an Honorary Doctorate from the New York School of Interior Design, and named an ASID National Design for Humanity recipient. She has also been honored as a HIP Designer for Good by Interior Design magazine, received the CREW Washington, DC Raise Up Your Voice Award, and was included in the Washington Business Journal's 40 Under 40 Class. Additionally, she is a recipient of the International Interior Design Association's Luna Textile/Anna Hernandez Visionary Award, among many other accolades. Kia is adamant that change is possible when difficult conversations happen. She has them every day as a female leader of color, speaker, educator, and mentor who exemplifies what's possible for those who are determined by design.

Ryan Welch develops tools and workflows that guide data-driven design thinking. He is a Principal and Research Director at KieranTimberlake, focusing on building performance through analysis, simulation, and software development. Ryan's notable projects include Roast™, a thermal comfort survey application, and Pointelist™, a wireless sensor network for real-time temperature and humidity measurements. He also led the development of Tally®, an LCA application for calculating the environmental impact of building materials. Ryan has worked with Rice University on master planning scenarios and developed digital workflows for the US Embassy in London. He is currently a Co-Principal Investigator on an ARPA-E-funded research project into 3D-printed carbon-negative structures with the University of Pennsylvania. Ryan has taught architectural design at Cooper Union, Yale University, and Princeton University and has conducted workshops at Harvard University, the University of Minnesota, the Royal Danish Academy of Fine Arts, and the University of Pennsylvania. He has lectured nationally and internationally.

So-Yeon Yoon is a Professor of Human Centered Design (formerly Design and Environmental Analysis) and the Director of Design-User Experience-Technology (DUET) Research Lab at Cornell University. Before joining academia, she practiced interior design and architecture in Korea and the US Yoon holds a PhD in Information Technology with an emphasis on Human-Computer Interaction. Her research focuses on understanding and optimizing user experiences through design in both physical and virtual environments. Leveraging emerging technologies, Dr. Yoon analyzes human responses to various design elements to enhance overall user satisfaction and engagement. Her primary research interests include the effects of design using simulations and user-technology interactions, providing valuable insights for design decision-makers and users.

PREFACE

A Collaborative Start

Amid a bustling university campus, a serendipitous encounter sparked a collaboration between two passionate individuals—a social and personality psychology researcher and an interior design educator. United by a common interest in the relationship between people and spaces, what began as a casual interaction quickly transformed into a dynamic exchange of ideas, blending curiosity with empirical research and practical design experience.

This book, *People and Spaces*, is a testament to the years of collaborative effort and shared insights that followed our initial meeting. From that first encounter, we realized that the study of people within built environments and the design of interior spaces are significantly enhanced by interdisciplinary dialogue. Our mutual understanding and combined expertise about people and spaces forms the foundation of this work.

In the following introduction, we provide rationale for why spaces are so critical to us as humans and explain the need for a holistic approach to practice and research, while also acknowledging the challenges. We are eager to share our point of view and a framework for creating and studying interactions between spaces and people. Finally, we offer tips on how to use this book effectively.

Together, as a designer and a psychologist, we aim to inspire and guide you in exploring the profound connection between people and the spaces they inhabit.

PART 1

Introducing People and Spaces

INTRODUCING PEOPLE AND SPACES

Setting the Stage

People have evolved to spend approximately 90% of their lives inside built environments—a striking truth that reveals the profound influence spaces have on how we work, live, and play. Designers, architects, engineers, and others often cite this statistic when discussing the importance of spaces, yet its origins are rarely referenced. To ground our understanding, we begin with a brief history of this data point.

From 1992 to 1994, the U.S. Environmental Protection Agency (EPA) conducted the National Human Activity Pattern Survey (NHAPS) to help scientists better understand the risks posed by different environments through the lens of where people spent their time. The findings, published in 2001 by the Lawrence Berkeley National Laboratory (see Figure 0.1), aimed to assess Americans' exposure to environmental pollutants (Klepeis et al.). The survey revealed that people spent a total of 86.9% of their time indoors, with the majority of that time spent in homes (68.7%), followed by smaller amounts of time inside a car (5.5%), at work (5.4%), at a bar or restaurant (1.8%), or in other interior spaces (11%). This leaves only 7.6% of people's time spent outside.

Shortly after the report was released, engineer and indoor air quality expert Richard Corsi (also a contributor to this book) offered a different way of looking at the 90% statistic in an effort to further underscore its impact on a person's life. Instead of using percentages or hours as in the original survey, Corsi communicates the total number of years, as shown in Figure 0.2. Based on the average life expectancy in the U.S. of 79 years, over their lifespan, Americans spend only about six years outside, compared to 69 years indoors, and another four years inside a vehicle (Bailes, 2018).

DOI: 10.4324/9781003004622-2

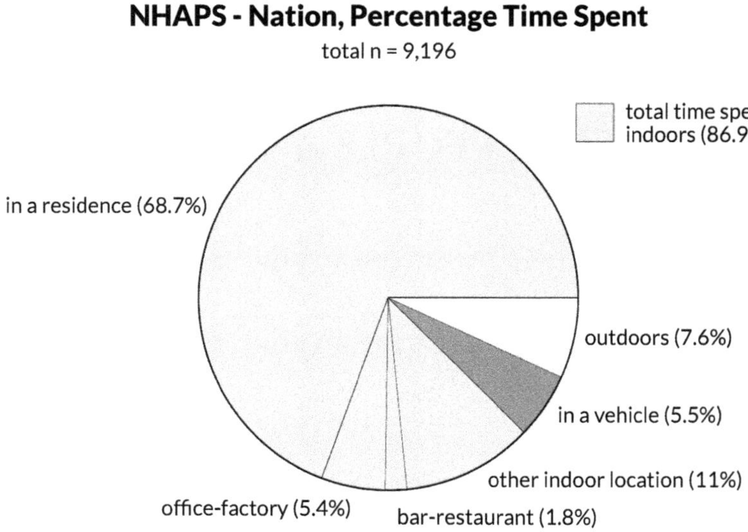

FIGURE 0.1 This pie chart from the NHAPS shows that Americans spent 86.9% of their time indoors in the 1990s, plus another 5.5% inside a vehicle. The NHAPS findings have been reinterpreted for 11 other countries, resulting in only slight variances (Klepeis et al., 2001).

Note: Diagram redrawn.

FIGURE 0.2 Referred to as the "Corsi Code," Richard Corsi translates the findings of the NHAPS into years based on the average American life expectancy. This figure illustrates that Americans spend approximately 69 years indoors, 4.3 years inside a vehicle, and only six years outside over a typical lifespan (Bailes, 2018).

Note: Diagram redrawn.

It has been over 30 years since the NHAPS survey and the Corsi Code interpretation. Since then, what has changed? In recent years, the locations where people spend their time budget at work have shifted significantly due to the impacts of the COVID-19 pandemic. In 2020, enabled by technology, the pandemic caused a massive shift to working from home, ultimately leading to a widespread change in workplace culture. As a result, a larger population of people do not go into the office five days a week, with many continuing to work from home. Industry polls and research indicate that flexible working between office and home is expected to be the main work arrangement in the future (McPhail et al., 2024). We speculate that even though this has been a major change, the percentage of time people spend in each indoor location has simply been reordered. So, on a typical day, most people still spend most of their time inside, with outdoor activities often still constituting the least significant part of their daily routine.

Given this context, it is not surprising that humans have been characterized as an "indoor species," alongside the poignant observation that "unlike the outdoor world, the indoor world is expanding" (Anthes, 2020, p. 6). To conceptualize the sheer scale of our life indoors, consider this—as of 2024, it is estimated there are currently around 2.7 trillion ft^2 (250 billion m^2) of interior area in constructed buildings worldwide (United Nations Environment Programme, 2024). Additionally, imagine that it's estimated that "*three-quarters* of the infrastructure that will exist in 2050 has yet to be built" (United Nations, 2021, para 7). This expansion will put us at a staggering 10.8 trillion ft^2 (1 trillion m^2). The next 25 years will see "the largest wave of building and infrastructure growth in human history" (Architecture 2030, 2023, para. 1), and is estimated to add the interior square footage equal to the size of Texas and New Mexico combined.

We share these statistics to convey how prevalent and integral spaces are to us all and the way we live. The numbers are illustrative, but what really matters is what happens when we are inside. According to the 2024 *Global Status Report for Buildings and Construction*,

> The built environment plays a central role in shaping social dynamics. Multiple aspects of people's lives, from health and well-being to human rights, are impacted at every stage of the building and construction lifecycle. Yet, the social implications of the buildings and construction sector rarely receive due attention....
>
> (United Nations Environment Programme, 2024, p. 22)

For all of us, as occupants of interior spaces for most of our days, what should we know? How do the individuals who help shape these spaces address the needs of future generations? What obligations do these people have in the ways spaces support us in the present moment? These questions highlight the need for holistic practice and research in understanding and designing the spaces we inhabit.

The Need for Holistic Practice and Research

Calls for holistic and integrated approaches to making spaces for people have been around for some time. Indeed, early philosophers, writers, scientists, and artists contemplated the importance of space and the human condition, recognizing that environments significantly impact people's wellbeing. For example in ancient Rome, the physician Asclepiades of Bithynia challenged the common practice of isolating the sick in dark rooms—a method rooted in the belief that darkness brought calm and aided in their recovery. Instead, he advocated for exposure to light and bright spaces (Rubin et al., 1998). Throughout history, diverse constituencies, doctors, city planners, anthropologists, and sociologists have followed suit. And while calls to combine empirical evidence from across our fields are longstanding, acknowledgement that interdisciplinary interventions offer a promising way forward has gained new momentum.

For the past hundred years or so, individuals from various fields and disciplines have been diligently working toward a better understanding of the influence that environments have on the human condition—as well as the ways people shape space. Unfortunately, professionals exploring those topics have often been operating solely within their realm of expertise to approach this area of inquiry. Though it is not fair or accurate to say this work has been done entirely in a vacuum, there is still a profound need to integrate the knowledge learned across multiple fields and disciplines. For continued and substantial progress in advancing these topics, leaders in specialized areas must begin to draw these worlds closer. It is only by putting together the puzzle pieces that each field and discipline has contributed that this broad domain can start creating a holistic picture of the person-place relationship.

Who Contributes to This Inquiry?

A diverse array of voices is invested in cultivating positive dynamics between people and spaces; all attempting to harmonize like a choir, but often singing solo from their unique perspectives. This critical line of inquiry does not, and should not, exclusively belong to any one field or discipline. Figure 0.3 offers a simple overview of the numerous voices engaged in informing and shaping the person-space relationship—and this is undoubtedly an incomplete list.

While enriching, the diversity represented in Figure 0.3 also poses significant challenges. One major issue is the lack of a shared language, which fortifies silos and impedes the advancement of knowledge. The language used to understand the dynamics between people and spaces shapes how this relationship is measured and how success is defined. Without common language, headway made by experts in one discipline may be lost or remain unknown in another. Such lack of cross-disciplinary communication can lead to duplicated efforts, missed opportunities to learn from others' mistakes, and potentially withholding solutions that could solve another group's problems. This reality stifles progress toward the larger goal of reaching a more comprehensive understanding of people and spaces. Professional conferences, symposia, and other interdisciplinary initiatives aim to bridge such gaps, but sustained collaboration requires continuous effort and supportive incentive structures. Fortunately, technological advancements offer new opportunities for

FIGURE 0.3 Diversity of Expertise Shaping People-Space Interactions. This figure illustrates the wide range of fields and disciplines that contribute to the study, design, and implementation of built environments working to understand people-space interactions. Collaboration across these areas is essential for holistic, integrated practice and research.

cross-disciplinary dialogue, providing platforms that can help ease communication and collaboration.

Why Are Holistic Approaches to the Built Environment Challenging?

First and foremost, the relationship between people and the spaces they inhabit is multifaceted, complex, and full of overlapping environmental, social, health, and human factors. Understanding how sustainability, socioeconomic status, culture, and physical ability affect people's spatial relationships often requires in-depth expertise rather than generalist perspectives. When combined with the multitude of responsibilities from psychological, architectural, and interior design standpoints, the challenges of adopting holistic approaches start to come into focus.

Architects Alvar and Aino Aalto's design for the Paimio Sanatorium serves as an early example. Through their 1932 design, the Aaltos drew on "quasi-scientific" design methods and biophilic principles to support tuberculosis patients in Finland. Their approach aimed to provide patients with access to natural light, fresh air, and control over their social interactions through access to numerous community spaces. Alvar Aalto likened the building to a "medical instrument" for healing and was quoted by journalist P. Morton Shand as saying, "The idea, it is perhaps hardly necessary to add, was an architect's not a doctor's...The doctors fail to understand it. Whether the medical profession will end by adopting it remains to be seen" (Woodman, 2016, para. 10).

The interdisciplinary quandary that the Aaltos faced a century ago is one that architects, interior designers, psychologists, and others continue to encounter today. Professionals often aim to center the human experience within the built environment and believe in integrating design and science but may lack the depth of knowledge and access to expertise to do so effectively. The architectural community regards the sanatorium as a success, but what if the Aaltos had worked with an interdisciplinary team that included an environmental psychologist, a neuroscientist, a pulmonologist, or an infectious disease specialist? How much farther might an integrated, evidence-based design approach have advanced the Aaltos' intuitive, empathy-based design approach? Finally, what might an interdisciplinary team have been able to test and prove to guide future built environments?

Uniting the Fields and Disciplines through Experience

In *People and Spaces*, we argue that each discipline brings unique insights and opportunities for synergy. Despite the challenges when working across disciplines, we gain remarkable benefits from this diversity—namely, a variety of perspectives and a breadth and depth of understanding of important topics. Each profession's deep dive into its specific focus areas has led to significant advancements in our broader shared goal. These varying viewpoints have also produced a plethora of methods to investigate the person-place connection. Technology has accelerated our ability to implement and utilize new modes of exploration. Researchers can now more accurately measure how individuals navigate, perceive, choose, and spend time in their environments than ever before. This progress presents new opportunities to combine efforts within and across fields. We are already seeing this emerge; for example, some designers incorporate virtual reality experiences to design and test new spaces, while psychologists use physiological metrics to measure people's real-time responses to environments. From our vantage point, technology has been a powerful "conversation starter" in bridging these divides and will hopefully continue to bring everyone working in this domain closer.

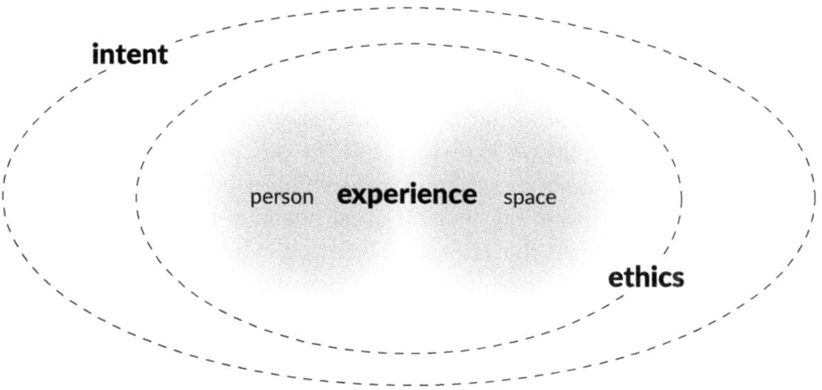

FIGURE 0.4 Framework for Positive Person-Space Relationships. This figure illustrates the core elements that foster positive interactions between people and their environments. It highlights the nested relationship of experience, ethics, and intent, which are fundamental for creating and maintaining supportive and enriching spaces.

In our assessment, human experience unites these diverse efforts, as all engagement within spaces hinges on it. Experience serves as the core from which both people and spaces interact—creating, enhancing, or eroding the relationship between the two. Ethical considerations naturally arise here, guiding experts and laypersons on how to best support both people and spaces. Consequently, the intent behind each action that shapes a human-centered experience becomes crucial. Figure 0.4 illustrates how these factors nest within one another, mirroring the structure of this book—from shaping experiences to considering ethics to crafting intent.

You can reference Figure 0.4 as a framework for achieving a positive person-space relationship by first defining the desired experience of the interaction between people and their spatial environment. This defined experiential outcome is then passed through an ethical lens. The ethical examination informs the development of purposeful intentions for research, design, and implementation to bring the experience to life. This process allows designers or makers of spaces to be responsibly creative when designing for people, and researchers or influencers of people to be creatively responsible when studying, planning for people in situ, and applying their learnings.

Navigating *People and Spaces*: How to Use This Book

This book is organized into three parts—*Shaping Experiences*, *Considering Ethics*, and *Crafting Intent*—and it is for anyone passionate about people and spaces. It serves as a catalyst for curiosity, inviting all of us to explore what others are doing and dismantle the barriers that separate us. This book offers an overview of how this domain is continuously growing, prompting further exploration in practice and scientific inquiry. Whether you are a practitioner, a scholar, or simply someone interested in the topic, exploring people and spaces is rarely linear, always evolving, and, in our professional experience, deepened through collaboration and interdisciplinary efforts.

As you read, we'll tackle big-picture questions like: How are spatial experiences shaped? What are the ethical obligations when creating inhabitable spaces? Ultimately, how does intent play out when designing built environments and studying occupants? We will explore how individuals across psychology, interior design, architecture, and other fields and disciplines conceptualize, examine, and address these questions. Finally, we reflect upon the book's entirety to impart what we view as Universal Truths that emerged throughout and to suggest where we can go next when working together.

With its 18 chapters, this book provides a window into a vast body of work that spans across fields and disciplines. Its primary aim is to underscore the significance of advancing the knowledge base and, in turn, elevating best practices in designing for and studying people and interior spaces. Each contributor has strived to present their viewpoints and endeavors in an accessible manner, irrespective of the reader's background. While each chapter stands alone, we organized them into the aforementioned framework consisting of three main sections: *Shaping Experiences*, *Considering Ethics*, and *Crafting Intent*. At the start and end of each part and prior to each chapter, we share our perspective to guide and inspire you through this book.

Shaping Experiences

This section highlights that regardless of whether engaging in a mundane task or a significant event, all human experiences are deeply intertwined with spatial contexts. This section examines how spaces influence human behaviors, thoughts, and emotions daily, consciously or unconsciously. Contributors explore the evolution of the person-space relationship, addressing questions about taste in design, the emotional impact of spaces, and strategies for designing environments that invite action. Each author demonstrates how different perspectives within their areas of study illuminate the intricacies of the human experience within the settings they explore.

Considering Ethics

Here, we examine how built environments can perpetuate or mitigate inequality, emphasizing that spatial experiences are not universally equal. This section explores how political, economic, and social systems influence our living environments and the ethical considerations arising from these interactions. Sharing framing from their respective disciplines, authors demonstrate how built environments can either safeguard or endanger systemic stability. Contributors highlight the need to address power imbalances and vulnerabilities to restore balance and equality in our societal systems. This section encourages all of us to view our surroundings through an ethical lens, considering how built spaces impact public health, inclusivity, diversity, and even the protection of personal data. It also stresses the importance of caring for the natural world and the interconnectedness of systems, urging us all to challenge the status quo and reconsider various aspects of our work and life.

Crafting Intent

Finally, in this section, we delve into the deliberate and thoughtful act of researching and designing spaces that adapt, evolve, and resonate with the dynamic human experience. Reflecting on the previously discussed themes of experience and ethics, the authors underscore the necessity of placing people's needs at the center of spatial design. It explores methods to ensure that design practices empower occupants to engage fully with their environments, allowing them to thrive. Contributors highlight using varying methods such as surveys, evidence-based design, interdisciplinary collaboration, and historical context to inform design. They also discuss the importance of including clients and occupants in the research and design process, and the role certification systems can play in supporting spatial and occupant needs. The section emphasizes that purposeful action and continuous iteration are vital in creating positive and ethical spatial experiences for a sustainable and resilient world.

Final Thoughts

We hope that *People and Spaces* inspires you to ask more questions, think more deeply, step outside your own worldview, and consider how you, too, can improve the person-place relationship in your world and for others. We encourage you to ponder: How do the spaces you occupy influence your daily interactions, emotions, behaviors, and overall health and wellbeing? And what might change if these environments were designed with a deeper understanding of those impacts? By weaving together diverse perspectives from multiple fields and disciplines, we aim to illustrate how integrated approaches to the design and research of people and spaces can profoundly enhance all of our understanding and interactions with the spatial environments we inhabit so frequently.

Bibliography

Architecture 2030. (2023). *Why The Built Environment – Architecture 2030*. www.architecture2030.org. https://www.architecture2030.org/why-the-built-environment/

Anthes, E. (2020). *The great indoors: The surprising science of how buildings shape our behavior, health, and happiness.* Scientific American/Farrar, Straus and Giroux.

Bailes, A. A. III. (2018, August 8). What percent of time do you spend indoors? *Energy Vanguard.* Retrieved from https://www.energyvanguard.com/blog/what-percent-time-do-you-spend-indoors/

Klepeis, N. E., Nelson, W. C., Ott, W. R., Robinson, J. P., Tsang, A. M., Switzer, P., Behar, J. V., Hern, S. C., & Engelmann, W. H. (2001). The National Human Activity Pattern Survey (NHAPS): A resource for assessing exposure to environmental pollutants. *Journal of Exposure Analysis and Environmental Epidemiology, 11*(3), 231–252. https://doi.org/10.1038/sj.jea.7500165

McPhail, R., Chan, X. W. (Carys), May, R., & Wilkinson, A. (2024). Post-COVID remote working and its impact on people, productivity, and the planet: An exploratory scoping review. *The International Journal of Human Resource Management, 35*(1), 154–182. https://doi.org/10.1080/09585192.2023.2221385

Rubin, H. R., Owens, A. J., & Golden, G. (1998). *Investigation to determine whether the built environment affects patients' medical outcomes.* The Center for Health Design. Retrieved from https://www.healthdesign.org/chd/research/investigation-determine-whether-built-environment-affects-patients-medical-outcomes

United Nations. (2021, October 21). UN Chief promotes 'enormous' benefits of greener cities. *UN News.* Retrieved from https://news.un.org/en/story/2021/10/1101992

United Nations Environment Programme. (2024). *Global status report for buildings and construction: Beyond foundations: Mainstreaming sustainable solutions to cut emissions from the buildings sector.* Nairobi. https://doi.org/10.59117/20.500.11822/45095

Woodman, E. (2016, November 17). Revisit: 'Aalto's Paimio Sanatorium continues to radiate a profound sense of human empathy.' *Architectural Review.* Retrieved June 25, 2024, from https://www.architectural-review.com/buildings/revisit-aaltos-paimio-sanatorium-continues-to-radiate-a-profound-sense-of-human-empathy

PART 2
Shaping Experiences

Framing Experiences

People do not encounter experiences in a silo. The first section of *People and Spaces* underscores this fundamental statement. The peaks and pits of life and every beat in between—from accomplishing mundane tasks to celebrating momentous occasions—occur within a spatial condition. Each of these moments involves a constellation of behavioral circumstances that have physical and often digital dimensions (Glass, 2018). Whether consciously or unconsciously, we all continuously select and craft spaces that support or sometimes hinder our daily lives. And often, hired professionals curate environments to promote the specific experiences we seek.

This section on *Shaping Experiences* brings together authors whose work explores the evolution of the person-space relationship. Collectively, they guide us in examining how spaces, furnishings, and objects can enhance or inhibit people's thoughts, feelings, and behaviors. Contributors tackle questions such as: What is taste in design, and can it be formularized and taught? How do spaces influence emotions such as awe? What are strategies for designing environments that invite action? Additionally, you will hear how furnishings and room layouts have shaped our world throughout political history. Then, looking ahead, contributors contemplate how new technologies shape our experience of physical space and what that means for us as inhabitants.

The following contributions reveal just some of the ways others are theoretically and pragmatically addressing these questions. You can expect to learn from a diverse group of researchers, academics, and practitioners representing a broad range of expertise ranging from sociology, psychology, and communication to architecture and interior design. Each author shares a unique perspective that draws on their knowledge of various subjects, such as neuroscience, new media, healthcare, and retail environments. These selections intentionally

DOI: 10.4324/9781003004622-4

come from varying viewpoints to inspire you to consider how to entwine disciplines and to help identify opportunities for new lines of inquiry. Given the magnitude of the human experience, we urge you to seek insights from different fields that can further inform and advance a greater understanding of the influential yet sometimes enigmatic relationship between people and spaces.

Reference

Glass, T. (2018). *Prompt: Socially Engaging Objects and Environments.* Birkhäuser.

CONNECTING 1

As occupants, our personal environments tell us and others something about our lives—what we did the days and weeks before, what we plan to do, and how we feel. Our spaces hold our past, present, future, and even who we aspire to be. Often, clues about one's true self manifest naturally and even unknowingly. For instance, few people choose to create clutter on their desks during a busy deadline period. Yet, at other times, people deliberately display information about their identities, values, beliefs, dreams, and goals throughout their environments. When we inhabit our homes, offices, cars, or even the spaces we visit, we constantly communicate about who we choose to be. Somewhere between these conscious and unconscious choices, we convey our self-expression, and what some may call our "taste" comes to light.

In the following chapter, sociologist Galen Cranz and co-author Chelsea Rushton take a deep dive into the concept of "taste." They explain what taste is and how it emerges in planned spaces and those spaces that evolve organically, and at all scales—from a room to an entire city. The authors also clarify why this, at times, polarizing notion is quite important and unavoidable when discussing people's relationship with space. Next, Cranz and Rushton propose a new model for taste that incorporates profiles to help you understand individual preferences devoid of hierarchical judgment. And likely most critical, the model debunks the idea of *good* and *bad* taste for people learning how to design. The benefit of this model is that rather than elevating design to something illusive and intuitive for a select few, this approach places taste into a realm that is more democratic, analytical, and, notably, teachable.

DOI: 10.4324/9781003004622-5

1

RE-EXAMINING TASTE IN DESIGN

Integrating Pragmatics, Symbols, and Aesthetics

Galen Cranz and Chelsea Rushton

Introduction

Taste is a metaphor that comes from our capacity to distinguish flavors and has evolved through centuries to mean an ability to discern good from bad aesthetically. As a sociologist of architecture, and more broadly of the arts and culture, I began thinking about the topic of taste and design with the seminal sociological literature that views taste as a form of social rank. Veblen (1899) wrote about "conspicuous consumption," that is, showing off through one's possessions. Chapin (1935) classified the material objects and their arrangements in residents' living rooms to measure their social class without having to ask them directly. Gans (1974) introduced the terms "high brow," "low brow," and "middle brow" taste to describe social classes in terms of their cultural preferences. Bourdieu's seminal study (1979) argued that the powerful and rich assume that they deserve their dominant position because of their superior taste. In common speech today, the word *taste* has evolved into more casual use, synonymous with *preference*. Even this usage of *taste* can still point to and uphold class differences and indicate judgments on someone's character or personhood.

Educators in architecture, planning, the arts, and beyond teach taste to students and junior colleagues indirectly, through nonverbal communication, much of which is derisive. Design theory is relatively mute on the topic of taste, since environmental design shifted away from the search for absolute standards, toward accepting the importance of social relativity. A recent collection of essays titled *After Taste: Expanded Practice in Interior Design* (Kleinman, et al., 2012) seeks to address issues of taste in design—primarily the aesthetic and the conceptual, and to a less extent the functional. However,

DOI: 10.4324/9781003004622-6

none of the authors acknowledge that taste is still used to judge and influence student work, create professional reputations, and shape the designs of everything from products to urban plans.

Taste in design needs a foundational re-examination. I offer a new, more democratic and analytic theory of taste. It integrates the three aspects of taste emphasized by other theorists—functional, conceptual, sensory. Most insist taste is one of the three, but here I show how all three dimensions are essential to defining and understanding taste and hence need to be integrated.

I view taste as a universal *process* of selection, assembly, and communication that *everyone* partakes in, not only gifted individuals.[1] My perspective comes from my education as a sociologist and my years as a professor of architecture at two major universities. In 1975, the State of New Jersey invited me to live for one week in a senior housing unit and photograph residents in their homes, as part of a sponsored study on housing for the elderly. What I started to learn there is that taste is the *outcome* of how a person balances its three components: *pragmatic* and *symbolic* objects, arranged using *aesthetic* principles. These are the three components of what I call the PSA Taste Model, which integrates methodological scientific thinking with artistic expression in a practical, applicable, and *teachable* way.

I will begin by describing the model and its components that I have presented earlier (Cranz, 2004). I will then illustrate the formula at all scales of the built environment. I conclude by discussing the advantages of this way of thinking about taste to encourage others to adopt this method in their teaching, professional, and everyday practices.

The Theoretical Model

Mathematical convention indicates the way taste works as a process. Two separate variables, pragmatics and symbols, are "added" together and then "multiplied" by aesthetic principles to produce taste as an outcome, that is, a composition:

$$\left(\textit{Pragmatics} + \textit{Symbols}\right)\textit{Aesthetic Integration} = \textit{Taste}$$

1 *Pragmatics* are objects and materials needed to make an environment functional: a fork is a utensil for eating; a door is a threshold into and out of a building; a tree provides food, shade, and wood; a crosswalk is a safety feature of urban circulation.

The pragmatic aspect of taste differentiates it from "pure" art. Without pragmatics, which brings utility, our discussion would shift from taste in design to the field of art criticism—judging the meaning of the symbolic references and the skill with which the artist communicated them aesthetically.

2 *Symbols* are objects and materials that represent a person, organization, institution, society, or culture. They communicate about relatives, activities, affiliate groups, achievements, travel, education, religion, values, and institutional, social, and cultural aspirations, and they non-verbally mark territory.

At the personal level, symbolic objects could include (but are not limited to) photographs, sports trophies, souvenirs, awards, diplomas, artworks, prized audio equipment, and religious objects. Real estate agents usually ask sellers to remove symbolic items from their houses when they are put on the market so potential buyers can envision their own things there. Symbolic building design elements include embellishments over doors and windows, building details and proportional schemes adopted from admired historical cultures (such as classical Greece, Rome, Japan, or China), planting schemes and statuary in gardens, and special gateways to urban complexes.[2]

Pragmatic and symbolic objects represent two different purposes: *utility* and *expression*, which people want to integrate. However, neither category—the pragmatic nor the symbolic—is fixed. The same object can—and almost always will—have both pragmatic and symbolic features, and it can code-switch to perform either function more dominantly, depending on context.[3]

3 *Aesthetic Integration* refers to the principles by which people combine pragmatic and symbolic objects or materials into compositions. Aesthetics, as a branch of philosophy, references knowledge that we gain through our five senses.[4] The aesthetic principles by which people organize objects and materials may or may not be conscious to them. These rules, as do the objects they organize, vary by cultural and historical context. Here I describe principles that I have commonly observed in 20th- and 21st-century North American and European design, as expressed in mainstream "shelter magazines," newspaper ads, calendars, and books that I have collected since 1975.

Most people first use **color** to make things match or contrast each other. Color schemes unify rooms in a home, building exteriors, gardens, and planned communities. **Texture** accounts for the sense of touch. The implied tactility of rich texture can be important to some, while others, especially modernists, deliberately understate texture by choosing smooth, shiny, or matte objects and surfaces. Similarly, using **pattern** to match, echo, or contrast plain surfaces can be used in interior decor, exterior building walls, and ground plane designs.

People also relate things by **shape**. Some people might collect circles, squares, or triangles together into a composition. A round shape might be composed of a square, triangle, or rectangle of roughly equivalent size. Others might assemble things of different shapes but of comparable **size**. Objects of the same size, like miniature figurines or paintings, might be placed together.

Symmetry or **asymmetry** are commonly used to arrange things. In a symmetrical design, left and right are likely to have identical objects or objects equal in size at the same level visually, such as matching nightstands on either side of a bed. Asymmetrical designs introduce dynamism to compositions (for instance, two framed pictures hung beside each other on a wall, with one higher than the other); these are generally considered less formal than symmetrical compositions.

Design happens at different **scales**. Some people compose only the top of a surface, such as a dresser or sideboard, while others include the segment of wall above it. Others might organize the entire wall, and still others compose all four walls of a room. Composing at larger scales becomes progressively more complex and difficult. Beyond the scale of what an individual might decorate in their living or work spaces, trained professionals usually take over: residential and commercial interior designers will integrate multiple rooms or spaces; architects design buildings; landscape architects work with gardens, parks, and public spaces; urban designers lay out the relationships between buildings; and city and regional planners account for the relationships among districts, other cities, and regions. At any scale of the built environment, the fundamental process of arranging is the same.

4 *Taste* in design involves combining and integrating pragmatic and symbolic objects through aesthetics. This unification is not necessarily permanent; things can be reassembled. Thus, taste communicates order and wholeness from a particular perspective, at a particular moment and location. Some people or compositions might give more importance to pragmatics, some to symbolics, some to aesthetics, and thereby create a taste "profile," which I will discuss in a later section.

Taste in Objects, Taste in People

Anthropologist Ellen Dissanayake has noted the importance of the relationship between things:

> I was intrigued with how much depended on *two* things and their relationship. One rock or one piece of wood is something (*some thing*), but once a second rock or piece of wood, or some other second thing, is placed with it, there is an immediate implicit connection between them that requires consideration.
>
> (Dissanayake, 2000, p. 4)

In a consumer world, what distinguishes people from one another is not so much the specific qualities of the things we have, but rather, how we constellate them with our other things. Status objects, like handbags, smart devices, computers, and cars, communicate their brand identity and reflect on the wearer or user, but even these items are judged in the context of the other things they own and the spatial conditions in which they are assembled. Therefore, questions about whether a single object is in good or bad taste, as well as issues of connoisseurship (a way to distinguish one object or creator from another), lose relevance in light of the importance of where and how they are placed, whether it is a dresser top or a city block.

Likewise, with people: a claim that a person "has taste" or "has no taste" does not offer much insight. Everybody composes, so everyone decorates. More information is revealed about a person in *how* and at what scale they assemble the many things in their environment. As I mentioned, some people will assemble more complex arrangements than others: some might use a greater number of principles for aesthetic integration or create order at larger scales than others. Some design professionals, such as famous architects like Frank Lloyd Wright and more contemporary Robert Venturi and Denise Scott-Brown, design at every scale, from spoon to master plan. Their ability to handle multiple scales does not necessarily indicate innate talent, but rather skill and training, which are teachable.

Teaching Taste

Taste *is* a skill that can be learned and applied through principles and examples. The phrases "good taste" and "bad taste" reflect principles of taste that are universally recognized but not standardized. In contrast, the PSA taste model makes it possible to discuss taste in more analytic terms, without hierarchical, moralistic, and even punitive qualifiers such as smirking and sneering. Teaching taste can mean (1) teaching oneself to know one's own design tendencies and (2) to become more empathetic to others' needs and preferences. The former is useful for everyone interested in learning about taste; the latter is particularly applicable for design professionals and educators who will be working with clients or teaching students.

Once, I asked each of the graduate architecture students in my Taste seminar to make an arrangement of all the things they had brought with them into the classroom (backpacks, books, notebooks, pens, computers, and other paraphernalia). The major distinction among their compositions was how much attention was paid to form (appearance) versus content (meaning). The differences related to what each student was trying to communicate—a slice of student life, painterly still life, form for form's sake, mystery—and did not fit the designations of "good" or "bad" taste. We also noticed marked differences in the scale of their compositions; some used a chair seat, some used the whole chair, others used a part of the wall or floor in relation to a chair. I was personally more attracted to some of the compositions than others, and I would say that some were more sophisticated than others or effective at communicating their intentions than others, but I took an analytic view. The PSA Taste Model aims to make people more aware of their own design inclinations, which form the basis of personal judgments of "like" and "dislike." The PSA Taste Model further aims to help people recognize the difference between like/dislike and good/bad: the former is a personal judgment; the latter is the universal application of that personal judgment, which is what the model helps to avoid.

Taste Profiles

To acknowledge skill differences and differences in interest in environmental expression, I offer the idea of taste "profiles." Taste profiles could show how people prioritize each of the three components of the PSA Taste Model:

- some people focus on pragmatic things,
- some focus on symbolic things,
- and some orchestrate multiple sensory qualities to create artistic unity.

Taste profiling would not provide a single high/low score, which could be perceived as measuring human worth or rank. Rather, it could map metrics in each of the three categories along a continuum, like the Meyers Briggs Type Indicator, for instance, to create unique types. Two people could end up with a numerically similar score but have very different profiles in terms of which elements of the model they prioritize in their compositions. Creating a taste profile indicator is an area of future research I hope to explore in my forthcoming book on Taste and Design.

Taste at All Scales of the Built Environment

The PSA Taste Model can be applied to all scales of environmental design. A table setting and a neighborhood, for instance, are arrangements at two different scales, but they do not require separate theories or disciplines to discuss how they are organized. I will discuss the PSA model at work in interior design, architecture, landscape architecture, and urban design and planning.

Interior Design

For most of us, our homes are the site of more everyday aesthetic activity than any other place. While the practice is general, it is more structured than we commonly assume.

My understanding of pragmatic and symbolic objects as elements of the taste process emerged during my early field research on decorating practices in a senior living facility's resident living spaces. In a week of living in the building, I was able to photograph over 20 units and interview their residents. I made a point of framing my photographs at the scales at which the residents made their compositions. An architect and I analyzed the photographs to look for common patterns. From this first sample, I developed the PSA model, and since then, I have continued to test my theory in culturally and economically diverse residences, as well as in public places, both indoors and outdoors, and cities as a whole.

While a resident in the facility, I interviewed those who volunteered, after the management asked me to start with the woman who had the reputation as the best decorator in the building (Figure 1.1). I also made a point of interviewing two residents who management told me to avoid because they were considered "dirty," and "not a good housekeeper." I thought that these "outliers" would show me a range of decorating approaches from best to worst—I was not yet thinking in terms of pragmatism, symbols, and aesthetics. The Pragmatic vs Symbolic dimensions were clarified in part by these two people, who were not dirty or poor housekeepers, but rather strictly pragmatic; the way they arranged their rooms lacked the symbolism that others expect (Figure 1.2).

It is also possible for design to lean in the other direction—of symbolism dominating pragmatism (one definition of *kitsch* is the absence of utility). Dominant symbolism might produce an interior bursting with so many sentimental objects that it is hard to move around or use the space for its intended purpose (work at a surface, make a meal, lie down, etc.) (Figure 1.3).

FIGURE 1.1 This interior set the standard of taste in this residence in New Jersey in 1975; color, texture, shapes, and symmetrical composition unite wall, furniture, and both practical and symbolic objects. Photograph by Galen Cranz.

FIGURE 1.2 The practical purpose of storing his files and providing light for her interest in plants were both more important than conventional symbolic displays for these two residents. Photographs by Galen Cranz.

FIGURE 1.3 Gordon McKay, Professor of Computer Science, Harry R. Lewis, in his office in Maxwell Dworkin Hall, Harvard John A. Paulson School of Engineering and Applied Sciences. Image by Cynthia Guo, https://commons.wikimedia.org/wiki/File:HarryLewis_Harvard_OfficeKnickKnacks.jpg, used under a Creative Commons Attribution-Share Alike 4.0 International license, https://creativecommons.org/licenses/by-sa/4.0/legalcode.

Buildings/Architecture

Buildings provide shelter from the elements and separate activities and social roles from one another. Roofs, walls, floors, windows, and doors are pragmatic basics at this scale. Symbolic elements might include decorative features, styles of execution, or the quality of building materials.

Examples of strictly—or primarily—pragmatic buildings include mid-20th-century high-density public housing and corporate office towers (Figure 1.4), and metal buildings, such as those by Butler or SteelMaster (Figure 1.5). In public housing, windows are not elaborated with lintels, shutters, or other elements that symbolize a single-family house. The colors are uniform to make painting easy and therefore less expensive, and similarly, using only one material for the exterior walls reduces costs. However, even strict pragmatism communicates symbolically. Public housing communicates that low-income people live here. Office towers show a strict economy of building materials and limit or eliminate decoration but their pragmatism has over time become a symbol of modernity, banality, and facelessness. The pragmatic simplicity of this steel building—one dominant material, no decorative embellishments nor color—supports the limited purpose of storage.

Buildings designed by strict modernist architects seek to avoid symbolism and recognizable decoration. However, this intentional avoidance of ornament can carry its own highly symbolic meanings: of efficiency, restraint, daring, "appropriateness," and rationality, in contrast to sentimentality. A well-known French architect who worked in this way, Le Corbusier (1887–1965), famously wrote that "a house is a machine for living in." His designs, such as Villa Savoye, rejected 19th-century decorative traditions and ornamentation (Figure 1.6).

FIGURE 1.4 Left: Public Housing, Hong Kong. Image by Flickr user Teddy Kwok, https://www.flickr.com/photos/bblkwok/8427327409/, used under a Creative Commons Attribution-NonCommercial-NoDerivs 2.0 license, https://creativecommons.org/licenses/by-nc-nd/2.0/legalcode. Right: XYZ Buildings, New York City. Image by Flickr user Peter Zoon, https://www.flickr.com/photos/peterzen/6125040110/, used under a Creative Commons Attribution 2.0 Generic license, https://creativecommons.org/licenses/by/2.0/legalcode.

FIGURE 1.5 SteelMaster Steel Storage Building. Image by Flickr user SteelMaster Buildings, https://www.flickr.com/photos/steelmastersteelbuildings/6878564850/, used under a Creative Commons Attribution-ShareAlike 2.0 Generic license, https://creativecommons.org/licenses/by-sa/2.0/legalcode.

The house defies most conventions for homes at the time (1928–1931): it is raised off the ground on columns (piloti); the windows create the appearance of a homogenous strip; the roof is flat, not gabled; the surface is smooth, not rusticated or crenelated; the entire building is concrete, not wood or stone; white, not colored. Ironically, Corbusier's efforts to make a house look like an efficient, practical machine generated a new aesthetic standard for modernity.

The California Building in San Diego, California, is a building very high on symbolism. Its extravagant and exuberant details draw from Plateresque, Baroque, Churrigueresque, and Rococo, Gothic, and Spanish-Colonial architectural styles. The building is so heavily decorated that its functional purpose could be eclipsed (Figure 1.7). The California Building uses the forms of religious cathedrals to symbolize the early connection of learning with monasteries. It is decorated with elaborate stone carvings, as well as tiles and glass beads. Only a knowledgeable viewer could read the meaning of the human figures, the busts, the crest, and non-figurative elements.

FIGURE 1.6 Le Corbusier, *Villa Savoye*, Poissy, France. Image by Wikipedia user Valueyou, https://en.wikipedia.org/wiki/File:VillaSavoye.jpg, used under a Creative Commons Attribution-ShareAlike 3.0 License, https://creativecommons.org/licenses/by-sa/3.0/legalcode.

Landscape Architecture

Humans lived most of the time outdoors until the rise of industrialization. Today we still value and need time outdoors—for food production and harvesting, fresh air, leisure, social life, exercise, and diurnal entrainment (synchronizing our hormone cycles with the sun). The pragmatic basics of landscape design include earth, sun, water, wind and air, trees and plants, and prospect and refuge. The symbolic elements include the layouts of trees, shrubs, and flowers to represent a variety of social orders—from agrarian (via pasture, ponds, and fences), paradisiacal (via fountains, fragrant flowers, and birds) to state hierarchical (via formal layout of vegetation with statuary and monuments including tombs).

A pragmatic approach to landscape can be seen in orchard, farm, or agribusiness planting schemes that are organized for ease of mechanical watering and harvesting. Gardens and parks, in contrast, represent idealized versions of nature and how humans can relate to nature. Nineteenth century American parks by Frederick Law Olmsted, such as his iconic Central Park in New York City (1876), symbolized and intended to create the feeling of being

FIGURE 1.7 Main entrance of the California Building, housing the Museum of Us, San Diego, California. Image by Wikimedia user Bernard Gagnon, https://commons.wikimedia.org/wiki/File:San_Diego_Museum_of_Man_03.jpg, used under a Creative Commons Attribution-Share Alike 3.0 Unported license, https://creativecommons.org/licenses/by-sa/3.0/legalcode.

in pastoral nature as tamed by human farming, in contrast to the city (Figure 1.8). Accordingly, the fields, woods, and ponds all carefully placed in Central Park harkened the landscape of the United States prior to industrialization, and pathways and trails were made curvilinear to avoid the experience of the

FIGURE 1.8 Aerial view of Central Park, New York. Original image from Carol M. Highsmith's America, Library of Congress collection. Image digitally enhanced by Flickr user rawpixel, https://www.flickr.com/photos/vintage_illustration/4625260246, used under a Creative Commons Attribution 2.0 Generic (CC BY 2.0) license, https://creativecommons.org/licenses/by/2.0/legalcode.

surrounding urban rectilinear grids. Olmsted's "Pleasure Grounds" emphasize the social, recreational, non-utilitarian purposes of these large parks.

In contrast, the more contemporary Parc de La Villette in Paris (1983) symbolizes urban culture and seeks to integrate with it (Figure 1.9). Architect Bernard Tschumi extended the urban grid pattern of Paris over Parc de La Villette to arrange its features, reversing the historic separation of park from city that led to many early Pleasure Ground designs that used curvilinear, not gridded, layouts and avoided urban views. The plan anchors the rhythm of Paris city blocks into the park by arranging buildings ("follies") in a grid; they are not camouflaged by trees or hills, but highlighted with glossy red paint. Lawns are clearly defined in large geometric forms—a circle split in half on both sides of the canal that bisects the land, a square, a triangle, and one free-form shape. Double rows of trees in the style of the French allée, not naturalistic clumps, marked circulation paths and symbolized French landscape traditions rather than English.

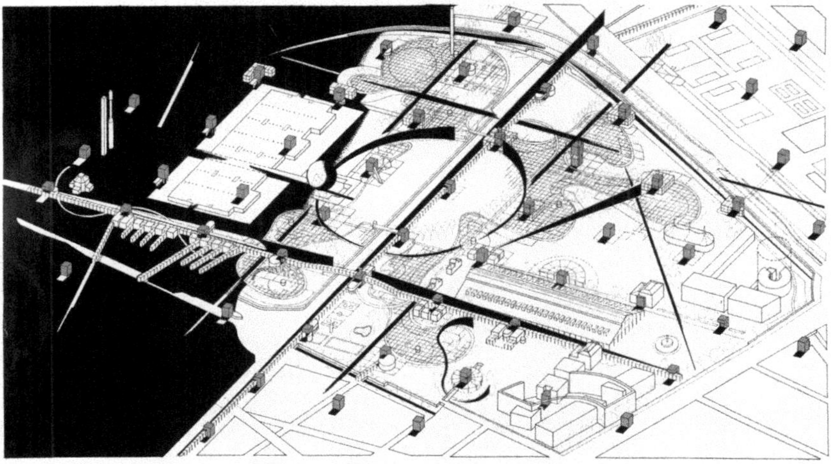

FIGURE 1.9 Plan drawing of Parc de la Villette, Paris, France. © Bernard Tschumi Architects.

Urban Design and Regional Planning

In cities, pragmatic considerations include the adjacencies of interdependent activities (e.g., elementary schools to residential districts), separation of incompatible activities (e.g., residential districts from noisy or dirty manufacturing), and circulation. Because equally sized and shaped blocks make it easy to sell real estate, the grid is the favored pragmatic urban scheme in most North American cities (Figure 1.10). In contrast, many old-world cities in Europe, Russia, and Asia were designed on radial patterns to connect the center to the periphery most directly (Figure 1.11).

Symbolism in urban planning expresses cultural, national, regional, and local ideals, including order itself (communicated through hierarchy in size, logic of placement of land uses—residential, commercial, industrial, recreational); productivity (size and location of buildings); power (government buildings, churches, large corporations); economic efficiency (usually the grid); natural beauty (public gardens and parks, maximizing views); commemoration of historical events (landmarks). City planners use the same aesthetic tools used at smaller scales—color, texture, pattern, shape, size, symmetry and asymmetry—to unite efficiencies with ideals at this large urban scale.

At the turn of the 20th century, advocates of the City Beautiful movement, which aimed to beautify cities in grand and monumental ways, had the ambition to create order at the scale of the entire city. Unfortunately, this order seldom extended beyond a central core because those values were abandoned during later decades of urban expansion. Postwar suburbs like the Levittowns

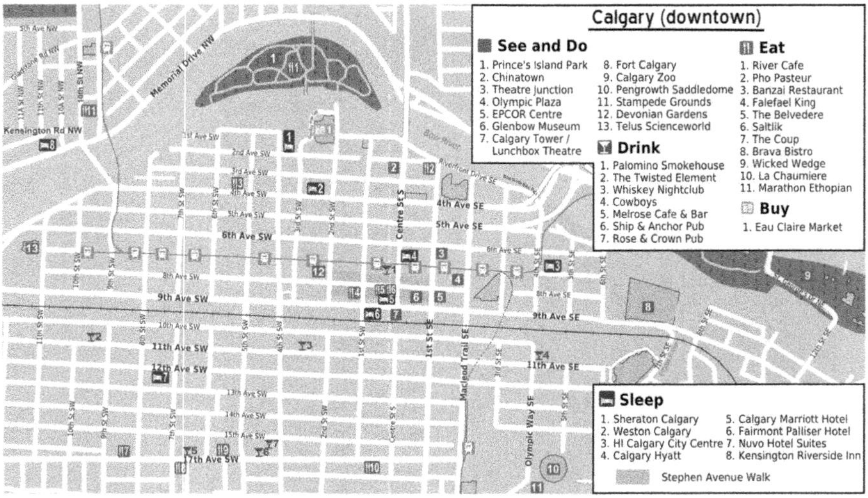

FIGURE 1.10 Wikivoyage-style map of downtown Calgary, AB, and the Beltline area. Image by Wikimedia user Shaund, https://commons.wikimedia.org/wiki/File:Calgary_downtown_map.png, used under a Creative Commons Attribution-Share Alike 4.0 International license, https://creativecommons.org/licenses/by-sa/4.0/legalcode.

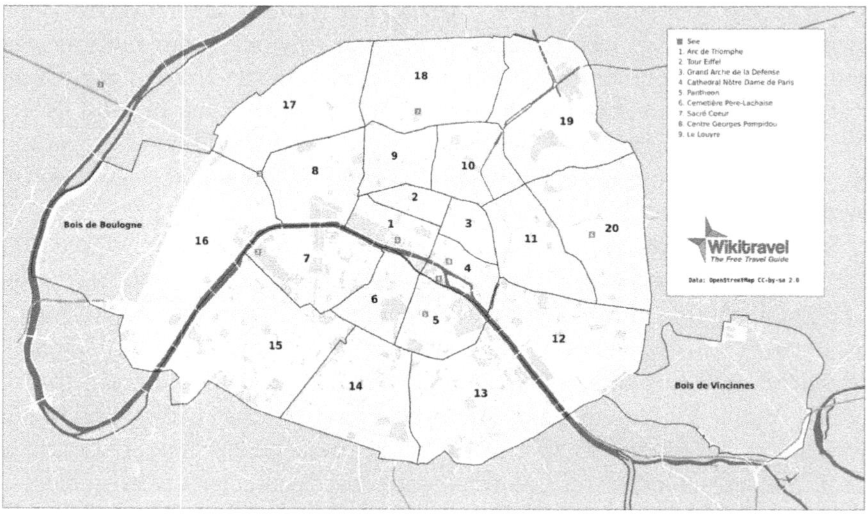

FIGURE 1.11 Map of the arrondissements of Paris. Image by Wikimedia user Mark Jaroski, https://commons.wikimedia.org/wiki/File:Paris_overview_map_with_listings.png, used under a Creative Commons ShareAlike 1.0 Generic license, https://creativecommons.org/licenses/sa/1.0/legalcode.

FIGURE 1.12 Seaside, a Florida Panhandle Beach Community. Image by Flickr user JR P, https://www.flickr.com/photos/ugardener/6861987144/, used under a Creative Commons Attribution-NonCommercial 2.0 Generic license, https://creativecommons.org/licenses/by-nc/2.0/legalcode.

of New Jersey and the Eichler suburbs in California used aesthetic qualities to symbolize relatedness and harmony. These Planned Unit Developments (PUDs) designed groupings of varied and compatible land uses within one subdivision. The regulatory ability to design houses, streets, sidewalks and pedestrian ways simultaneously allowed them to work together to enhance the whole. New Urbanist developments, such as Seaside, Florida, arose in the US in the 1980s from an intention among developers to create communities akin to old world villages (Figure 1.12). These developments employ features including a central meeting place, walkable streets, and visually coherent buildings. The latter is achieved by the use of matching colors and materials, which creates a recognized harmony, harking to the material palettes of historic towns. In this image of Seaside, we see houses of uniform height with gabled roofs, porches, and varied pastel colors within a limited palette that create a common space, enhanced by trees and two white entry columns, for recreation, parking, bicycling, children's play, and informal neighboring.

Advantages of the PSA Taste Model

The harmonization of the pragmatic and symbolic through aesthetics is a richly detailed nuanced process, different in almost every context, but its principles are consistent. By using the PSA model of taste, all scales of the environment—interiors, buildings, landscapes, and cities—can be characterized by their relative emphasis on the expression of pragmatic, symbolic, and aesthetic concerns. One could go on to analyze even larger entities like regions.

You, the reader, could consider the pragmatic and symbolic features of the block or building where you live, or how you yourself have arranged your things inside your home. In the case of neighborhoods, how much attention has been given to making aesthetic unity out of the street, sidewalk, building facades, building height, driveways, cars, telephone poles, sign posts, trees, flowers, and planting strips? Some neighborhoods will have more aesthetic unity than others. Socio-economic class significantly influences neighborhood design, landscaping, and maintenance, but two comparable neighborhoods can have different taste profiles from one another. In the case of buildings and houses, how many symbolic references can you identify? There are so many possibilities—Cape Cod, King Tut, classical Greece, space travel, alpine, sierran, desert ecologies, and more. How many aesthetic dimensions have been used, and are they consistent with the cultural epochs being referenced?

As for the way you arrange your objects, are you a modernist, a romantic, a colonial purist, an eco-freak, someone who has curated away most anything that would distract from a single message? Most likely, you probably have a mix of things—gifts, things you inherited, things you have chosen including contemporary high-tech kitchenware or digital items. Have you put similar colors together? How many other aesthetic dimensions like texture, shape and size have you engaged? Your friends and relatives may assemble things in the same way if you come from a subculture with established norms for display, but today they are more likely to do so differently since friends and even family are likely to come from different backgrounds.

The PSA model allows us to appreciate such differences because it is analytic, democratic, and nonjudgmental. You may not *like* or understand the way a space is decorated or designed, but if you can become aware of what the space is expressing, whether consciously or not, you may be able to contemplate with equanimity why those design choices were made. This is a significant cultural application of the PSA Taste Model. Because the model is not confined to contemporary American or European cultures, it can be used to analyze taste in other historical periods, including pre-industrial civilizations, as well as in contemporary global settings. The PSA Taste Model has the capacity to mitigate moralistic judgment, class discrimination, and even racism.

As the world continues to globalize, and as design programs in universities everywhere accept greater numbers of international students and more people join design professions abroad, the PSA Taste Model's cultural applications are particularly relevant. It places professional designers and laypersons on a continuum: designers can account more thoroughly for their clients' social contexts and needs, and feel confident that their clients and audiences understand the principles of practicality, expression, and composition. Conversely, clients can better understand what motivates designers' decisions, and speak with them more confidently about their visions. Further, the simplicity of the PSA Model gives design educators a comprehensible way to make explicit the taste rules they are teaching; in turn, students can feel less intimidated or confused, and more confident to learn about and develop their own taste profile, to express taste in their own designs, and to discuss taste in others, using a common language.

Notes

1 Anthropologist Ellen Dissanayake (Dissanayake, Ellen. 2000. "Two Orphans and a Dog: Art and Transformation." *Haystack Mountain School of Crafts*, 4) believes that artistic assembly may be inherent to humans because of our impulse to order things even before the process gets connected to social status.
2 Symbolism is one way to establish cultural importance and dominance. What gets promoted culturally and historically generally only encompasses dominant values and therefore leaves out (and can oppress) swathes of people.
3 Even a single object can be viewed through the PSA framework if we consider that any given object is made of selected and assembled materials to meet an intended purpose in a distinctive composition.
4 Peter Lamarque, "The first use of the term *aesthetics* in something like its modern sense is commonly attributed to Alexander Baumgarten in 1735." *Oxford Encyclopedia*, "History of Aesthetics," accessed October 6, 2020. https://www.oxfordbibliographies.com/view/document/obo-9780195396577/obo-9780195396577-0002.xml#:~:text=The%20first%20use%20of%20the,and%20Francis%20Hutcheson%20mark%20the.

References

Bourdieu, Pierre. (1984). *Distinction: A Social Critique of the Judgment of Taste*. Cambridge: Harvard University Press. (Original work published 1979).
Chapin, F. Stuart. (1935). "A Measurement of Social Status." In *Contemporary American Institutions: A Sociological Analysis*, 373–397. New York: Harper & Brothers Publishers.
Cranz, Galen. (2004). "A New Way of Thinking about Taste." In *The Nature of Craft and the Penland Experience*, 130–136. Lark, NY. Republished in 2013 in *Environmental Design Research: The Body, the City, and the Buildings in Between*, edited by Galen Cranz and Eleftherios Pavlides. San Diego: Cognella.
Dissanayake, Ellen. (2000). "Two Orphans and a Dog: Art and Transformation." *Haystack Mountain School of Crafts*, 4.
Gans, Herbert. (1974). *Popular Culture and High Culture*. New York: Basic Books.
Gans, H. J. (1999). *Popular culture and high culture (Rev. ed.)*. Basic Books. (Original work published 1974).
Gartman, David. (1991). "Culture as Class Symbolization or Mass Reification? A Critique of Bourdieu's Distinction." *American Journal of Sociology*, 97, no. 2 (September): 421–447.

Kleinman, Kent, Merwood-Salisbury, Joanna, and Weinthal, Lois, editors. (2012). *After Taste: Expanded Practice in Interior Design*. New York: Princeton Architectural Press.
Lamarque, Peter. "History of Aesthetics." *Oxford Encyclopedia*, accessed October 25, 2012. https://www.oxfordbibliographies.com/view/document/obo-9780195396577/obo-9780195396577-0002.xml#:~:text=The%20first%20use%20of%20the,and%20Francis%20Hutcheson%20mark%20the
Veblen, Thorstein. (1899). *The Theory of the Leisure Class*. New York: Modern Library.

CONNECTING 2

As Cranz and Rushton highlighted in the previous chapter, the artifacts we place and design decisions we all make within our spaces, or those we create for others, reflect our identities and preferences. Moreover, these decisions also have the power to influence our thoughts, feelings, and behaviors. In psychology, "emotion regulation" refers to the ability to control our emotions (Gross, 2001). Typically, this control is internal and occurs when interacting with other people or learning to process our thoughts and feelings. However, some scholars speculate that people can intentionally use their environments to impact how they regulate their emotions (Graham et al., 2015). Spaces can aid in this process through the personal items chosen for display, like keeping a favorite photo of our pet beside our desk, ready to help soothe after a stressful email exchange.

The colors, textures, and materials selected for environments can also help set the stage. For example, a hotel lobby might incorporate overstuffed seating in boldly contrasting patterns surrounded by colorful artwork to create a lively atmosphere that encourages conversation. Conversely, a spa might include warm woods, plush white towels and robes, and muted wall colors to evoke a sense of calm and restoration. These design choices reflect not only taste but are meant to elicit specific feelings and behaviors from guests. Further, these decisions translate across contexts—from private homes to small shared public spaces such as offices, hotels, and bars to grand spaces like museums, cathedrals, outdoor plazas, and even entire cityscapes.

In the next chapter, data strategist Hanna Negami and neuroscientist Colin Ellard delve into the influence of spaces on our emotions by focusing on the experience of "awe." Through this lens, Negami and Ellard illuminate the relationship between space and emotion, tracing back through theories

DOI: 10.4324/9781003004622-7

and scientific findings to explain how this connection occurs and how it may manifest in contemporary times.

References

Gross, J. J. 2001. "Emotion Regulation in Adulthood: Timing Is Everything." *Current Directions in Psychological Science*, 10: 214–219. https://doi.org/10.1111/1467-8721.00152

Graham, L. T., Gosling, S. D., and Travis, C. K. 2015. "The Psychology of Home Environments: A Call for Research on Residential Space." *Perspectives on Psychological Science*, 10, no. 3: 346–356. https://doi.org/10.1177/1745691615576761

2

FROM THE SUBLIME TO THE VERTIGINOUS

The Psychology of Awe-chitecture

Hanna Negami and Colin Ellard

Introduction

One of the earliest known human construction projects can be found in south-east Turkey at Göbekli Tepe (see Figure 2.1). The site consists of massive stone columns depicting fantastical monsters constructed about 10 to

FIGURE 2.1 Göbekli Tepe Site

Note: Photo by Teoman Cimit/CC BY-SA 3.0.

DOI: 10.4324/9781003004622-8

12,000 years ago. This dating suggests that these columns were erected prior to human sedentation, which means that they would have required the coordinated effort of large numbers of people who did not live together but who congregated specifically to build the structures. This realization led Klaus Schmidt, the discoverer of the ruins at Göbekli Tepe, to assert that "first came the temple, then the city" (MacLeod, 2019; Schmidt, 2000). Schmidt's meaning was that there was evidence for an inversion of the conventional way of thinking that humans build to satisfy ordinary affordances of everyday life such as organizing and containing behavior. Instead, this archeological evidence suggests that the original purpose of building may have had as much to do with sculpting human emotion as it did with facilitating the pragmatic aspects of our lives. Though the site's function is not clear, our best guesses are that it served as a place of refuge, healing, or relief from the anxieties of a species newly arising to full awareness of its fragility and mortality. Though architecture has advanced over subsequent millennia, our modern buildings may not be so different in this respect. *Intentionally or not, buildings influence how we feel.*

How Spaces Influence Emotions

Recently, there has been growing interest in deconstructing with more precision the relationship between the design of a space and the emotional state that it inspires. Some progress has been made in developing scientific methods to study such relationships (see reviews by Ellard, 2015 and Goldhagen, 2017). Not only can we use refined psychological methods to assess mental state through questionnaires, but we can also use biometric measures like skin conductance, heart rate, brain waves and eye movements to appraise the manner in which physiological state is influenced by our surroundings. Measurement of such physiological variables can give us a window into a person's emotional state. State-of-the-art developments in sensor technology allow us to collect such data on-the-fly in field settings (Ellard, 2017). Immersive virtual reality provides opportunities for measurement of such relationships in simulations (Mazumder, Spiers & Ellard, 2020). What has become clear through these efforts is that there are powerful and measurable relationships between architectural design elements and the palette of human emotion.

Some of the environmental factors that influence emotion are related to simple perceptual properties like geometry or pattern. For example, according to prospect-refuge theory (Appleton, 1975), we find the most comfort in locations that afford us both information about our surroundings (prospect) and protection from risk (refuge). In other words, the geometric shape of an environment, as defined by its outer contours, can influence psychological state. This notion, rooted in the biology of habitat selection (Tinbergen, 1952), has been taken up in design and architecture (Dosen & Ostwald, 2013). In particular, it has been argued to form the basis of some aesthetic elements of the designs of Le Corbusier (Unwin, 2010), Alvar Aalto (Roberts, 2003), and Frank Lloyd Wright (Hildebrand, 1991), among others. In addition, there is empirical support for a human preference for particular locations even in featureless virtual environments with varying geometries that provided differing degrees of prospect and refuge (Wiener & Franz, 2005).

Expanding on Appleton's observations and taking into account findings that suggest a powerful impact of views of nature on human thought and feeling, Eleanor and Stephen Kaplan developed a more comprehensive framework called attention-restoration theory to describe the relationship between settings and behavior (Kaplan & Kaplan, 1989). Their framework included not only the influence of natural views but also certain aspects of the geometry of space. For example, scenes that contained "mystery" were those in which the viewer was invited to explore a setting more deeply. Think of the alluring bend in a trail or even an urban landscape that invites the viewer in. Their work is part of a broader interest in the importance of having a sense of vitality in scenes both built and natural, as has been described both by architectural theoreticians (Alexander, 2003; Salingaros, 2006), planners (Jacobs, 2016), and psychologists (see review by Ellard, 2020). Recent work suggests that such responses to vitality may be undergirded by low-level perceptual properties of nature scenes, such as spatial frequency—a rough proxy of the level of fine detail present in an image, which is captured to some extent by the mathematical construct of self-similarity or fractality (Biederman & Vessel, 2006; Coburn et al., 2019; Valtchanov & Ellard, 2015), and so likely biologically based.

There is little doubt that the physical features of a setting can influence emotional state through mechanisms that may be biologically rooted. However, it is also obvious that our associations with a place, its role in our culture, and our memories will also have a potent impact on our emotional response to it (Smith et al., 2009). Much of the abundant literature on place attachment refers to such factors, perhaps shown most clearly in our attachment to religious places (Mazumdar & Mazumdar, 2004). Ultimately, it would be a mistake to see the two realms of cultural and historical influences on place-related behavior and their biological roots as entirely separate. Even at the level of neurobiology, there is evidence for interplay between the two (Causadias et al., 2017).

The Psychology of Awe

One example of a particularly powerful emotion that mediates the relationship between the built environment and elicited response is awe. Contemporary psychology defines awe as a complex emotion provoked by a sense of perceptual vastness that results in cognitive accommodation, or a need to readjust one's existing mental schemas (Keltner & Haidt, 2003).

Like many ideas in psychology, the study of awe has its roots in philosophy. In 1757, Edmund Burke published his writings on the sublime, on which Keltner and Haidt (2003) based their psychological definition of awe. Burke wrote that sublime experiences are characterized by two components: the power and the obscurity accompanying the sublime stimulus. Power translated to vastness; and obscurity, or the inability to understand the stimulus, translated to a need for cognitive accommodation. Power in the sublime "derives all its sublimity from the terror with which it is generally accompanied" (p. 60)—for Burke, terror was central to the sublime experience.

Since the 2003 publication of Keltner and Haidt's paper defining awe in psychological terms, the study of awe in psychology has flourished. However, while Keltner and Haidt (2003) and Burke (1757/1990) explicitly characterized awe (or the sublime, in Burke's case) as a fundamentally mixed-valence emotion (one that has both positive and negative qualities), most research on awe treats it as a primarily positive emotion; and most of the findings on the psychological effects of feeling awe have been benefits of feeling awe. For instance, researchers have found positive associations between feeling awe and wellbeing (Gordon et al., 2017), prosocial behavior (Piff et al., 2015; Prade & Saroglou, 2016; Rudd et al., 2012; Stellar et al., 2017), spirituality (Van Cappellen & Saroglou, 2012), feeling connected to other people (Bai et al., 2017; Hornsey et al., 2018), memory (Danvers & Shiota, 2017), and immune health (Stellar et al., 2015).

More recently, however, researchers have begun to explore the darker side of awe and its potential negative psychological effects. While Keltner and Haidt (2003) described awe as existing "in the upper reaches of pleasure and on the boundary of fear" (p. 297), they also theorized the existence of variants of awe, based on different appraisals of the awe-inducing stimulus, such as of beauty or threat. In a 2017 paper, researchers Gordon et al. explored one of these variants, threat-based awe (awe resulting from an appraisal of threat in the awe-inducing stimulus), and how its psychological effects compare to positive awe. Through several studies, they found that participants who felt threat-based awe, compared to participants who felt positive awe, gave lower ratings of wellbeing and higher ratings of powerlessness and fear. Both forms of awe result in feeling small (Bai et al., 2017; Gordon et al., 2017; Piff et al., 2015). This "small self" effect goes beyond the physical comparison between oneself and a large stimulus; it also translates to a feeling of reduced significance in the world (Piff et al., 2015) and has been found (in the study of positive awe) to promote prosocial behavior (Piff et al., 2015) and humility (Stellar et al., 2018). As with most work on awe, the findings on threat-based awe were based on awe elicited using nature imagery (e.g., a video about the formation of tornadoes; Gordon et al., 2017).

To induce awe in the laboratory, most work relies on images or videos of natural scenes and phenomena or participants' memories of their experiences in nature. Architecturally induced awe presents an important area of investigation. Being imbued with social meaning, the spaces we occupy hold great potential to powerfully shape our social psychology. Indeed, there is a nascent line of research investigating awe in the built environment. For instance, Joye and Verpooten (2013) constructed a theoretical argument that religious monumental architecture has been designed to provoke awe to fulfill social functions of religion across history. Specifically, they argue that by provoking awe and making people feel small, religious monumental structures increase community cohesion and openness to religious ideas. Although there is not enough evidence to determine the function of the Göbekli Tepe with certainty, Joye and Verpooten's (2013) work presents the possibility that this structure was purposefully designed to inspire a sense of awe, perhaps thus fostering community or religious experience. Research on awe-inspiring architecture thus builds on psychological work on awe as well as on existing work on the relationship between architecture and emotion.

Current Research on Awe in the Built Environment

As one of the few teams working on examining architecturally induced awe, we have investigated factors that predict awe in the built environment, as well as psychological effects of architecturally induced awe. In one project, we looked at what architectural features might predict awe in building interiors (Negami & Ellard, 2021). To do this, we had a set of photographs of various building interiors rated on objective architectural properties, such as ceiling height, the proportion of windows, and the amount of ornamentation. We had the same photographs rated by a separate group of participants on the spaces' emotional qualities—how the spaces made them feel after imagining occupying each space (see Figure 2.2). When we modeled the architectural features together with the elicited emotions, we found that features that reflected the size, adornment, and sanctity of the interior significantly predicted a feeling of awe. Beyond being one of the only studies showing that we may elicit awe through images of architecture in a laboratory setting, this study also reveals *how* buildings induce awe architecturally—specifically, that the perceptual vastness of architectural interiors (both in physical size and level of ornament) plays a significant role in provoking awe through built space.

More recently, we have begun to extend work on positive and threat-based awe by Gordon et al. (2017) to architectural environments. Although previous work by Joye and Dewitte (2016) used images of skyscrapers to evoke awe and a threat response (measured through freezing, or a slowed motor response), we were not successful in provoking threat-based awe using video of tall skyscrapers. Instead, participants indicated that they felt positive awe

FIGURE 2.2 Example of Photographic Stimuli Used in Experimental Study.

Note: Indoor pool at Hearst Castle. This image was given the highest average awe rating in the study. © 2011 Kay Gaensler Photography (Detail)/CC BY-NC-SA 2.0.

in response to this video, along with another video of architectural environments meant to elicit positive awe, which included shots of buildings such as museums and cathedrals. While this finding can be interpreted optimistically, suggesting that people generally have positive responses even to tall, corporate buildings, it shows the need for more work to determine what about our stimuli led to a positive awe response. It questions whether the original Joye and Dewitte (2016) finding can be replicated in a different context.

We have also compared social effects of natural and architectural spaces that elicit positive awe. Specifically, as previous work has found that positive awe evoked through natural scenes promotes greater engagement with social collectives (Bai et al., 2017; Hornsey et al., 2018), we wished to see whether awe-eliciting architectural environments would do the same. We predicted that because architecture has social meaning that natural environments lack, awe-eliciting built environments would facilitate collective engagement with smaller social groups (e.g., one's community). In contrast, we predicted that natural environments would facilitate integration among larger groups (e.g., people all over the world). We found that both natural and built environments similarly promoted feelings of universality and engagement with larger social groups compared to a control condition. This preliminary finding suggests that architecture, by provoking awe, can promote social cohesion, just as Joye and Verpooten (2013) theorized regarding religious monumental architecture.

More research is needed to fully understand the psychological impact of awe-inspiring architecture. Further research on the antecedents and effects of awe-inducing built space could help designers build new structures that facilitate wellbeing, positive affect, and prosocial behavior, such as places of healing and refuge. On the other hand, are there certain environments in which a feeling of awe would *not* be beneficial—whether through as-yet unknown effects associated with awe, or an undesirable focus on the space itself (such as, perhaps, an operating room, or spaces people must move quickly through)? Much has yet to be uncovered through empirical work, including the dynamic or temporal effects of feeling awe through architecture—such as the experience of architecture revealing itself in stages or experiencing rhythm through architecture. One related question we often receive is the sustained effect of awe or repeated exposure to awe-evoking spaces, including architectural ones. Though there is not yet data to speak to this question, effects of an awe-inducing environment over time may be divergent. For instance, in certain contexts, familiarity over time could dull or decrease a feeling of awe after repeated exposure to the same stimulus, whereas in another context, the knowledge of a stimulus gained through that familiarity could increase a feeling of awe (for example, through learning how much power or material it took to construct a building).

Conclusion and Implications

Empirical work could also help us understand architectural history, such as the architecture of fascist regimes, from a psychological perspective. Adolf Hitler and his architect, Albert Speer, designed monumental architecture for the Nazi regime purposefully to "stun" the masses and make people politically passive (Gordillo, 2015). Are there specific architectural elements that distinguish monumental, awe-eliciting structures that facilitate passivity and conformity from those that facilitate prosocial behavior and wellbeing? If so, what are those elements, and if not, what additional factors might moderate those outcomes?

More recently, the Trump administration issued an executive order called "Make Federal Buildings Beautiful Again," which proposed that all new federal government buildings be built in a neoclassical style (Chicago Sun Times, 2020). Though the order's ostensible purpose is to prevent modernist designs for federal buildings on simple aesthetic grounds, the move is reminiscent of earlier tyrannical efforts to stifle creativity, promote homogeneity, and impose dubious aesthetic standards on institutional architecture. Given the advancing state of our understanding of the relationship between built form and emotional response, it becomes a legitimate concern that such a mandate crosses the line. It moves from being a guideline that might promote beautiful, awe-inspiring architecture to favoring gaudy monuments commissioned by dictators, primarily as a kind of atmospheric propaganda tool. This contemporary example shows that the growing body of theoretical and empirical work on the psychological impact of built space is not strictly confined to academia, but it has direct implications for the world we build for ourselves.

Yet while research on psychological impacts of built space has real-world implications, as the field develops, we must work with architects toward translating findings into design guidelines and avoid prescribing rigid rules that may come from overgeneralizing results. Research in environmental psychology helps us understand the various and subtle ways the spaces we inhabit and occupy shape how we feel and behave. The more recent work on awe-inducing architecture has begun to demonstrate findings and implications as rich and complex as the emotion itself. As we continue to understand architecturally induced awe from a psychological perspective, we can strive to inform the design of healthier buildings that promote feelings of awe and wellbeing in general.

References

Alexander, C. (2003). *The Phenomenon of Life*. CES Publishing.

Appleton, J. (1975). *The Experience of Landscape*. Wiley.

Bai, Y., Maruskin, L. A., Chen, S., Gordon, A. M., Stellar, J., McNeil, G. D., Peng, K., & Keltner, D. (2017). Awe, the diminished self, and collective engagement: Universals and cultural variations in the small self. *Attitudes and Social Cognition*, 113(2), 185–209. https://doi.org/10.1037/pspa0000087

Biederman, I., & Vessel, E. (2006). Perceptual pleasure and the brain. *American Scientist*, 94(3), 249–255. https://doi.org/10.1511/2006.59.247

Burke, E. (1757/1990). *A Philosophical Enquiry into the Origin of our Ideas of the Sublime and Beautiful*. Oxford University Press.

Causadias, J. M., Telzer, E. H., & Lee, R. M. (2017). Culture and biology interplay: An introduction. *Cultural Diversity and Ethnic Minority Psychology*, 23(1), 1–4. https://doi.org/10.1037/cdp0000121

Chicago Sun Times Editorial Board. (2020, February 5). Make federal buildings 'beautiful again?' Trump declares war on modern architecture. *Chicago Sun Times*. https://chicago.suntimes.com/2020/2/5/21124236/architecture-making-federal-buildings-great-again-trump-executive-order-design

Coburn, A., Kardan, O., Kotabe, H., Steinberg, J., Hout, M. C., Robbins, A., MacDonald, J., Hayn-Leichsenring, G., & Berman, M. G. (2019). Psychological responses to natural patterns in architecture. *Journal of Environmental Psychology*, 62, 133–145. https://doi.org/10.1016/j.jenvp.2019.02.007

Danvers, A. F., & Shiota, M. N. (2017). Going off script: Effects of awe on memory for script-typical and -irrelevant narrative detail. *Emotion*, 17(6), 938–952. https://doi.org/10.1037/emo0000277

Dosen, A. S., & Ostwald, M. J. (2013). Prospect and refuge theory: Constructing a critical definition for architecture and design. *International Journal of Design in Society*, 6(1), 9–23. https://doi.org/10.18848/2325-1328/CGP/v06i01/38559

Ellard, C. (2015). *Places of the Heart*. Bellevue Literary Press.
Ellard, C. G. (2020). Neuroscience, wellbeing and urban design: Our universal attraction to vitality. *Psychological Research on Urban Society*, 3(1), 6–17. https://doi.org/10.7454/proust.v3i1.81
Goldhagen, S. W. (2017). *Welcome to Your World: How the Built Environment Shapes our Lives*. HarperCollins.
Gordillo, G. (2015). Nazi architecture as affective weapon. *The Funambulist Papers*, 2, 54–63. https://doi.org/10.21983/P3.0098.1.00
Gordon, A. M., Stellar, J. E., Anderson, C. L., McNeil, G. D., Loew, D., & Keltner, D. (2017). The dark side of the sublime: Distinguishing a threat-based variant of awe. *Journal of Personality and Social Psychology*, 113(2), 310–328. https://doi.org/10.1037/pspp0000120
Hildebrand, G. (1991). *The Wright Space: Pattern & Meaning in Frank Lloyd Wright's Houses*. University of Washington Press.
Hornsey, M. J., Faulkner, C., Crimston, D., & Moreton, S. (2018). A microscopic dot on a microscopic dot: Self-esteem buffers the negative effects of exposure to the enormity of the universe. *Journal of Experimental Social Psychology*, 76, 198–207. https://doi.org/10.1016/j.jesp.2018.02.009
Jacobs, J. (2016). *Vital Little Plans: The Short Works of Jane Jacobs*. S. Zipp, & N. Storring (Eds). Random House.
Joye, Y., & Dewitte, S. (2016). Up speeds you down: Awe-evoking monumental buildings trigger behavioral and perceived freezing. *Journal of Environmental Psychology*, 47, 112–125. https://doi.org/10.1016/j.jenvp.2016.05.001
Joye, Y., & Verpooten, J. (2013). An exploration of the functions of religious monumental architecture from a Darwinian perspective. *Review of General Psychology*, 17(1), 53–68. https://doi.org/10.1037/a0029920
Kaplan, R., & Kaplan, S. (1989). *The Experience of Nature: A Psychological Perspective*. Cambridge University Press.
Keltner, D., & Haidt, J. (2003). Approaching awe, a moral, spiritual, and aesthetic emotion. *Cognition and Emotion*, 17(2), 297–314. https://doi.org/10.1080/02699930302297
Macleod, D. (2019). The architecture hypothesis: Göbekli Tepe and the origins of civilization. *Intertwining*, 2, 24–41.
Mazumdar, S., & Mazumdar, S. (2004). Religion and place attachment: A study of sacred places. *Journal of Environmental Psychology*, 24, 385–397. https://doi.org/10.1016/j.jenvp.2004.08.005
Mazumder, R., Spiers, H.J., & Ellard, C.G. (2020). Exposure to high-rise buildings negatively influences affect: Evidence from real-world and 360-degree video. *Cities and Health*, 6(6). doi: 10.1080/23748834.2020.1839302
Negami, H., & Ellard, C. (2021). How architecture evokes awe: Predicting awe through architectural features of building interiors. *Psychology of Aesthetics, Creativity, and the Arts*. https://doi.org/10.1037/aca0000394
Piff, P. K., Dietze, P., Feinberg, M., Stancato, D. M., & Keltner, D. (2015). Awe, the small self, and prosocial behavior. *Journal of Personality and Social Psychology*, 108(6), 883–899. https://doi.org/10.1037/pspi0000018
Prade, C., & Saroglou, V. (2016). Awe's effects on generosity and helping. *The Journal of Positive Psychology*, 11(5), 522–530. https://doi.org/10.1080/17439760.2015.1127992
Roberts, J. W. (2003). Prospect-refuge theory and Alvar Aalto's experimental house at Muuratsalo: 'What is it that we like about Aalto's site-related architecture and why?'.

In *Progress: The Proceedings of the Twentieth Annual Conference of the Society of Architectural Historians*, Australia and New Zealand, SAHANZ, Sydney. https://hdl.handle.net/1959.13/35452

Rudd, M., Vohs, K. D., & Aaker, J. (2012). Awe expands people's perception of time, alters decision making, and enhances well-being. *Psychological Science*, 23(10), 1130–1136. https://doi.org/10.1177/0956797612438731

Salingaros, N. A. (2006). *A Theory of Architecture*. Umbau-Verlag.

Schmidt, K. (2000). "Zuerst kam der Tempel, dann die Stadt" Vorläu-figer Bericht zu den Grabungen am Göbekli Tepe und am Gürcütepe 1995–1999 ["First came the temple, then the city" Preliminary report on the excavations at Göbekli Tepe and at Gürcütepe 1995–1999]. *Istanbuler Mitteilungen*, 50, 5–41.

Smith, M., Davidson, J., Cameron, L., & Bondi, L. (2009). *Emotion, Place and Culture*. Routledge.

Stellar, J. E., Gordon, A., Anderson, C. L., Piff, P. K., McNeil, G. D., & Keltner, D. (2018). Awe and humility. *Journal of Personality and Social Psychology*, 114(2), 258–269. https://doi.org/10.1037/pspi0000109

Stellar, J. E., Gordon, A. M., Piff, P. K., Cordaro, D., Anderson, C. L., Bai, Y., Maruskin, L. A., & Keltner, D. (2017). Self-transcendent emotions and their social functions: Compassion, gratitude, and awe bind us to others through prosociality. *Emotion Review*, 9(3), 200–207. https://doi.org/10.1177/1754073916684557

Stellar, J. E., John-Henderson, N., Anderson, C. L., Gordon, A. M., McNeil, G. D., & Keltner, D. (2015). Positive affect and markers of inflammation: Discrete positive emotions predict lower levels of inflammatory cytokines. *Emotion*, 15(2), 129–133. https://doi.org/10.1037/emo0000033

Tinbergen, N. (1952). *Social Behaviour in Animals*. Springer.

Unwin, S. (2010). *Twenty Buildings Every Architect Should Understand*. Routledge.

Valtchanov, D., & Ellard, C. G. (2015). Cognitive and affective responses to natural scenes: Effects of low level visual properties on preference, cognitive load and eye-movements. *Journal of Environmental Psychology*, 43, 184–195. https://doi.org/10.1016/j.jenvp.2015.07.001

Van Cappellen, P., & Saroglou, V. (2012) Awe activates religious and spiritual feelings and behavioral intentions. *Psychology of Religion and Spirituality*, 4(3), 223–236. https://doi.org/10.1037/a0025986

Wiener, J. M., & Franz, G. (2005). Isovists as a means to predict spatial experience and behavior. In C. Freksa, M. Knauff, B. Krieg-Brückner, B. Nebel, & T. Barkowsky (Eds.), *Spatial Cognition IV: Reasoning, Action, Interaction* (pp. 42–57). International Spatial Cognition 2004. Lecture Notes in Computer Science, vol. 3343. Springer. https://doi.org/10.1007/978-3-540-32255-9_3

CONNECTING 3

When did you last need instructions for sitting in a chair or climbing stairs? While people may need guidance to operate a sophisticated piece of furniture or navigate a complex building, most intuitively understand how to traverse the spaces, furnishings, and objects around them. In their thought-provoking essay, social psychologists and researchers Kerry Marsh, Benjamin Meagher, and Cassidy Burt explain that people are culturally conditioned to know how to inhabit everyday environments. However, what happens when encountering a space or object that does not fit within mental schemas or cultural norms?

When experiencing an unfamiliar setting, people are much like toddlers who employ social learning by observing and modeling the behavior of others around them. Occupants need help, guidance, and instruction when navigating novel spaces; the same goes for social interaction within these environments. For example, an art museum might intentionally create a provocative environment to prompt visitors to pause and reconsider their surroundings, challenging them to view traditional art in a new way. However, needing to process and explore ambiguity is not helpful in an emergency room where lives depend on doctors and nurses being able to work seamlessly and efficiently (Glass, 2018). As such, it is possible to tune the design of places to enable specific interactions with others and the built environment.

When devising new and familiar experiences, Marsh et al. emphasize the significance of designing spaces that strategically invite action. They advise scaling them to match individual capabilities and incorporating readily detectable features and qualities—also known as affordances—to nudge behavior. Additionally, the authors encourage using sight lines to pique a person's

DOI: 10.4324/9781003004622-9

innate curiosity and provide opportunities for them to transform their spaces. Consider employing these evidence-based approaches in the future to create purposeful spatial experiences.

Reference

Glass, T. (2018). *Prompt: Socially Engaging Objects and Environments.* Birkhäuser.

3

DESIGNING MEANINGFUL ENVIRONMENTS POST-DARWIN

How Spaces Affect Perceptions & Behaviors

Kerry L. Marsh, Benjamin R. Meagher and Cassidy J. Burt

When we pass through a building, our experience of perceiving the environment's features—its walls, doorways, and furnishings—is simply that we directly see what is there. If objects obscure our view of furniture or openings, we discover the rest of the space by walking around in it or by merely moving our heads. If you *think* about how we perceive space, which is not something we typically do, it does not feel as if it involves complex mental puzzles that require piecing together incomplete images of the world. Nevertheless, this common-sense understanding contrasts with many theories of perception grounded in pre-evolutionary, early 19th century notions of how animals perceive, which wrongly inflict great inferential challenges on the perceiver's brains. The only 21st century theory of perceiving and acting that is genuinely post-Darwinian (Heft, 1997) is James Gibson's ecological approach. It posits that people's naïve understanding of what they perceive about the physical world is vastly more correct than traditional views would argue (Gibson, 1966, 1979).

The ecological perspective is grounded in the fact that humans co-evolved with their environments (Swenson & Turvey, 1991). Because of this, humans have perceptual and motoric systems exquisitely adapted to detect the informational regularities in our environments that allow us to act adaptively within them. Although beyond the scope of this essay to unpack, unchanging aspects of our environment—the edges where a chair begins, or where a surface drops off to create a step—are properties of the world that are mathematically specifiable as "invariants" to a moving observer. Thus, even though what we see changes with each millisecond we move, we are nevertheless perceptually attuned to the environmental invariants that inform us about the world. What we are able to detect is in fact "*necessarily specific* to the facts of

DOI: 10.4324/9781003004622-10

FIGURE 3.1 The End of Sitting. Artwork created by Rietveld Architecture-Art-Affordances and Barbara Visser, Photo by Jan Kempenaers. Reproduced with permission from Withagen & Caljouw (2016). In a comparison between workers in a conventional office setting and The End of Sitting environment, Withagen and Caljouw found that 83% of participants in The End of Sitting worked in more than one non-sitting posture, and that participants in this environment felt more energetic and reported higher well-being. No differences were reported between the two office settings in participants' concentration levels and satisfaction with their created product.

the environment and of an animal's movements relative to the environment" (p. 103, Turvey & Shaw, 1999).

Pre-Darwinian theories of perception, however, assume that perceptual systems (e.g., vision) provide only ambiguous and impoverished information about the external world. Such an approach implies that people's use of a space and their reactions to it are learned. How people respond to an environment is based on arbitrary inferences and aesthetic reactions toward it—based mainly on the symbols evoked by a design, past associations, and the social rules of one's culture. Reactions to space are therefore highly normative and arbitrary; if raised in a different culture that did not have chairs and stairs one would not see that these features of a space are for sitting or walking up and down. Such an approach suggests that those who design spaces would need to follow well-established conventions, and rules about symbolism and aesthetics. And if one designed a completely unfamiliar space as depicted in Figure 3.1 or

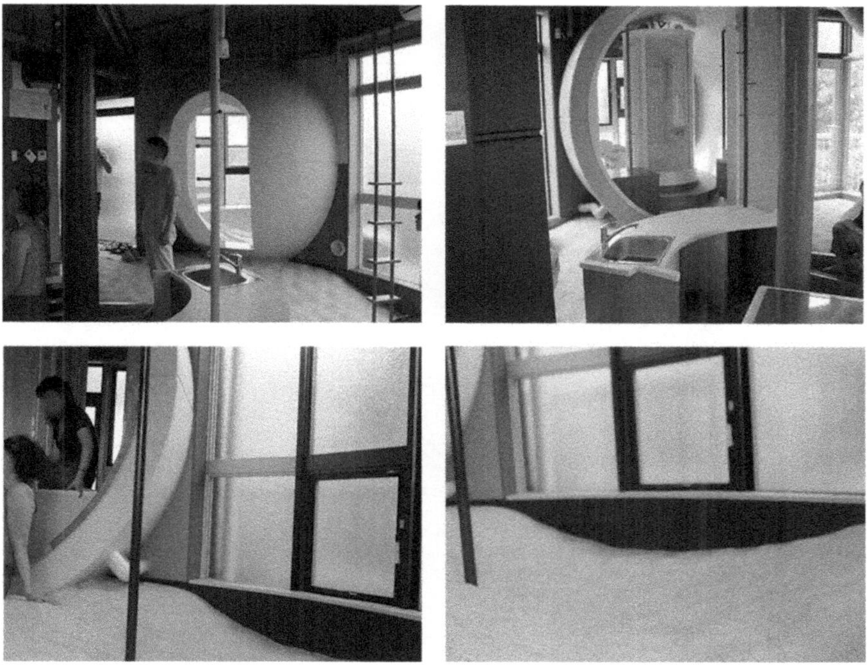

FIGURES 3.2A, 3.2B, 3.2C, AND 3.2D (CLOCKWISE) Arukawa & Gins Reversible Destiny Lofts. Photos taken July 6, 2007 by first author in Mitaka, Tokyo, Japan. The Reversible Destiny Lofts were designed under the philosophy of "procedural architecture," said to give guests the opportunity to discover the full potential of the body and experience challenging environments. These environments may include ladders (Figure 3.2a), rounded rooms and curved floors (Figures 3.2b, 3.2c, and 3.2d), vertical poles for grabbing while moving throughout, and surfaces for multiple purposes like sitting, eating on, or leaning.

Figure 3.2, they would need to provide instructions (e.g., add signs) for how the space should be used.

To evaluate one's novel design, the conventional approach would suggest that a designer could simply show still images of a space, and ask people their judgments and emotional responses to it. In contrast, an ecological perspective would see responses to still images as uninformative. Instead, they would determine the adequacy of a depicted space by observing how successfully people move around in and fully use it (e.g., Withagen & Caljouw, 2016). From an ecological perception perspective such actions will be driven by how well a designer has ensured that *information specifies opportunities to act for individuals and multiple interacting individuals.* From a design perspective,

FIGURE 3.3 Black Lives Matter protest at the steps of the Philadelphia Art Museum steps. Taken by the third author in Philadelphia on June 6, 2020. The design of location allows for solo action such as walking, sitting, or cycling, as well as group action such as making and holding large signs, and standing in groups at different levels on the stairs.

this means thinking hard about whether the features of a complex workspace (in Figure 3.1) or an unusual apartment (in Figure 3.2) match the needs and bodily capabilities of the individuals who inhabit it. Space design should invite people to engage in actions.

Moreover, because human life is fundamentally social, it is important for designers to consider the ways in which the physical environments they create guide or constrain different types of interpersonal interactions. One basic distinction, coined by the English psychiatrist Humphry Osmond (1957), is between *sociopetal* and *sociofugal* settings, i.e., places that facilitate or inhibit social interaction, respectively (see Figure 3.3 for an example of an outdoor, sociopetal space). Osmond, who originally discussed these terms in the context of psychiatric institutions, argued that patients need both: communal rooms that help them form beneficial relationships with staff and other patients, as well as places to retreat to for privacy. Such spaces need to be consciously designed to afford these different types of social experiences, in order to allow occupants to effectively use the environments to help regulate their thoughts, emotions, and behavior (Meagher & Marsh, 2017; Nguyen et al., 2018; Ren et al., 2020; Taylor & Ferguson, 1980). In this essay, we suggest three principles to help guide a socioecological approach to *designing spaces to invite action*.

Principle 1: Design Action-Scaled Spaces

The first principle follows from a Gibsonian position that has become a common refrain in modern psychology: People perceive in order to act. Gibson hypothesized that the changing "flow" of information across the eye's retina as we move directly specifies the functional properties of surfaces and objects.[1] For instance, as young children begin to crawl or walk, they become attuned to information that indicates an object's reach-ability, or a floor's crawl- or walk-ability. By moving around to explore a space, humans determine what actions they can safely complete given the features of the environment. Thus, it is through direct engagement with a space that a child or adult becomes attuned to these features.

Because perception functions to facilitate action, it is important for designers to scale their environments to the action capabilities of those who will wander through it. Spatial designers should determine what action possibilities, or *affordances*, a space provides to the desired inhabitants, whether adults, children, those using a walker, or those pushing a stroller or a wheelchair. Crucially, research reveals that people's individual perceptions and actions in an environment are keenly scaled to one's bodily capabilities.[2] For example, stairs that are of a perfect height for comfortably climbing in a typical gait for adults will be too high for a young child's optimal comfort, because "climb-ability" of stairs is determined by the height of the riser considered *in relation to* the length of one's legs (Warren, 1984).

In the same way, sociopetal spaces must be optimally scaled for the type of social interaction the designer seeks to facilitate. For example, developmental differences dramatically alter the way in which children interact with their peers. A daycare room designed to promote cooperative sharing will be of little use to toddlers only capable of parallel play. Similarly, for adults, settings can be designed in ways that maximize their use for the type of relationships present. The distance between people differs in systematic ways based on their relationship (Hall, 1966) as Figure 3.4 reveals. Interacting at distances of 3 feet or less is comfortable for close friends or family but results in discomfort when interacting with an acquaintance. A space designed for interacting with colleagues should therefore differ from one designed for friends. Space designed to support solitary activity can also vary, based on the motives driving a person's desire for privacy. For example, an individual who wishes to be alone may opt to enter an environment with a large number of people, provided it affords them a sufficient amount of anonymity (Leino-Kilpi et al., 2001).

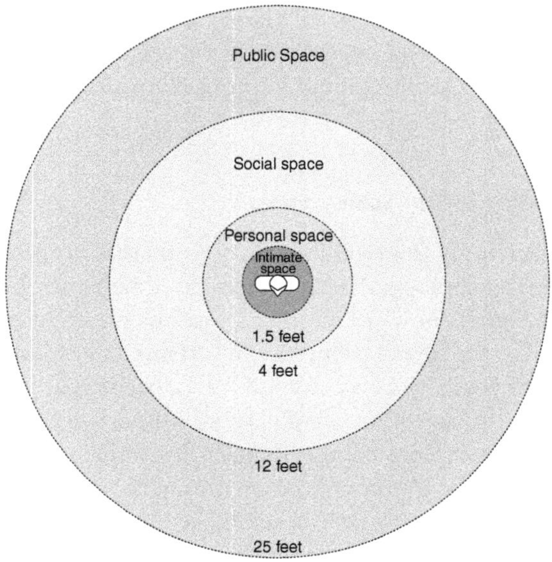

FIGURE 3.4 E. T. Hall's (1966) analysis of personal space suggests that an intimate distance is used with close relationships and allows for behaviors such as hugging or whispering. Family members or close friends interact within the range of personal distance. People who are casual acquaintances will typically interact at a social space distance; in contrast, people typically give public presentations at a public distance from the audience.

Principle 2: Make Affordances Readily Detectable

Other animals discover the affordances of their natural environment through exploration, and humans are no different. To invite action in a space, the affordances need to be readily perceivable with vision or other perceptual systems (e.g., Marsh & Meagher, 2016; Meagher, 2020; Withagen et al., 2012). But a space is likely to fail if a designer relies on the patience or curiosity of humans who must work hard to discover its affordances. As those who design products (such as technological devices) readily find, the actions one can do with a new object can often be difficult to detect at a glance (Norman, 2013).

In general, a designer needs to consider the perspective of those entering a space through different paths. Those who enter a space from different directions have different "isovists" (Benedikt, 1979), which refers to what one can see of the space (in all directions) from a particular point in the space. From some vantage points within a room, certain possibilities for exploration may be impossible to see, as Figure 3.5 illustrates. Moreover, some features that are relatively prominent as one enters a place from one point of entry may be less

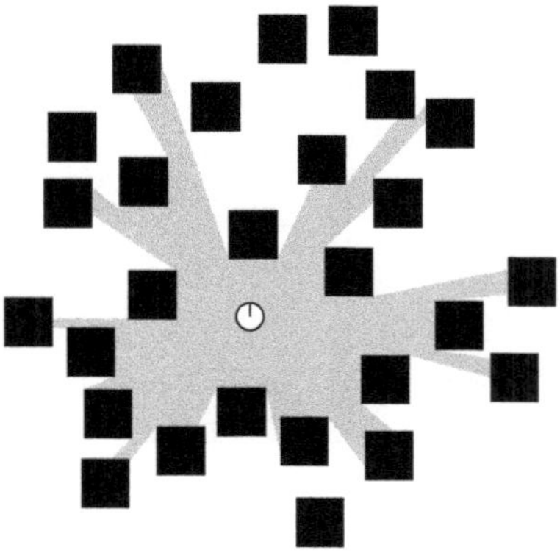

FIGURE 3.5 From a single vantage point in space, a person's 360 degree view (indicated in blue) of their environment is termed the isovist of that point. Here the isovist indicates the person can see all but one of the objects depicted in the lower half of the diagram. In contrast, several more objects in the upper half of the space will be occluded from view until the person shifts their vantage point.

obvious—further away—than from other entries. Features directly in front of our natural line of sight take up a larger visual angle and should be more likely to tempt action.[3] Features that are lit, stimuli that are moving, or features that stand out from the background in other ways should also garner more attention (Taylor et al., 1979).

For designing a space to facilitate social experiences, our second principle suggests that the information specifying social affordances must also be easily detectable to perceivers. That is, people need to be able to recognize the opportunities for interaction in that setting. Likely the greatest source of such information is, quite simply, other people. After all, the capacity to "people watch" is among the chief draws of popular public spaces (Whyte, 1980), and being able to see others can be critical for recognizing an opportunity to communicate. (See Figure 3.6.) A clear example comes from Frank Gehry (2004), who describes how he designed an academic building to promote faculty interaction:

> Just putting the cafeteria in the middle and putting their breakout spaces in view of the cafeteria means they can see when other professors are going to lunch and say, 'Oh Good, I'd like to talk to that guy. He's going to lunch, I'm going to lunch'.
>
> (p. 24)

Thus, the design of the building can itself help its occupants detect social affordances when they become available.

FIGURES 3.6A (LEFT) AND 3.6B (RIGHT) Before and after photos of an affordance-redesign of Slayter Plaza at Denison University, Granville, Ohio. Designed with input from Professor Harry Heft. Photos used by permission, Denison University Communications and Archives. Left, benches are placed in a way that is *sociofugal,* or not encouraging social interaction between students. Right, new benches and chairs are installed in the plaza in a manner that promotes a richer array of social interaction possibilities.

Principle 3: Invite Further Exploration of Affordances

Perceiving and acting are tightly intertwined; what we see in the environment impels us to act. Moreover, our actions illuminate more information to perceive: as one turns a corner, new inviting features of the environment appear. Decades of research in environmental psychology have provided evidence that people tend to like environments more when they provide the opportunity for discovery, a quality referred to as *mystery* (Kaplan et al., 1989; Kaplan & Kaplan, 1989). Perceiving provides new opportunities to act, which in turn provides new possibilities for action that can be seen, or heard, smelled, or felt. In this way, settings that have much to see require actions to see them, and the more one explores the space the more behavioral opportunities one discovers.

How might the affordances of a space be staged in such a way that completing one action (e.g., moving further into the room) yields perceptions that invite further action? Some suggestions come from considering how people move through natural environments. In natural environments, vistas—an opening, semi-enclosed from which one looks out and sees some expanse of nature—are likely to be particularly remarkable and inviting places. Heft's (1997) work on wayfinding reveals that finding one's way through a space involves a sequence of vistas punctuated by key transitions between those vistas. We would expect that those points of transition strongly impel us to move forward (to see the vista fully revealed) more so than other pathway segments.

Thus, designers might structure built environments with an eye on pulling people toward a "reveal," where visual and auditory information in the transition from one space to another tantalizingly suggests a new vista. For instance,

FIGURES 3.7A (TOP) AND 3.7B (BOTTOM) Stairs and escalators inside the Central Library in Seattle, Washington. Photos used with permission from the Seattle Public Library. Designed by architect Rem Koolhaas and LMN Architects. Photos used with permission from the Central Library. The stairs in Figure 3.7a are bright red, a unique feature of the actionable space which invites library visitors to explore the upper and lower floors. The escalator in Figure 3.7b is bright yellow, as are many other areas which invite visitors to explore each floor of the library.

a path forward might lead to detecting an increased volume of sound indicating a different activity underway in front of us, or glimpses might be seen of new structures and potential affordances that draw us toward that doorway. Unfortunately, wayfinding through many buildings involves passing through a series of uninformative opaque hallways between rooms. If major pathways through a space, such as the stairways and escalators in Figures 3.7a and 3.7b, are designed to reveal new affordances as one passes through it, it invites travel along the pathway and may aid navigation as well.

Additionally, our actions might not merely uncover new possibilities for action, but actually change the setting in some way, promoting still further actions—for oneself or others nearby. Indeed, this may explain the power of movable features of the environment (Whyte, 1980): individuals create new possibilities by choosing where to place a movable chair. And this transformation also changes the interaction opportunities for others as well. A series of studies by Withagen and colleagues (Jeschke et al., 2020; Jongeneel et al., 2015; Sporrel et al., 2017; Withagen & Caljouw, 2017) demonstrates these ecological principles in the context of children's playground behavior. When given the opportunity to create their own playground design using jumping stones, children do not create configurations with aesthetic considerations or patterns in mind. Instead, stones were placed with varying widths. However, these placements were not arbitrary: the gap widths were instead scaled to the jumping ability of the child (Jongeneel et al., 2015). By being able to explore and adapt their environment, the children regulate their own play behavior in ways that are actually more active and more challenging (Sporrel et al., 2017).

Conclusion

The proof of an environment's adequacy is whether it is experienced as welcoming to the people (solo or collectively) who enter and spend time in it. Stripping a space down to the barest of features, perhaps in some form of minimalist modernist architecture, is therefore not what is suggested here. Instead, the socioecological approach emphasizes that aesthetic qualities are not the only components of a welcoming space. Rather, the act of accurately scaling to the behavioral needs of a setting's users will inherently contribute to creating a more inviting and engaging environment. Spaces can invite appropriate action by making salient the opportunities, or indeed, barriers to action, and by supporting continued perceptual exploration that reveals new information and behavioral opportunities about the setting.

Notes

1 Gibson hypothesized that people can detect regularities—what he referred to as *invariant* structures—in optic flow that specifies the functional properties of surfaces and objects.

2 Research focusing on both simple solo actions like walking up a staircase (Warren, W. H. (1984). Perceiving affordances: Visual guidance of stair climbing. Journal of Experimental Psychology: Human Perception and Performance, 10(5), 683–703), or joint actions like moving objects together (Richardson, M. J., Marsh, K. L., & Baron, R. M. (2007). Judging and actualizing intrapersonal and interpersonal affordances. Journal of Experimental Psychology: Human Perception and Performance, 33(4), 845), verifies Gibson's hypothesis that people are sensitive to information that specifies affordances. Research demonstrates that there are objective features of the environment, that when considered in relation to an objective feature of an individual, critically determine the point at which a behavior is possible or impossible such as stair climbing or moving an object alone. Moreover, people's perceptions and attempts to engage in action are precisely predicted by the mathematical function of these two variables.

3 This concept is supported by social cognitive research exploring how attentional factors affect our perceptions of other people. Specifically, distinctiveness is important: a unique feature that stands out in the visual display will reap more attention, much like being the only male or female in a group of people accentuates others' perceptions of their causal impact (Taylor, S. E., & Fiske, S. T. (1978). Salience, attention, and attribution: Top of the head phenomena. In L. Berkowitz (Ed.), Advances in Experimental Social Psychology (Vol. 11, pp. 249–288). Academic Press). People who are salient are more likely to be remembered as having talked more or had more impact on the decision-making of a group for instance. Features that are lit, stimuli that are moving, or features that stand out from the background in other ways should garner more attention (Taylor, S. E., Crocker, J., Fiske, S. T., Sprinzen, M., & Winkler, J. D. (1979). The generalizability of salience effects. Journal of Personality and Social Psychology, 37(3), 357–368).

References

Benedikt, M. L. (1979). To take hold of space: isovists and isovist fields. *Environment and Planning B: Planning and Design*, 6(1), 47–65.

Caljouw, S. R., de Vries, R., & Withagen, R. (2017). RAAAF's office landscape The End of Sitting: Energy expenditure and temporary comfort when working in non-sitting postures. *PLoS ONE*, 12(11), e0187529. https://doi.org/10.1371/journal.pone.0187529

Gehry, F. O. (2004). Reflections on design and architectural practice. In R. J. Boland Jr., & F. Collopy (Eds.), *Managing as Design* (pp. 19–35). Stanford University Press.

Gibson, J. J. (1966). *The Senses Considered as Perceptual Systems.* Houghton Mifflin.

Gibson, J. J. (1979). *The Ecological Approach to Visual Perception.* Houghton Mifflin.

Hall, E. T. (1966). *The Hidden Dimension* (First Paperback Edition edition). Anchor. Doubleday & Company: Garden City, NY.

Heft, H. (1997). The relevance of Gibson's ecological approach to perception for environment-behavior studies. In G. T. Moore, & R. W. Marans (Eds.), *Advances in Environment, Behavior, and Design, Vol. 4: Toward the Integration of Theory, Methods, Research, and Utilization.* (pp. 71–108). Plenum Press

Jeschke, A. M., de Lange, A. M. M., Withagen, R., & Caljouw, S. R. (2020). Crossing the gap: Older adults do not create less challenging stepping stone configurations than young adults. *Frontiers in Psychology*, 11. Article number 1657. https://doi.org/10.3389/fpsyg.2020.01657

Jongeneel, D., Withagen, R., & Zaal, F. T. J. M. (2015). Do children create standardized playgrounds? A study on the gap-crossing affordances of jumping stones. *Journal of Environmental Psychology*, 44, 45–52. https://doi.org/10.1016/j.jenvp.2015.09.003

Kaplan, R., & Kaplan, S. (1989). *The Experience of Nature: A Psychological Perspective* (1989–98477-000). Cambridge University Press; psyh.

Kaplan, R., Kaplan, S., & Brown, T. (1989). Environmental preference: A comparison of four domains of predictors. *Environment and Behavior*, 21(5), 509–530. psyh. https://doi.org/10.1177/0013916589215001

Leino-Kilpi, H., Välimäki, M., Dassen, T., Gasull, M., Lemonidou, C., Scott, A., & Arndt, M. (2001). Privacy: A review of the literature. *International Journal of Nursing Studies*, 38(6), 663–671. psyh. https://doi.org/10.1016/s0020-7489(00)00111-5

Marsh, K. L., & Meagher, B. R. (2016). Affordances and interpersonal coordination. In P. Passos, K. Davids, & J. Y. Chow (Eds.), *Interpersonal Coordination and Performance in Social Systems* (pp. 245–258). Routledge.

Meagher, B. R. (2020). Ecologizing social psychology: The physical environment as a necessary constituent of social processes. *Personality and Social Psychology Review*, 24(1), 3–23.

Meagher, B. R., & Marsh, K. L. (2017). Seeking the safety of sociofugal space: Environmental design preferences following social ostracism. *Journal of Experimental Social Psychology*, 68, 192–199. https://doi.org/10.1016/j.jesp.2016.07.004

Nguyen, T. T., Ryan, R. M., & Deci, E. L. (2018). Solitude as an approach to affective self-regulation. *Personality and Social Psychology Bulletin*, 44(1), 92–106. https://doi.org/10.1177/0146167217733073

Norman, D. (2013). *The Design of Everyday Things* (Revised & Expanded Ed.). Basic Books.

Osmond, H. (1957). Function as the basis of psychiatric ward design. *Mental Hospitals*, 8(4), 23–27. https://doi.org/10.1176/ps.8.4.23

Ren, D., Wesselmann, E. D., & van Beest, I. (2020). Seeking solitude after being ostracized: A replication and beyond. *Personality and Social Psychology Bulletin*, 47(3), 426–440. 0146167220928238. https://doi.org/10.1177/0146167220928238

Richardson, M. J., Marsh, K. L., & Baron, R. M. (2007). Judging and actualizing intrapersonal and interpersonal affordances. *Journal of Experimental Psychology: Human Perception and Performance*, 33(4), 845.

Sporrel, K., Caljouw, S. R., & Withagen, R. (2017). Gap-crossing behavior in a standardized and a nonstandardized jumping stone configuration. *PLoS One*, 12(5), e0176165. https://doi.org/10.1371/journal.pone.0176165

Swenson, R., & Turvey, M. T. (1991). Thermodynamic reasons for perception--action cycles. *Ecological Psychology,* 3(4), 317–348.

Taylor, S. E., Crocker, J., Fiske, S. T., Sprinzen, M., & Winkler, J. D. (1979). The generalizability of salience effects. *Journal of Personality and Social Psychology*, 37(3), 357–368.

Taylor, R. B., & Ferguson, G. (1980). Solitude and intimacy: Linking territoriality and privacy experiences. *Journal of Nonverbal Behavior*, 4(4), 227–239. psyh. https://doi.org/10.1007/bf00986199

Taylor, S. E., & Fiske, S. T. (1978). Salience, attention, and attribution: Top of the head phenomena. In L. Berkowitz (Ed.), *Advances in Experimental Social Psychology* (Vol. 11, pp. 249–288). Academic Press.

Turvey, M. T., & Shaw, R. E. (1999). Ecological foundations of cognition: I. Symmetry and specificity of animal-environment systems. *Journal of Consciousness Studies*, 6, 95–110.

Warren, W. H. (1984). Perceiving affordances: Visual guidance of stair climbing. *Journal of Experimental Psychology: Human Perception and Performance*, 10(5), 683–703.

Whyte, W. H. (1980). *The Social Life of Small Urban Spaces*. Conservation Foundation.

Withagen, R., & Caljouw, S. R. (2016). 'The end of sitting': An empirical study on working in an office of the future. *Sports Medicine*, 46(7), 1019–1027.

Withagen, R., & Caljouw, S. R. (2017). Aldo Van Eyck's playgrounds: Aesthetics, affordances, and creativity. *Frontiers in Psychology*, 8. Article number 1130. https://doi.org/10.3389/fpsyg.2017.01130

Withagen, R., De Poel, H. J., Araújo, D., & Pepping, G. J. (2012). Affordances can invite behavior: Reconsidering the relationship between affordances and agency. *New Ideas in Psychology*, 30(2), 250–258.

CONNECTING 4

In the previous chapter, Marsh et al. unpacked how affordances (our perception of opportunities for interaction) provide information about a space. In this next chapter, researcher and interior designer Susan Sung Eun Chung takes this concept further, venturing deeper into the realm of spatial cognition. More specifically, Chung examines how people's understanding of spaces can unlock the hidden potential of their environments.

Throughout *People and Spaces*, authors discuss the dual qualities of the person-place relationship, encompassing ways people shape environments and how environments shape people. Here, Chung introduces an essential theory that explains the directionality of this dynamic relationship, distinguishing between reactive and proactive approaches. Chung also expertly navigates how a places' spatial, ambient, and symbolic attributes affect an individual's sensory, cognitive, and psychosocial processes. What is the ultimate goal?—to achieve a harmonious and purposeful outcome.

Chung demonstrates the application of these theories through case studies on workplace design. Employing these projects, she poses critical questions: How can a workplace be designed for creativity? And how can a workplace support and enable innovation versus serve as a disruptor? These examples illustrate theory in action and help guide all of us to intentionally optimize our spaces.

DOI: 10.4324/9781003004622-11

4

EXPLORING PLACE POTENTIAL

Understanding Purpose, Perception and Activation

Susan Sung Eun Chung

Place can be defined as a space that has purposeful meaning. Space is created from physical boundaries but, when a person establishes an emotional connection with it, it is perceived as a meaningful place that offers opportunities through its design. A large open room in a high school may provide students opportunities to run around, play games, read, complete assignments, etc., but these activities are best enabled through design. Citizen HKS (a public interest design and global social impact initiative of the architecture and engineering firm, HKS) reimagined a corner in a large classroom space at Lane Technical College Preparatory High School in Chicago and transformed this 456 square foot space into a sensory well-being hub that could calm students with developmental disabilities (Figure 4.1). Using data-driven insights, the demountable frames that are assembled as a high-tech playset include different activity zones with sensory affordances that have proven to improve neuro-divergent adolescents. To the students, faculty, and parents, this sensory well-being hub is a place being actively sought to find equilibrium. While space provides the physical dimension of our existence, place takes this further by shaping context and experience within the physical area and layers in contextual meaning associated with it through time and emotion.

We strive to create boundaries around limitless expansion—time and space—to better process and comprehend the world around us. We scan for cues to orient ourselves within the situation and context. The psychological field of spatial cognition looks at how we acquire information and use knowledge about our environment to determine where we are, how to obtain resources, and how to navigate geographies to find our way to destinations. Spatial information not only provides us with basic information on our surroundings but also has the potential to empower us to thrive in performing

DOI: 10.4324/9781003004622-12

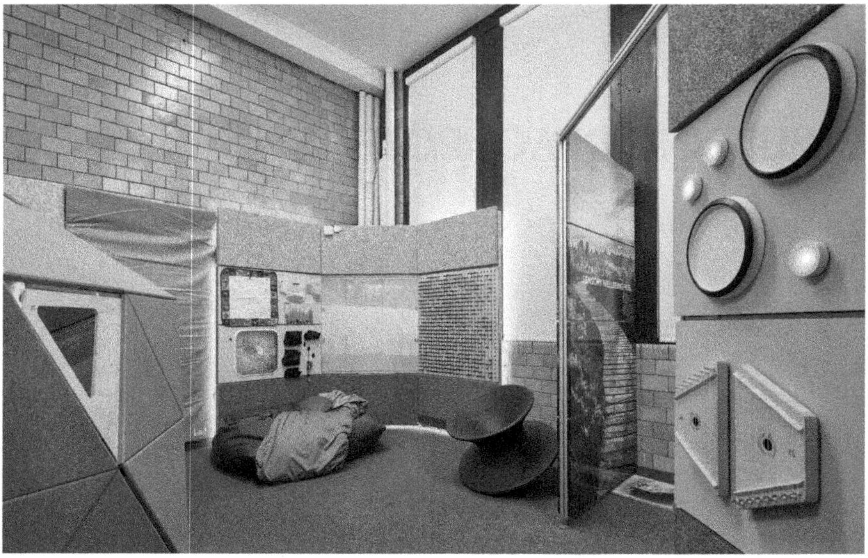

FIGURE 4.1 Sensory Well-being Hub at Lane Tech High School in Chicago, Designed by Citizen HKS (Photo Credit: Hannah Jaggers).

activities within space and time. But how much do we activate these spaces to enrich our experiences?

Purpose of Place Established: Connecting with Space

People and their innate and learned characteristics shape their perceptions of space. Some are more aware of, or attentive to, their surroundings and develop an understanding of the purpose of the space that transcends beyond what is seen. For example, the Unity Health Care Brentwood waiting room has a quilt wall with triangles wrapped in fabric with visually complex patterns and bright, saturated colors and with some that have inspirational words, collected from input by the community, silk-screened onto the fabric (Figure 4.2). For the Brentwood community located in Washington, D.C., this detail is not just a designed element that adds visual interest in the waiting room but a symbolic gesture of care toward the patients and their caregivers. Participants in this community exercise may feel a direct connection to this wall due to their contribution but, for those that are reading the words for the first time, their attention to the words on the wall and the meaning extrapolated from them also has the potential to lead to a positive emotional response toward the care they are awaiting.

A place comes to life through the interactions between people and place—how people experience and spend time in the place they inhabit. Spaces may be designed with purpose but until these spaces are activated and used accordingly, the intention is dormant. When people and place come together in thoughtfully designed spaces, people's experiences can transform the place

FIGURE 4.2 Unity Health Care Brentwood Waiting Room, Designed by Gensler (Photo Credit: Wray Ward).

with purposeful interactions. We know from past visits that libraries are typically quiet areas to read, write, or study. We can do these activities in other environments such as at home, in a classroom, and in coffee shops, but they each provide a different atmosphere and opportunity. The theory of affordances is founded on this relationship between a person and their interaction with the surrounding objects in the space. The theory argues that people perceive space through affordances, or opportunities for action, not specific qualities (Gibson, 1986). Affordances refer to an object's perceived and actual properties, especially those that determine its use (Norman, 2002). We go to libraries when we desire a quiet environment among people using the space similarly versus coffee shops when we seek background noise and the opportunity to be in the presence of others who are doing dissimilar activities. The spatial properties perceived by the individual are interpreted and then acted upon, resulting in an interaction between people and place.

Place Potential Unleashed: Perception and Activation

The designed space is a multi-faceted construct consisting of many parts that come together in creating place potential. The layout and functionality of fixtures, furnishings, and equipment compose the *spatial attributes*, the physical stimuli that is intangible in space (e.g., lighting, temperature, sound, and color) determine the *ambient attributes*, and implicit and explicit messages that add interpretation of the social setting through signs, symbols, and artifacts create the *symbolic attributes* (Davis, 1984; Bitner, 1992; McCoy, 2005; Chung, 2015). Each of these place attributes can impact sensory, cognitive, and psychosocial processes that result in a desired outcome (e.g., creative performance): *sensory processes* are simple behavioral responses from the sensory modalities, *cognitive processes* include perceptual and intellectual processes that shape behavioral responses to environmental stimuli, and *psychosocial processes* are emotional and social behavioral responses (Chung, 2015).

Environmental perception is the initial gathering of information as we assess our surroundings. For example, in Figure 4.3, we may notice the space has good daylight streaming in through the windows, that also provide access to views including nature, technology to support collaborative work in a casual setting due to the large monitor accompanied by a sofa and lounge chairs, and opportunity to read individually or converse socially in a relaxed environment. Our initial response to a space is in its entirety as we imagine ourselves as a part of the environment and connect to the specific goal or purpose for being there. We then choose to take notice of the details, and possibly make changes to the space, or transition our focus to non-spatial details such as the activity or task conducted and/or the people in the space. Some people have an innate

FIGURE 4.3 Multi-use Space at the American Society of Interior Designers Headquarter Office, Designed by Perkins & Will (Photo Credit: Eric Laignel).

awareness of their surroundings and quickly recognize environmental details, whereas some pay little attention overall. We process and interact with environmental information differently which can result in different spatial experiences.

Our Attitude Toward Perceiving Environmental Information (Passive vs. Active)

We may enter a space and do a quick scan of environmental cues but be more attentive to *what* is happening and less about *where* it is happening (Figure 4.4). People who have a *passive* view of the environment either have already processed environmental stimuli as unnecessary information and blocked out these distractions or have put more emphasis on other contextual factors such as the situation, the activities at hand, and the social environment instead. On the other hand, some people may briefly scan the environment for initial bearings and then switch focus back and forth between the situation and environment to gather and utilize cues as necessary. In this instance, a person may be using an *active* view of the environment to enhance their understanding of the situation by scanning for more contextual cues. However, individuals who are consciously aware of their surroundings may be easily distracted by environmental stimuli and prefer a place with less visual complexity.

Our Behavior When Activating the Environment (Reactive vs. Proactive)

Another perspective on perceiving the environment is in how we interact with environmental cues and factors (Figure 4.5). Our attitude toward the environment and how the experience is controlled dictates these views.

A *reactive* approach looks at the transaction between people and place from the lens that the environment changes people and their behaviors. The *locus of control* is in the environment. In this approach, people respond to environmental conditions without making changes to the environment. This

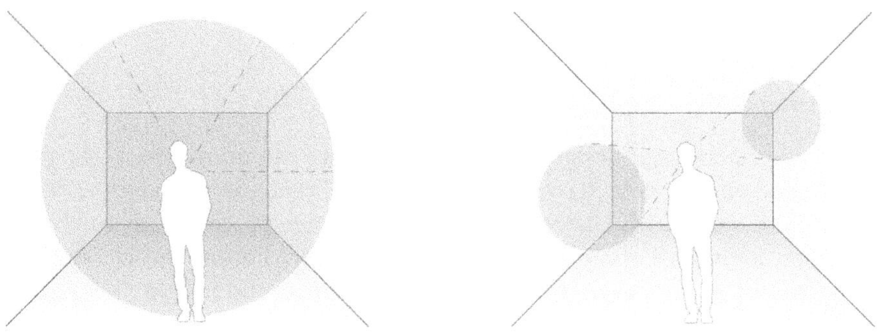

FIGURE 4.4 Passive and active view in perceiving environmental information. Diagram by Xie Maggie Hill.

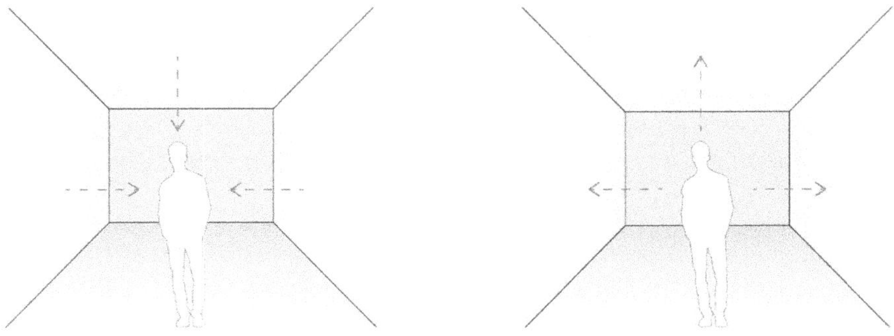

FIGURE 4.5 Reactive and proactive approach in activating the environment. Diagram by Xie Maggie Hill.

approach could be related to ***environmental determinism***, which poses that culture and society have been developed by the environment rather than by human choice. A ***proactive*** approach looks at the transaction between people and place from the lens that people have the ***self-determination*** to change the environment. The locus of control is in the people. In this approach, people shape environments into places with purpose and continue to make changes according to their needs. This allows a person to rely on the environment and actively gather information and/or utilize resources within the environment to better adapt to the situation. For example, an office worker may enjoy their desk near the window but notice that the sun light in the afternoon creates a glare. The worker may adjust the computer screen, pull down the shades, and/or use this time to change scenery and work from another space.

The act of designing a space itself is a proactive step; however, oftentimes, the designed space is left alone, without change, switching this to a reactive relationship between people and place. Only when active users of the environment choose to make changes to fit evolving needs does the relationship transition back into a proactive one. When the interactions between people and place become iterative, the full place potential is unleashed and becomes a living, evolving, organic space.

Advancing Designed Space

Our understanding of designed space and how we can utilize space as part of our desired outcomes need to expand to users. For example, aligning the design of an office space with characteristics of the creative process leads to creativity. Both communal and private spaces support preparation and elaboration, while privacy and seclusion better support incubation and insight (Kristensen, 2004; Meusburger, 2009). Collaboration is better facilitated in open-plan offices, whereas creative thinking happens in places that provide moments of relaxation (Haner, 2005). Unplanned interaction and rapid transfer of ideas are fostered in centrally located spaces, whereas tasks are better executed in segregated spaces (Penn, Desyllas, & Vaughan, 1999). Continued research on designed spaces and how they lead to desired outcomes can evolve into designing optimal places with strong purpose and meaningful experiences, equipping people with a valuable resource that can support their needs.

Creative Application: Supportive Enabler vs. Innovative Disruptor

The potential of place can be activated by thoughtful design solutions considering the purpose of the place and the different individuals' perceptions of place. How we perceive place and its potential can lead to other ways of responding to designed space. In many cases, the physical space is designed to minimize distractions and support the primary function and purpose of the space (i.e., supportive enabler). The designer's role is to extract details of the desired purpose, the characteristics of its inhabitants, and potential uses beyond the shared information. The main aim is to create a space that supports people and function, enabling people to successfully fulfill their goals. Designed space is not intended to become a stressor for its inhabitants and is usually perceived as unsuccessful when it is identified as so. Continuous inquiry can help identify these environmental stressors, and a design can be refined to eliminate or reduce them.

People also thrive when they have control over their settings, accompanied by a moderate amount of change. Office design has incorporated a variety of spaces for employees to choose to work in and this autonomy in the workplace brings empowerment (Hoskins, 2014). People in need of change oftentimes look to refresh or renovate their spaces, seeing new design as an advantageous opportunity to spark energy and excitement (i.e., innovative disruptor). Personal preferences and changing different spatial settings, activities and cognitive intensity can impact how the physical workplace supports creativity (Martens, 2011). More specifically, this "dislocation" effect in which users diverge from traditional norms and are surrounded with design elements that communicate opportunities that are different from typical activities (e.g., lounge chair facing outdoor scenery instead of work desk; Figure 4.6), along with eliminating hierarchy and encouraging participation, are central to bolstering creativity (Lewis & Moultrie, 2005). This "getting away from the workplace" helps to think differently and creatively (Magadley & Birdi, 2009). The benefits of generating stimuli, or introducing new stimuli, in the environment can provide opportunities for innovation.

Both scenarios acknowledge the significant role that designed space plays in creating purposeful experiences. The key is to understand people and their interaction with place, constantly examining this dynamic relationship to continue with thriving outcomes. Our experiences within a space are an iterative process, just as design should be.

FIGURE 4.6 Perkins & Will Minneapolis Office supporting a dislocation effect (Photo Credit: Corey Gaffer).

Acknowledgments

The project examples are award recipients of the ASID Outcome of Design program. Susan Sung Eun Chung was affiliated with ASID at the time of this work and is currently affiliated with HKS, Inc.

References

Bitner, M. J. (1992). Servicescapes: The impact of physical surroundings on customers and employees. *Journal of Marketing*, 56(2), 57–71. https://doi.org/10.1177/002224299205600205

Chung, S. E. (2015). *Effects of Lighting on Creative Performance* (Publication No. 3690585) [Doctoral dissertation, Cornell University]. ProQuest Dissertations Publishing.

Davis, T. R. V. (1984). The influence of the physical environment in offices. *Academy of Management Review*, 9(2), 271–283. https://doi.org/10.5465/amr.1984.4277654

Gibson, J. J. (1986). *The Ecological Approach to Visual Perception*. Hillsdale, NJ: Erlbaum.

Haner, U. (2005). Spaces for creativity and innovation in two established organizations. *Creativity and Innovation Management*, 14(3), 288–298. https://doi.org/10.1111/j.1476-8691.2005.00347.x

Hoskins, D. (2014, January 16). Employees perform better when they can control their space. *Harvard Business Review*. https://hbr.org/2014/01/employees-perform-better-when-they-can-control-their-space.

Kristensen, T. (2004). The physical context of creativity. *Creativity and Innovation Management*, 13(2), 89–96. https://doi.org/10.1111/j.0963-1690.2004.00297.x
Lewis, M., & Moultrie, J. (2005). The organizational innovation laboratory. *Creativity and Innovation Management*, 14(1), 73–83. https://doi.org/10.1111/j.1467-8691.2005.00327.x
Magadley, W., & Birdi, K. (2009). Innovation labs: An examination into the use of physical spaces to enhance organizational creativity. *Creativity and Innovation Management*, 18(4), 315–325. https://doi.org/10.1111/j.1467-8691.2009.00540.x
Martens, Y. (2011). Creative workplace: Instrumental and symbolic support for creativity. *Facilities*, 29(1/2), 63–79. https://doi.org/10.1108/02632771111101331
McCoy, J. (2005). Linking the physical work environment to creative context. *Journal of Creative Behavior*, 39(3), 167–189. https://doi.org/10.1002/j.2162-6057.2005.tb01257.x
Meusburger, P. (2009). Milieus of creativity: The role of places, environments, and spatial contexts. In Meusburger, P., Funke, J., & Wunder, E. (Eds), *Milieus of Creativity – An Interdisciplinary Approach to Spatiality of Creativity*. Berlin: Springer.
Norman, D. A. (2002). *The Design of Everyday Things*. (1st 1990 ed.). New York: Doubleday/Currency.
Penn, A., Desyllas, J., &Vaughan, L. (1999). The space of innovation: Interaction and communication in the work environment. *Environment and Planning B: Planning and Design*, 26(2), 193–218. https://doi.org/10.1068/b4225

CONNECTING 5

You are not alone if you have ever wondered what motivates people and their behaviors. As humans, we have fundamental needs, values, and individual differences—such as our personalities and experiences—that drive our actions. These also naturally manifest in how we structure and organize our spaces. For example, a young adult might move into an apartment to assert their independence from a parent. Going beyond individual needs, a new company may incorporate an elaborate lounge space into its office to foster social connection among employees. These embedded motivations are also evident on much larger scales, such as built environments that represent and influence the political values of entire nations.

While it may be commonplace for people to strive for power and social status in their daily lives (Reiss, 2004), this is magnified in the political sphere. In the following chapter, architect and academic Kevin Nute draws our attention to examples that span history and political settings to convey the intriguing interplay between furniture and room arrangements and how they shaped acts of governance and diplomacy. Nute explains how intentionally designed layouts established equality, leading to collaboration on the one hand, or hierarchy and adversarial relations on the other. The mere shape of a table or the positioning of people around it makes a difference, giving physical presence to intangible motivations.

In turn, these seemingly inconsequential decisions can significantly impact the overall perception, interpersonal interactions, and ultimately, *outcomes* of a situation. While many may view the furnishing of a room as purely functional in some spaces, or serving a superficial stylistic purpose in others, Nute demonstrates how furnishing a room may be far more critical, especially amid

DOI: 10.4324/9781003004622-13

world wars and dueling political powers. While most of us don't usually find ourselves in these high-intensity circumstances, imagine how this level of motivational intention might shape even the most basic day-to-day experiences.

Reference

Reiss, S. (2004). The multifaceted nature of intrinsic motivation: The theory of 16 basic desires. *Review of General Psychology*, 8(3), 179–193.

5
SPATIAL POLITICS

Kevin Nute

In a speech to the British Parliament in October 1943, Winston Churchill famously declared "We shape our buildings and afterwards our buildings shape us." His statement implied a two-way relationship between patterns of human being and built space. This essay suggests that, as Churchill implied, built forms designed to accommodate aspects of human being do seem to reinforce those characteristics, and that spaces originally conceived for quite different purposes can also shape behaviors and institutions.

What emerges is confirmation that relationships between patterns of human being and built forms are far from the simple one-to-one model implied in Louis Sullivan's much misunderstood motto "form follows function." This essay focuses in particular on how the arrangement of seating in political assemblies and at international peace conferences both reflected and affected political relations.

The Politics of Opposition

The purpose of Churchill's 1943 speech was to make the case for rebuilding the House of Commons as it had been before it was destroyed in May 1941. Churchill argued that the arrangement containing two facing ranks of seating most effectively supported the established two-party British political system (Figures 5.1 and 5.2). This configuration, he suggested, had proved itself more effective than other spatial arrangements that did not differentiate members along party lines, which he implied led to deadlocked votes and ineffective government (Churchill, 1943):

> Logic has been applied in the design of many countries' semi-circular assemblies. These buildings give every member, not only a seat to sit in but often a desk to write at, with a lid to bang, has proved fatal to Parliamentary Government as we know it here in its home and in the land of its birth.

DOI: 10.4324/9781003004622-14

FIGURE 5.1 The pre-WWII House of Commons chamber designed by Charles Barry, completed in 1852.

Churchill seems to have been suggesting that chambers that were not spatially divided along party lines gave individual members too much freedom to vote their conscience, rather than according to the party whip. He did not elaborate on why this might be the case, but one can speculate that being surrounded by other members of a given group and prevented from mixing with members of another group would make voting against your party more difficult. In other words, the proximity of peers discouraged independent voting, and a divided chamber facilitated political control of party members.

Churchill dismissed the semi-circular assembly as appealing "only to political theorists," but acknowledged that the case for retaining the divided chamber was founded more on custom than logic. It seems worthwhile briefly revisiting the history of political assemblies to examine where the bifurcated assembly chamber originated, and how it compares to its primary alternative, the semi-circular form.

FIGURE 5.2 Churchill inspecting the destroyed House of Commons chamber in May 1941.

The earliest purpose-built political assembly chamber we have records of is the Athenian Bouleuterion, dating from the end of the 6th century BCE. It was designed to accommodate meetings of the Boule, a council of 500 elected citizens with advisory, legislative and administrative responsibilities in the Athenian Democracy. The building consisted of a rectangular main hall with tiered seating on three sides. There were no political parties at the time, but each of the ten "tribes" of Athens was represented by 50 delegates. Although two of the sides of the original Bouleuterion faced each other, there was no official division of delegates, nor any evidence that this configuration was intended to symbolize any kind of allegiance to particular groups. In fact, in the sequence of new, larger Bouleuterions built adjacent to the original over the next four centuries any such implied division gradually disappeared until, by 200 BCE, the chamber had effectively become the spatial equivalent of a roofed theater (Figures 5.3–5.5).

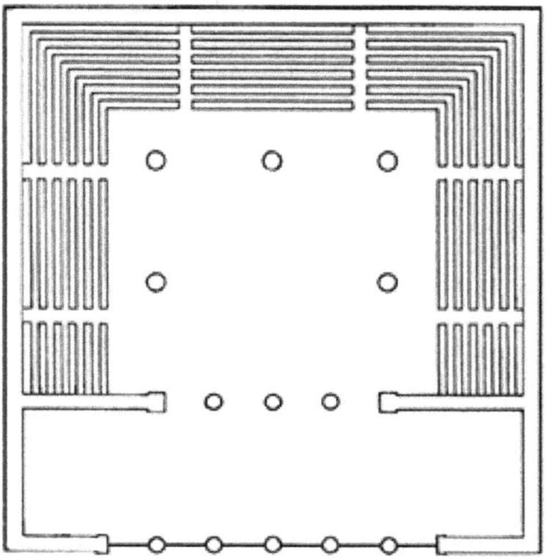

FIGURE 5.3 The Bouleuterion, Athens, Greece, ca 600 BCE.

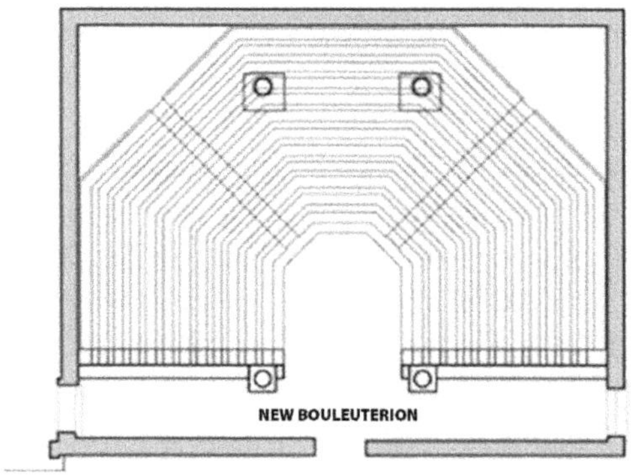

FIGURE 5.4 The Bouleuterion, Athens, Greece, ca 400 BCE.

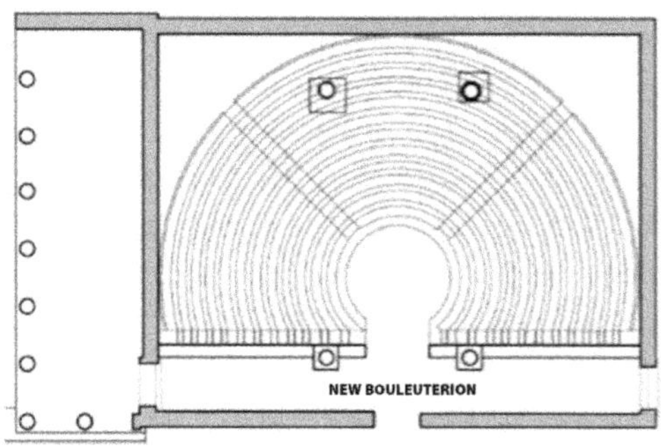

FIGURE 5.5 The Bouleuterion, Athens, Greece, ca 200 BCE.

The similarities with the theater are not coincidental, although the progression toward rather than away from its semi-circular form may be. Before the first purpose-built chamber was constructed to accommodate the Boule, its meetings were often held in theaters. The Pnyx, the home of the larger popular Athenian assembly, the *Ecclesia*, was also initially shaped much like a theater. Although its orientation was later reversed to project from the hillside, at each stage of its development the terraces of this assembly, which in this case accommodated 6,000, were focused on a central speaker's platform, and it is this spatial emphasis on the speaker that distinguishes the theater form of assembly from the two-sided version that would not appear until centuries later in Rome. Anyone wishing to address the Greek assemblies could only do so from this privileged central position (Figure 5.6).

It is not until the development of the Curia, the home of the Roman Senate between 130 and 36 BCE, that we see the first signs of political parties in the form of the Optimates, who broadly-speaking represented the interests of conservative landowners, and the Populares, who saw themselves as representing the wider public. This division had not existed before 130 BCE, however, so the bifurcated form of the Curia was clearly not designed to manifest it. The disappearance of this political schism after only 80 years suggests that in this case, at least, the division of the chamber also seems to have had no direct political effect (Figure 5.7).

It has been generally assumed that the bifurcated form of the British House of Commons chamber derived from the fact that from 1548 until 1834 meetings of the Commons were held in the Chapel of St. Stephens, in which the choir seating was divided bilaterally in the traditional manner of Christian churches (Dovey 1999) (Figure 5.8). Since the division of the early Christian church was itself derived from the Roman basilica, however, either way, the bifurcation of the British House of Commons can be seen as ultimately Roman in origin (Uro, Day, Demaris and Roitto 2019).

Kim Dovey has suggested that the division of St. Stephens Chapel "presupposed two opposed parties" (Dovey 1999, 87). Yet there was no political division of the members of the Commons into parties for more than a century after they moved into St. Stephens Chapel, and the first such split was actually created by a famous political division. In 1678 the then heir to the throne, James Duke of York, was revealed to be a Catholic, creating a rift among parliamentarians that effectively established the Tory and Whig parties according to whether one was for or against having a Catholic king. Moreover, it was not until more than a century after the formation of the two parties, in the 1780s, that they actually began sitting separately on opposite sides of St. Stephens Chapel. When a purpose-built chamber was finally constructed for the Commons in 1852, however, both the bifurcated seating arrangement of the Chapel and the spatial separation of the parties were retained (Figure 5.9).

None of the earliest bifurcated political assembly spaces seem to have been intended to accommodate opposing groups, then. In the case of the House of

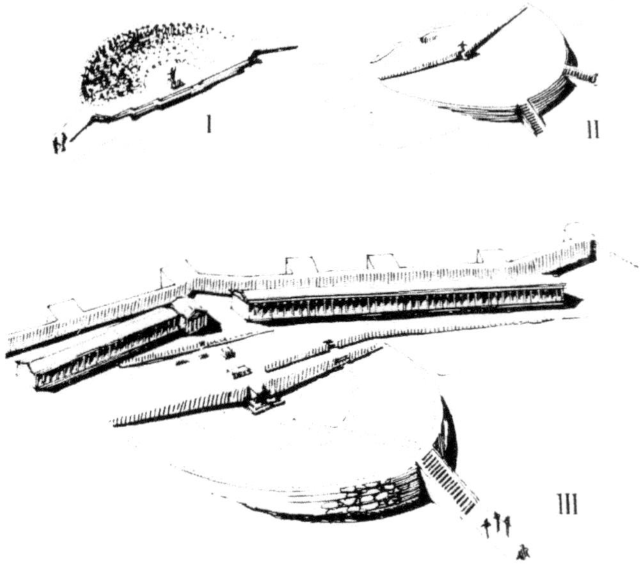

FIGURE 5.6 The development of the popular Athenian assembly, the Pnyx.

FIGURE 5.7 Digital reconstruction of the bifurcated Curia Julia, Rome, 1st Century CE.

Commons, however, as Dovey argues, the divided form may well have served to reinforce political divisions. When you are a member of the "Opposition," a title that has distinctly spatial implications, your default stance is likely to be confrontational.[1]

FIGURE 5.8 Meeting of the House of Commons in St. Stephens Chapel, Palace of Westminster, London, England, 1808.

The Shape of International Relations

In contrast to the arrangement of seating in political assemblies, a great deal of forethought over political relationships seems to have gone into the design of international conference tables.[2]

Paris (1919)

The peace conference intended to ensure that WWI would be "the war to end all wars" was dominated, both politically and spatially, by its three major victors, France, the United States and Great Britain, whose delegates sat at the head of the conference table. As long ago as the 16th century, Francis Bacon had pointed out that "at a long table a few at the upper end, in effect, sway all the business" (Bacon 1940), and that was exactly how the Versailles conference proceeded (Figure 5.10).[3]

There were actually five victorious allies present at the Congress, but the seating arrangement expressed a clear hierarchy within them, with the president of France running proceedings as the host, seated between the president of the United States and the prime minister of Britain, Italy was placed to one side, and

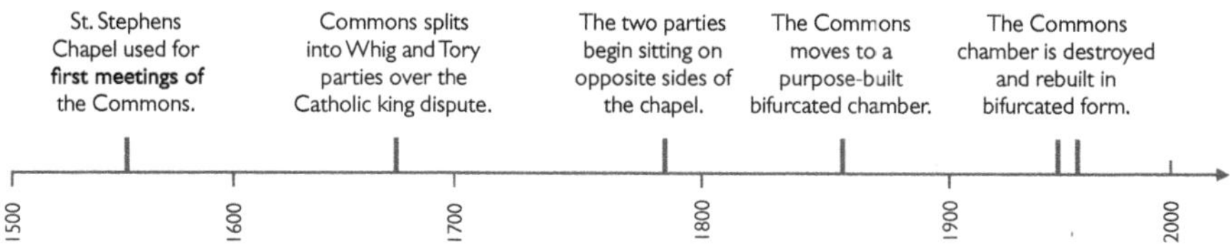

FIGURE 5.9 Key events affecting the House of Commons.

Japan was confined to the fringes (Figure 5.12). This arrangement was a conscious expression of the perceived power relations between the nations, and its message was to have direct effects, both immediately at the conference and over subsequent decades.

The thinly veiled colonial attitude manifested in the seating arrangement, which refused to acknowledge Japan as even the equal of Italy, was further compounded when Japan's racial equality proposal for the League of Nations was voted down by Britain and Australia. It is impossible to know whether the seating arrangement played a role in the Japanese eventually walking out of the Congress and their increasing hostility to the Western powers over the following decades, but the message was clear: Japan was marginal. What the Western organizers of the conference failed to understand was that there are few greater insults in Japanese culture than being treated as an outsider.

Potsdam (1945)

As in King Arthur's mythical court, the message of the round table used at the Potsdam conference of the three major WWII allies, the USA, the USSR and the UK, was one of unity and equality. The reality could hardly have been further from this image. As the only nuclear nation at the time, the US was effectively the lone superpower, the Soviets were now viewed as the West's most likely future adversary, and Britain was largely irrelevant militarily, having been effectively bankrupted by the war (Figure 5.11).

At Potsdam, as in Paris a quarter century earlier, then, the shape of the conference table was intended to convey a message. In France, it had been one of differential power among allies. Here it was the opposite. Paris had been intended to retain an existing order, but its inherent inequities quickly exploded into a new conflict. At Potsdam, the intention was keep the allies together long enough to end WWII, which it succeeded in doing, just.

Geneva (1954)

On May 8, 1954, representatives of the Democratic Republic of Vietnam (the Vietminh), France, China, Laos, Cambodia, the State of Vietnam, and the United States met in Geneva to work out an agreement to end the war

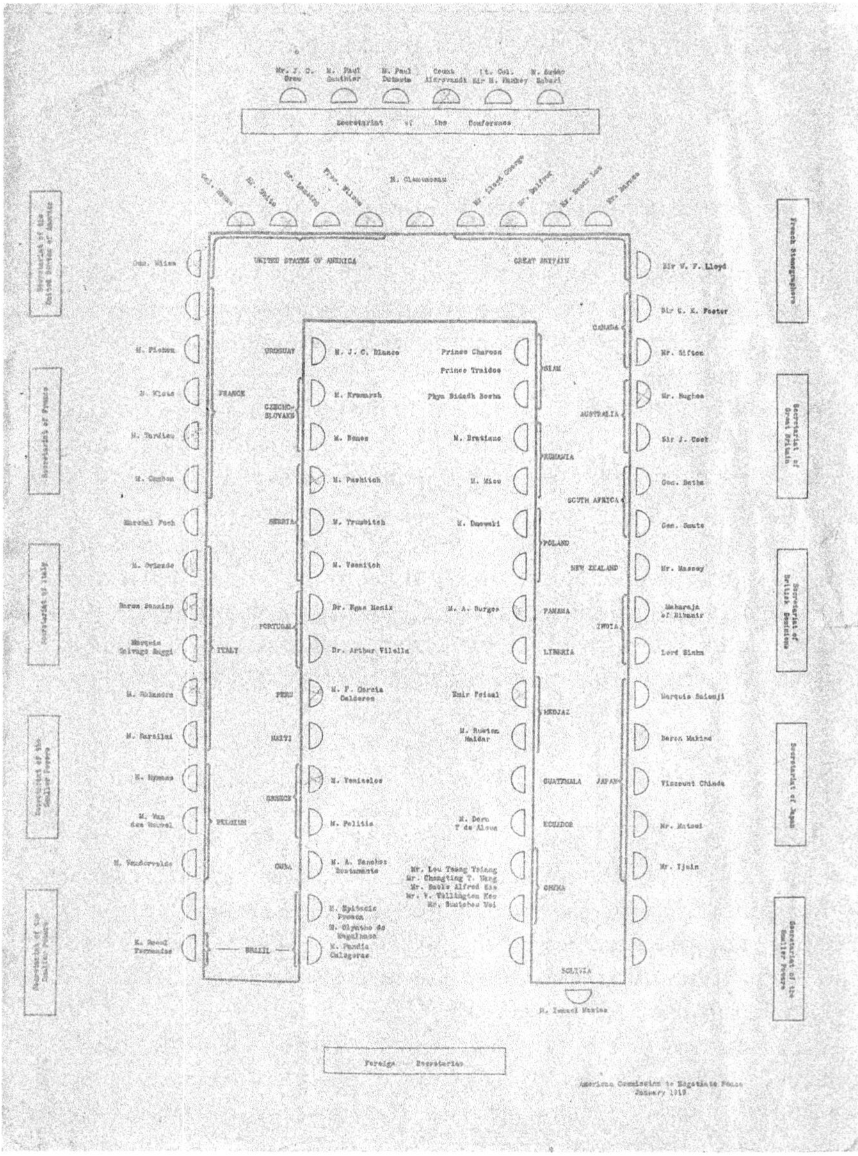

FIGURE 5.10 Perceived hierarchy within the victorious allies expressed in the seating plan at the opening meeting of the Peace Congress, Ministry of Foreign Affairs, Paris, France, 1919.

for independence between the Vietminh and colonial France. The seating of the delegations directly reflected their degree of political interest in the outcome, their relative power, allegiances, and antipathies. The Soviet Union and Britain were invited as independent brokers, and sat on a separate table from the other delegations. As direct military allies, China and the

FIGURE 5.11 Potsdam 1945. Stark contrasts in political ideology, wealth and military capabilities between the three major WWII allies were concealed beneath the unifying symbol of a round table.

Democratic Republic of Vietnam sat together, and were separated from their adversary, France, by the non-aligned Laotian delegation. The State of Vietnam was seated between its two allies, France and the United States, with the non-aligned Cambodian delegation acting as a buffer between the two cold-warring superpowers, the Americans and the Soviets. The newly communist People's Republic of China was seated opposite the United States, and, revealing its estrangement from Moscow at the time, also distant from the Soviet Union (Figure 5.12).

The overall shape of the table was that of a square, like the circle at Potsdam, an expression of the unity and equality of all the participants. The gap on the left expressed the assumed independence of the British and Soviet delegations, who had no direct interest in Vietnam. The defeated colonial power, the French, were at the center, with the newly emerging adversaries, the Vietminh and the US directly confronting each other and flanked by their closest allies. The Cambodian and Laotian delegations were treated as peripheral, but interested parties, and were sandwiched between the primary antagonists, as their nations would be in the new conflict that would soon follow.

Paris (1968)

The shape of the table used at the 1968 Vietnam peace talks in Paris infamously took months to agree, and is a prime example of how political and

FIGURE 5.12 Political interests, allegiances and antipathies expressed in the seating arrangement of the 1954 Geneva peace conference.

power relations are read into spatial configurations.[4] The bickering over shape of the table hinged on whether it should reflect four equal participants, or two opposing groups. The North Vietnamese wanted a square table, affording equal status to all four parties, but the South refused to accept the Vietcong as equals. The North then proposed a circular table, but this was again rejected by the South on the same grounds. The US and the South then proposed two semicircles separated by a neutral zone as a means of delineating the two sides of the conflict. This was rejected by the Vietcong, who insisted on an undivided table to express their equal status with the other participants. The deadlock was finally broken by the Soviet Union, who pressured the North Vietnamese to compromise. The final agreement was for a round table, expressing the equality of the four delegations, but with two smaller side tables placed precisely 18 inches away on either side, which the South Vietnamese interpreted as indicating the two sides to the conflict, but which the North and the Vietcong considered meaningless (Figures 5.13–5.15).

The refusal of the parties to accept seating arrangements they felt misrepresented their relationship to the others, even as their own people continued to die in the war, illustrates the very real meanings attached to spatial relationships. Unlike the design of traditional political assembly chambers, then, which were originally apolitical in nature, the seating arrangements of international

COMPLETE RACING

Los Angeles Times FINAL

VOL. LXXXVIII SEVEN PARTS—PART ONE MONDAY MORNING, DECEMBER 16, 1968 138 PAGES DAILY 10¢

PARIS CONFEREES TOLD TO 'STOP SQUABBLING'

Black Students Seek Skills to Aid Own People

BY WILLIAM TROMBLEY

Clifford Urges Saigon, Hanoi to Begin Dealing With Issues

U.S. JETS STIR UP MISSILE EXCHANGE IN NORTH VIETNAM

NEW PROF MEETS THE STUDENTS—Vice President Hubert Humphrey is greeted at Macalester College, St. Paul, after he accepted a shared professorship there and at the University of Minnesota in Minneapolis.

A 'SOFT GRADER,' HE JESTS

Humphrey Accepts Teaching Assignments at Two Colleges

200 Reported Seized in Continuing Wave of Arrests in Brazil

FIGURE 5.13 Report on the deadlock over the shape of Vietnam Peace Conference table, *The Los Angeles Times*, December 16, 1968.

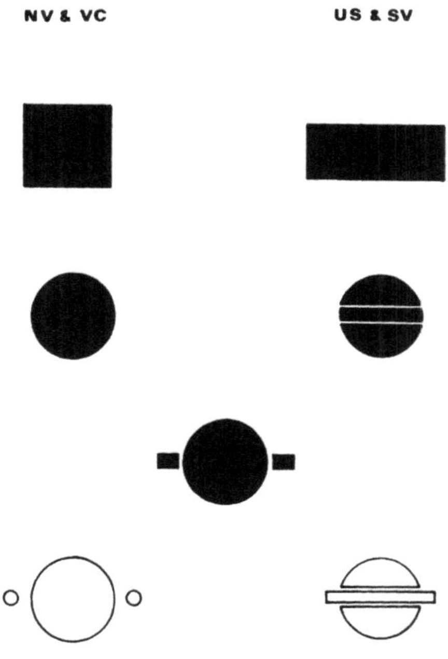

FIGURE 5.14 The evolution of the Paris Peace Conference table (Klaus Herdeg, 1983).

FIGURE 5.15 The finally agreed table in use.

conferences have frequently been deeply political in both their configuration and perceived meanings.

Where one should sit during meetings has long been the subject of popular theories.[5] In today's online world, however, many of the disparities of in-person gatherings have disappeared. It is too early to say how this "flattening" of space has affected the way we interact. In theory, though, since now everyone faces everyone else, and no one is in a dominant position, or on anyone's "side," it might be expected that meetings might be somewhat more confrontational but also less tribal.[6] Whatever the actual effects of remote meetings turn out to be, however, history suggests that the characteristics of this new space will affect how we relate to one another.

Notes

1 See Kim Dovey, "Traces of Democracy," *Framing Place: Mediating Power in Built Form* (London: Routledge, 1999), p. 103. Paul Crosby has since made a similar argument in "Is the Architecture of Westminster Bad for Politics?" *The Conversation*, February 29, 2016. https://theconversation.com/is-the-architecture-of-westminster-bad-for-politics-55427.

2 On the wider topic of peace negotiation spaces, see Andrew D. Seidel "The Use of the Physical Environment in Peace Negotiations," *Journal of Architectural Education*, 32(2), 1978: 19–23. DOI: 10.1080/10464883.1978.10758169

3 The first published discussion of the effects of different seating arrangements on human behavior was Francis Bacon's 16th century account of the impact of the relative positions of a king and his counselors, in which he suggests that "A long table and a square table, or seats about the walls, seem things of form, but are things of substance; for at a long table a few at the upper end, in effect, sway all the business; but in the other form there is more use of the counsellor's opinions that sit lower." Francis Bacon, "Of Counsel," *Essays* (New York: Oxford University Press, 1940), p. 89, quoted in Klaus Herdeg, *The Decorated Diagram: Harvard Architecture and the Failure of the Bauhaus Legacy* (Cambridge, MA: MIT Press, 1983), p. 26.

4 See Jeffrey Michaels, "Stuck in Endless Preliminaries: Vietnam and the Battle of the Paris Peace Table, November 1968–January 1969," *Defence-In-Depth*, Research from the Defence Studies Department, King's College London, May 19, 2017. https://defenceindepth.co/2017/05/19/stuck-in-endless-preliminaries-vietnam-and-the-battle-of-the-paris-peace-table-november-1968–january-1969/; also Klaus Herdeg, *The Decorated Diagram: Harvard Architecture and the Failure of the Bauhaus Legacy* (Cambridge, MA: MIT Press, 1983), pp. 27–28.

5 Over the past 50 years, there have been many empirical studies on seating and power relations. See, for example, Bernardo Tirado, "The Power Seat: Where You Sit Matters," *Psychology Today*, October 15, 2012: https://www.psychologytoday.com/us/blog/digital-leaders/201210/the-power-seat-where-you-sit-matters. Also "How to Pick the Right Seat in a Meeting EVERY Time," *Science of People*, https://www.scienceofpeople.com/seating-arrangement/

6 Several studies have identified downsides to virtual meetings. See, for example, Petr Slovák, "Effect of Videoconferencing Environments on Perception of Communication," *Cyberpsychology: Journal of Psychosocial Research on Cyberspace*, 1(1), 2007. https://cyberpsychology.eu/article/view/4205/3246, and, more recently, Matt Southern, "Study Finds 4 Negaive Effects on Too Much Video Conferncing," *Search Engine Journal*, February 15, 2021. https://www.searchenginejournal.com/study-finds-4-negative-effects-of-too-much-video-conferencing/397301/.

Reference

Churchill, W. (1943, October). *Speech to the British Parliament.* UK Parliament. Retrieved October 4, 2024, from https://www.parliament.uk/about/living-heritage/building/palace/architecture/palacestructure/churchill/

CONNECTING 6

Observing and examining the past shows how built environments have shaped and informed different ways of life. As Nute articulated, furniture types, spatial arrangements, and the overall structural organization of a place can profoundly influence social behaviors, even those of great consequence, such as global politics. However, the potential effects on society become even more critical when looking ahead. Nute concluded the last chapter by discussing how technology's impact on spatial and interpersonal relationships is in flux. This transitional period exists in part because it is now feasible to technologically enhance spaces to do more for people. And suddenly, there is also the opportunity to fully immerse people into a new digital dimension of space where they can live, work, and play. The virtual world introduces uncharted design territory, novel occupant experiences, and endless possibilities for innovation. With that, it of course, also presents an entirely new set of challenges and dangers to ponder.

We conclude *Shaping Experiences* by directing your attention toward the future. In this next chapter, researcher, interior designer, and new media expert Leah Scolere offers a fascinating tour of how technology and design merge to influence experiences within physical and virtual spaces. Scolere highlights the convergence of digital information and physical environments and how that is changing expectations of the tangible world. For example, people have long considered architectural spaces as platforms or stages where interactions occur. But, with technological advancements such as smartphones and wearable devices that can now locate and connect us in new ways, physical spaces have evolved into "platformed places" where multiple

DOI: 10.4324/9781003004622-15

digital technologies intertwine with physical architecture. This scenario creates a dynamic data exchange, enabling two-way interactions between people and places, enhancing experiences while yielding data and valuable insights into space utilization. This new reality undoubtedly brings trade-offs alongside unprecedented opportunities that will one day soon become commonplace.

6

ARCHITECTURE AS PLATFORMED PLACES AND MEDIATORS OF DATA EXCHANGE

Leah Scolere

Introduction

While visiting ARTECHOUSE's (n.d.) seasonal exhibition *In Peak Bloom* (Figure 6.1), I was immersed in a series of interactive experiences, which included digital projections of cherry blossoms that responded to my gestures (Figure 6.2). The life-size tree bloomed based on the perceived intimacy between participants detected through biometric sensors and an enchanted garden story installation experienced through a phone-based augmented reality app. In particular, the augmented reality experience allowed me to use my phone to discover layers of digital information and artistry in the physical installation. As I moved my phone around the installation, physical tags revealed blooming flowers, and physical landmarks in the enchanted forest revealed digital animals and characters as well as a narrative about Japanese folklore (Figure 6.3a and 6.3b). This museum/exhibition example illustrates the potential to use the digital world to enhance the experience of physical environments and provides ideas for expanding how we create more immersive spaces across digital and physical environments.

Emerging digital practices and behaviors have changed consumers' and building occupants' expectations of physical spaces—requiring the physical environment to be increasingly multipurpose, interactive, and continuously connected (Neubert, 2019). These connected environments are often supported through a variety of platform technologies.

The following sections highlight several key aspects of designing for experience. These include the convergence of digital information and physical space, the trade-offs of platformed places, and ultimately, the opportunities for critical design.

DOI: 10.4324/9781003004622-16

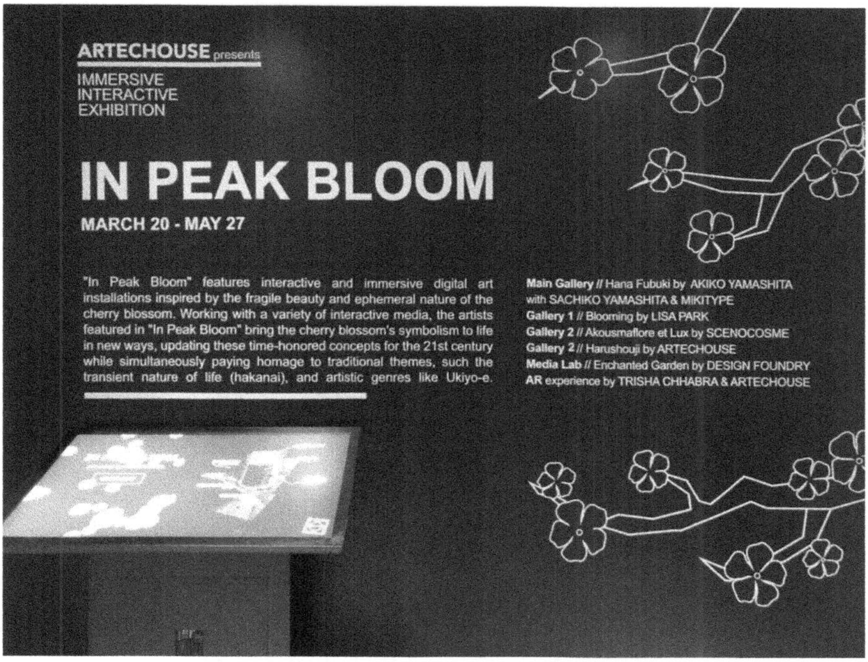

FIGURE 6.1 ARTECHOUSE IMMERSIVE INTERACTIVE EXHIBITION. Location: ARTECHOUSE, Washington D.C. In Peak Bloom, 2019. Photo taken by Leah Scolere.

FIGURE 6.2 View of gesture-responsive projections of cherry blossoms. Location: ARTECHOUSE, Washington D.C. In Peak Bloom, 2019. Photo taken by Leah Scolere.

FIGURE 6.3A View of AR experience with physical tags that when viewed through a phone reveal visual graphics such as this blooming flower. Location: ARTECHOUSE, Washington D.C. In Peak Bloom, 2019. Photo taken by Leah Scolere using ARTECHOUSE app.

Convergence of Digital Information + Physical Space

The increase in *locative media*—mobile devices, wearable technology, and other connective technologies that are able "to be located in physical space and provide information about the device's surrounding space"—has blurred the boundaries between physical and digital spaces (Frith, 2017, p. 537; Frith, 2015). The term "hybrid spaces" is a useful concept to understand the convergence of "social interaction, digital information, and physical space" as an integral part of spatial experiences (De Souza e Silva, 2006; see also Frith, 2017). Interior designers and architects are increasingly being called upon to design building architecture and interior environments for this hybridity. Therefore, designers must envision hybrid spaces where visitors and building occupants use their mobile devices as an integral part of the experience

FIGURE 6.3B View of AR experience with moving graphics and text overlaid on the physical exhibition space. Location: ARTECHOUSE, Washington D.C. In Peak Bloom, 2019. Photo taken by Leah Scolere using ARTECHOUSE app.

by receiving location-based information that encourages specific interactions (Scolere & Malinin, 2023). Extending this concept of hybridity to interior architecture, we can understand contemporary and future-oriented interiors as *connected places;* designed for increasing interaction between mobile devices, digital information, and the building architecture.

Integral to this notion of designing *connected places*, is the role of digital information or data collected from building systems and building occupants. Kitchin and Dodge (2014) identified the role of software in creating spaces and socio-technical systems such as the "code/space" of airports enabled by software. The growth surrounding the Internet of Things (IoT)[1] has enabled these connected places, which leverages networked devices to transfer data about designed environments. Increasingly, buildings are becoming platforms for a staggering number of technology systems including entry and security systems, data-sensing systems (occupancy, lighting, environmental), lighting control systems, meeting room reservation systems, digital wayfinding, and many more. For occupants or visitors these technology systems accessed through personal devices and apps may provide convenient services or enhancements to everyday experiences, such as building access, space reservations, or wayfinding. For building operators though, these technology systems provide endless sources of data that may inform decisions about building system performance and space utilization.

Platformed Places

When referring to connective technologies, platforms can be understood as "digital infrastructures that enable two or more groups to interact" (Srnicek, 2017, p.43). Communication and new media scholars define *platforms* as "sociotechnical assemblages" which serve to structure exchanges between different parties and are "oriented toward data collection and retention" (Gillespie, 2018, p. 18–22). Platforms are intermediaries between different groups of users and span different types such as *advertising platforms* (social media), *cloud platforms*, *product platforms*, *industrial platforms*, and *lean platforms* (Srnicek, 2017, pp. 48–49). Rather than being neutral, platforms are built with intentionality, politics, goals, and priorities that shape use and activity (Gillespie, 2010).

While places have always provided a platform for social interaction, building architecture is now tightly interwoven with digital infrastructure, such that an entire ecosystem of interactions and data-sensing is being mediated through a multitude of connective technologies. Rather than a series of individual technologies, the future of designing building architecture and interiors is moving toward integrated and centralized software systems that link an ecology of devices. As such, buildings are becoming *platforms* that mediate data between building systems and occupants.

Thinking of building architecture as a *platform* helps examine issues of these connected places such as the types of interactions that are being structured, the types of data being exchanged, the way data is interpreted and managed, and the role of occupants in shaping the platform. Supported by platform technologies, these connected spaces may provide opportunities for *enhanced*, *shareable*, and *augmented* experiences of interior environments.

Enhanced Experiences

Experimentation with the role of technology to enhance the experience of space is happening across various industry sectors, including retail, entertainment/hospitality, healthcare, and workplace. Enhancements often take the form of providing visitors opportunities to learn context-specific information about the space or products within the space, to simplify their navigation of a space, to participate in services that streamline their experience with spaces, and to unlock features of a space.

In retail environments, this convergence of digital and physical often takes the form of an app log-in which may allow consumers to find and reserve products as they move throughout the store, scan products to look up features and sizing, self-checkout, and unlock special deals to members. For example, in Nike's flagship House of Innovation, along with other retail locations, customers can use the "in-store mode" feature of the Nike app to scan the barcode of a product to check product availability and have your size brought to you (see Figure 6.4).

The case of Disney's MagicBand bracelet, worn by guests at the Walt Disney World Resort, is an example of how this wearable device moves beyond giving access and opportunities for convenient payment to providing constant communication with sensors throughout the park. Disney's MagicBand uses Radio Frequency (FR) technology—the same tech used in credit cards, keyless car entry, and fitness bands—to allow guests to tap their band at resort touchpoints for short-range readers to unlock experiences (Disney World, 2024). These include hotel room entry, park admission, and purchases. In addition to these short-range readers, guests' MagicBands can be read by long-range readers in specific locations across the resort to provide personalized experiences, photos, and videos while collecting information about interactions related to experiences, rides, and restaurants (Disney World, 2024). This data is generated so that Disney can tailor experiences to visitors, offering suggestions about rides, etc. Guests can use the wrist-worn MagicBand[2] or download the "My Disney Experience" app on their phones to use the MagicMobile experience to unlock features at specific access points in the resort.

This example illustrates how an entire physical environment can be connected to a virtual platform and can provide a personalized experience for navigating an environment, while affording convenience, interactivity, and the ability to unlock experiences. We can easily imagine the experiential opportunities to take a MagicBand approach to interior environments where the entire interior environment has opportunities to unlock immersive experiences.

Virtual tours of spaces across residential and commercial sectors allow visitors to explore more information about their physical environments before or during their visit to the space. 3D capture platforms such as Matterport (2024) allow everyday users and design professionals to scan physical environments with a 3D or 360 degree camera or mobile device to transform spatial data into a photo-realistic digital twin of a space. Enabled by artificial intelligence and machine learning technologies, the resulting 3D digital model carries dimensionally accurate information about the actual physical environment.

FIGURE 6.4 View of Nike App Scan and try-on in-store mode service. Location: Nike House of Innovation 650 5th Ave, New York, NY. Photo taken by Jonathan Scolere.

Furthermore, the digitized environment can serve as an immersive 360 degree virtual tour with embedded graphic tags, audio, video, links, and information about the interior environment that can be experienced remotely via a browser link without visiting the site or accessed while in the physical space to learn more about specific features. For example, we used this 3D capture technology to create a virtual tour of our Design Materials Library at Colorado State University, where digital graphic tags allow visitors to learn about the features of the space and the intent behind some of the material collections (see Figure 6.5). On small and large scales, this technology[3] is expanding how

FIGURE 6.5 View of 3D Capture Technology: Virtual Tour with overlaid information to explore the space. Location: Design Library, Nancy Richardson Design Center at Colorado State University. Photo taken by Leah Scolere through Matterport.

environments can be experienced virtually and the types of information about physical spaces that can be exchanged during the design process, construction management process, or facilities management process.

Shareable Experiences

Social media platforms like Instagram have become spaces where users share their experiences of places, including restaurants, museums, retail stores, hotels, and workplaces. This fits into broader conversations of designing for what Novarini and Mendez (2018) and others in the industry have referred to as "shareable moments" within interior environments. These shareable moments are unique features of a space such as a graphic mural, floor tile pattern, logo, or vignette designed to entice visitors into a photo-op (see Figure 6.6a). In response to the affordances (Gaver, 1991; Scolere & Malinin, 2023) of these location-based connective technologies, designers are increasingly asked to create interior environments which invite consumers and users to share their spatial experiences via image-sharing platforms. For example, a Fast Company (2018, November 21) tour of Nike's House of Innovation on New York's Fifth Avenue, described how the lighting settings in the fitting rooms were intentionally designed to enhance the way users photograph and share their experiences with products. Sean Madden, Senior Director of Product Nike

FIGURE 6.6A View of digital screen in Nike's House of Innovation. Location: Nike House of Innovation 650 5th Ave, New York, NY. Photo taken by Jonathan Scolere.

Direct, explained, "People take a lot of selfies in fitting rooms, so a good room and interesting light really helps with that" (Fast Company, 2018, November 21) (see Figure 6.6b) Moreover, selfie walls, distinct branded elements, or interactive experiences encourage users to participate and share their experiences across a *social media platform ecology* (Zhao, Lampe & Ellison, 2016) made up of numerous platforms.

FIGURE 6.6B View of fitting rooms with adjustable lighting for better selfies. Location: Nike House of Innovation 650 5th Ave, New York, NY. Photo taken by Brooke Leff.

Moving beyond curated photo-moments, platforms that emphasize videos such as TikTok or Instagram Stories provide a venue for sharing dynamic movement experienced in spaces. Digital walls with moving imagery and interactivity are becoming integral building materials that are experiential and translate to shareable and exciting experiences of place.

Augmented Experiences

The increasing user expectation for interactive environments has given way to experimentation with augmented reality (AR) technology across a variety of spaces. AR technology is composed of a real-time, digital overlay on the physical environment (Azuma, 1997; Liao, 2019). This AR content or digital overlay can take various forms including video, audio, 3D models or animations, and text allowing for unique real-time interactions with the physical environment. As such, AR technology sets itself apart with its place-based interaction with physical environments (Graham et al., 2013; Liao & Humphreys, 2015; Liao, 2019). While AR can be experienced through both head-worn devices (such as Microsoft Hololens) and mobile devices, many everyday experiences of AR that engage users in learning and interacting with their physical environments are accessed through mobile devices such as phones or tablets.

While common uses of AR technology include things like social media photo and video filters (e.g., in Snapchat and Instagram), the concept of an AR digital overlay on physical spaces has the potential to continue to expand how we experience and understand spaces. The interiors products industry has been experimenting with AR to help consumers and designers visualize furniture, lighting, paint, wallcovering, and more in interior environments. For example, the IKEA Place app was an early adopter that leveraged AR technology to allow users to digitally place accurately scaled furniture in their homes to help visualize and test out selections prior to purchasing (Figure 6.7).

In addition to experiential storytelling through AR in exhibitions such as those by ARTECHOUSE (n.d.), mobile AR applications have enabled a variety of other interactions. In these instances, mobile AR is used to communicate through place whereby users and content creators augment spaces that ultimately impact people's perception and relationship to those places (Liao & Humphreys, 2015). For example, AR applications such as the brush app used at the Facebook Headquarters by artist Heather Day[4] allow painterly marks to be digitally overlaid on a building and collectively experienced by building occupants (Figure 6.8a and 6.8b). This AR installation opens the door to the potential of creating experiences that might let other users leave their mark digitally on a space or collectively contribute to a digital community wall within an interior. Future visitors or building occupants would be able see these contributions and add their own.

Beyond a medium for digital art and immersive environments for entertainment, AR technology can amplify *engagement* between people and spaces. For example, post-occupancy evaluations (POEs) have long been used to assess building performance, occupant satisfaction, and the effectiveness of design decisions (Shepley, 2011; Hosey, 2019). Now, AR can expand the goals of the POE to engage users with contextual building feedback and educate occupants about resource opportunities within a facility in real-time. As such, in a grant-funded project, alongside Dr. Laura Malinin, our team is piloting a beta exploratory AR mobile application in an academic incubator building[5] (Scolere et al., 2023). As the building occupant moves through the interior environment, certain spatial locations activate an AR digital overlay of contextually-specific information and graphics (Figure 6.9). For example, responding to a question will unlock enhanced digital information about the intention of the interior setting to help participants learn how to use the building more effectively by making specific features more salient and suggesting intended uses. This capability becomes even more important as designers and building owners rely on building rating systems such as LEED and the WELL Building Standard to guide design strategies that encourage occupant physical activity, cognitive and emotional well-being, thermal comfort, exposure to light, and many others. Conceptualized around the idea of a "building that teaches,"[6]

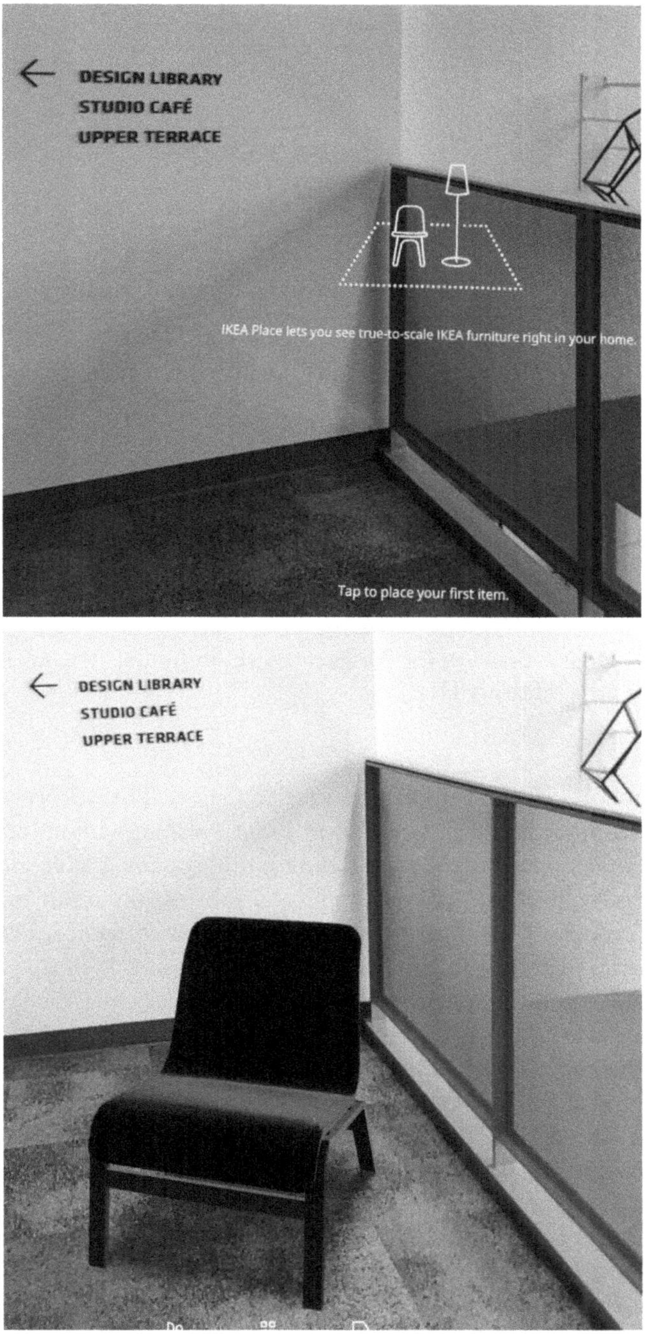

FIGURE 6.7 View IKEA Place app interface and virtual chair overlaid on the physical environment. Location: Nancy Richardson Design Center. Screenshots of IKEA Place app taken by Leah Scolere.

FIGURE 6.8A Digital drawing for Augmented reality mural. Digital Drawing by artist Heather Day.

this AR application and future iterations can move POE processes beyond evaluation to engagement and education about the design intention of specific building features related to these building rating systems (Scolere & Malinin, 2023). Thus, technology will communicate information about building features, and occupants will provide contextually situated feedback in real time about using the features.

We can rely on future projects to expand these ideas further. For example, AR experiences could provide a digital material ingredient label to communicate the sustainable properties of materials used in the building construction or highlight specific interior products and how they contribute to acoustics, material health, or function. Taken even further, AR technology has the potential to communicate post-occupation how buildings were designed to be disassembled and how materials fit into the projected building life-cycle. Independent research and design labs such as Space10 by IKEA were dedicated to speculating on the future of AR and spatial mapping technologies through a series of everyday experiments focused on prompts around using AR to edit rooms, visualize effects of light, trace an object's lifespan, and many more. In simple terms, AR continues to be poised as a gamechanger for how we design, assess, and experience hybrid places in the architecture and interior design industry.

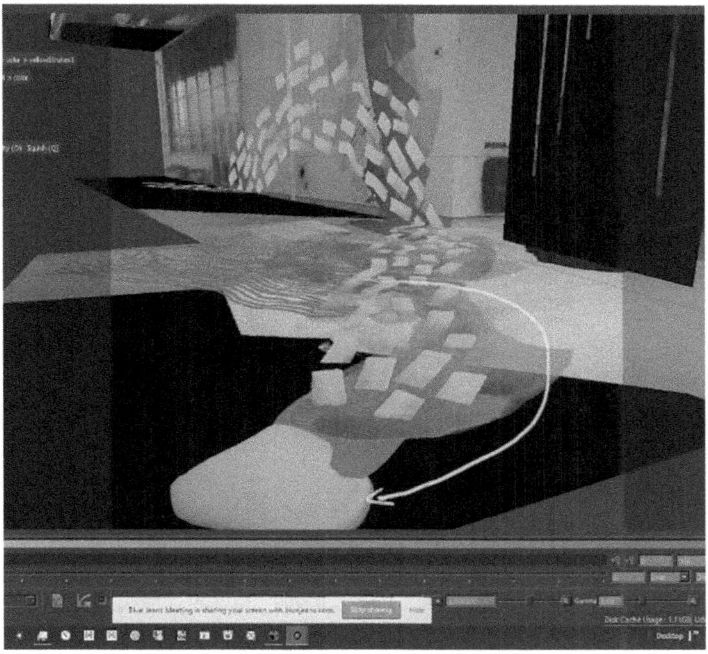

FIGURE 6.8B Behind the scenes development with animators to bring Heather Day's digital sketch to life for the Augmented Reality (AR) application. Screenshot of process by artist Heather Day.

Platformed Places and Trade-Offs

As discussed, there is potential for building architecture to be a platform for digital and physical integration where occupants' interactions and feedback become a more intentional component of the ongoing shaping of spatial experience. There is also the opportunity to re-imagine the goals of these platforms and to incorporate opportunities for engagement, creative expression, and community building. However, as we design for and navigate platformed environments increasingly composed of an ecology of connected physical spaces, we need to consider the emerging tensions between experience, privacy, and access.

Data, Privacy, and Context

In what ways does the context of an interior environment matter? For example, many consumers readily accept the trade-off of sharing data with convenience and personalized information in retail interiors. There have been ongoing advances with in-store data collection technologies such as Bluetooth sensors, WiFi, 2D cameras, video analytics, and radio frequency identification (RFID). These evolving technologies have the ability to provide retailers with data about customers such as "gender, age, range, location, movement, and

FIGURE 6.9 Light and Color location and digital interaction in a mobile AR application for Nancy Richardson Design Center. Location: Nancy Richardson Design Center. Screenshot from Augmented Reality App taken by Leah Scolere.

shopper mood" (Terry, 2019, n.p.; Cron & Noble, 2023). This data combined with opt-in mobile app log-in data from consumers means more tailoring of content to consumers but may also mean more granular monitoring of customers' in-store spatial experience. In corporate workplace design, the discussion of continuous data collecting is often promoted through the promise of "optimizing building performance" and "informing space utilization."

For example, this convergence of digital and physical may take the form of sensors for utilization and environmental monitoring. Combined with badge swipe or biometric access, these sensors and a whole host of mobile apps can be tied into building management systems to understand user preferences better and inform decision-making for the building owner or operator. Often in IoT-enabled environments or smart buildings, occupants may not be aware of how technologies are interacting and how that aggregated data might impact one's privacy (Pappachan et al., 2017; Harper, Mehrnezhad & Mace, 2021).

There are often unintended consequences of data collection in one context having implications in another context. For example, Levy and Barocas (2018) introduced the term "refractive surveillance" to explain how data collection from consumers in retail environments also contributed to the tracking of employees and their interactions, resulting in "new forms of managerial control" over retail employees based on this data (p.1). In this instance, experience-enhancing, tech-driven design for the customer had a negative trade-off for the people serving them. Designers and operators alike have an ethical obligation to consider context, including all occupants whose privacy may be impacted by data collection.

As we consider the complexity of issues related to privacy in connected IoT-enabled interiors, Helen Nissenbaum's (2009) foundational theory of "contextual integrity" provides a framework for understanding privacy as being regulated through context-relative norms for the appropriateness of information transmission. In other words, contextual factors play a large role in how people evaluate privacy concerns. Designers and building owners can develop or use established frameworks to be more thoughtful about the role of occupants' privacy in the larger socio-technical system of building design. This contextual approach can help further efforts around developing more "privacy-aware smart buildings" that focus on the communication of policies, technologies, and user preferences (Pappachan et al., 2017; Pathmabandu, Chhetri, & Baig, 2020)

Inclusion and Access

As the *digital divide* becomes larger (DiMaggio et al., 2004; Norris, 2001), how can designers ensure that connected environments are inclusive to all users? In these connected environments, not having access to a mobile device may mean not being able to access the full experience of that environment. In other situations, there may be only one way to access information and resources such as a restaurant only offering access to the menu through a QR code that relies on your phone to scan that code to access the menu. Ultimately, this impacts the inclusivity of our interior environments, too. While designers have tended to focus on designing inclusive physical environments *or* designing for inclusive technologies (apps, digital screens, platforms), underexplored has been the dedication to designing for *inclusivity across digital and physical environments.* Designing for inclusivity across environments requires an experience journey approach of thinking about how information, resources, and features are intentionally integrated and overlaid as part of the design process and how we can give users multiple ways to participate in the spatial experience. The increase in designing for hybrid spaces suggests the need for developing tools for accessing inclusivity on a digital-physical spatial continuum for interior environments.

Opportunities for Critical Design

While buildings are increasingly designed as platforms and mediators of data to optimize spatial environments toward improving user satisfaction, collaboration, productivity, and building performance, it is less typical to engage building occupants with data, sensor technology, or real-time dashboards. There is the potential for a more *participatory* approach for how designers, stakeholders, and building occupants co-design how data-sensing technologies are implemented, presented to users, and influence spatial utilization approaches. Furthermore, the future of designing connected environments will require designers to be thoughtful advisors, providing guidance about the role of place-based data and ethical considerations for data collection and management. However, guidelines for how designers can navigate tradeoffs between connectedness and respite, convenience and privacy, have not been widely developed or adopted. Design practice areas could benefit from a more in-depth understanding of users' perceptions of data-sensing technologies and the impact on behavior, critical reflection on the ethical implications of designing for connected environments, and the development of toolkits to guide designers' conversations with stakeholders, building manager, and building occupants from pre-design to post-occupancy.

In addition to equipping professional designers to guide conversations about data-sensing technologies, it is also essential to prepare future designers who will considerably expand upon the integration of technology into physical environments. Thus, there is a vital need to provide design and architecture students with curricula dedicated to ethical considerations and robust best practices for conceiving and implementing connected environments.[7] Many design and architecture schools use critical design, employing design to provoke conversation, as an exploratory approach to tackle controversial issues (Dunne & Raby, 2001; Dunne & Raby, 2013). One of these issues most definitely should be discussing data ethics. We all must ask this question: how might we make building and occupant data monitoring and sensing salient to users while avoiding unintended negative implications? This essay is a call to all designers and stakeholders to initiate more explicit opportunities to discuss considerations for designing connected places and the future of buildings as platforms for data exchange.

Notes

1 Postcapes, Internet of Things Platforms, 2014.
2 The technology is continuously evolving with Disney offering an even more enhanced and connected experience with the option of MagicBand+. https://privacy.thewaltdisneycompany.com/en/resortfaqs/
3 Matterport technology continues to be advanced by AI with recent features leveraging generative AI to allow users to "defurnish" existing spaces to feature an idealized view of the virtual interior by digitally removing aspects of the interior. https://matterport.com/blog/bringing-generative-ai-to-digital-twins-matterports-three-pillars-of-ai
4 For more infomation about artist Heather Day's work refer to https://www.heatherday.com/
5 This ongoing project is part of an ASID Research Foundation grant-funded project titled *Post-Occupancy Engagement: Exploring Augmented Reality Technology as a Tool for Assessing and Enhancing Effectiveness of Building Design Strategies.* The Colorado State University team is composed of Dr. Leah Scolere (PI), Dr. Laura Malinin (Co-PI), and collaborators Dr. Francisco Ortega (Computer Science), and Dr. Jeni Cross (Sociology) along with the support of the Institute for the Built Environment and an interdisciplinary team of undergraduate and graduate students in Interior Architecture and Design, Computer Science, and Art. The beta AR-application was tested through a testflight link for a limited time. Further iterations are required to create a more stable application for users as well as to reliably collect POE feedback through the application.
6 The term 'buildings that teach' has been used in interior design to refer to the positive lessons we can learn from buildings (Cole, L. B., & Altenburger, E. (2019). Framing the teaching green building: Environmental education through multiple channels in the school environment. Environmental Education Research, 25(11), 1654–1673. https://doi.org/10.1080/13504622.2017.1398817; Wiebenson, J. (1998). Buildings that teach. Educational Leadership, 55(7), 61–64)
7 With the rise in Artificial Intelligence (AI) and experimentation within the design industry, there will be a continual push for design education curriculum that contextualizes AI for design related to ethical practices.

References

ARTECHOUSE (n.d.) *Washington DC. In Peak Bloom.* ARTECHOUSE. https://www.artechouse.com/program/in-peak-bloom/

Azuma, R. (1997). A survey of augmented reality. *Presence*, 6(4), 355–385.

Cole, L. B., & Altenburger, E. (2019). Framing the teaching green building: Environmental education through multiple channels in the school environment. *Environmental Education Research*, 25(11), 1654–1673. https://doi.org/10.1080/13504622.2017.1398817

Cron, A. & Noble, G. (2023, August 18). *Unlocking new retail insights with scaled video analytics.* Chain Store Age (CSA). https://chainstoreage.com/unlocking-new-retail-insights-scaled-video-analytics

De Souza e Silva, A. (2006). From cyber to hybrid: Mobile technologies as interfaces of hybrid spaces. *Space and Culture*, 9(3), 261–278.

DiMaggio, P., Hargittai, E., Celeste, C., & Shafer, S. (2004). Digital inequality: From unequal access to differentiated use. In K. Neckerman (Ed.), *Social Inequality* (pp. 355–400). Russell Sage Foundation.

Disney World (2024). *My Disney Experience FAQs Privacy.* Retrieved November 17, 2024 from: https://privacy.thewaltdisneycompany.com/en/resortfaqs/

Dunne, A., & Raby, F. (2001). *Design Noir: The Secret Life of Electronic Objects*. Springer Science & Business Media.
Dunne, A., & Raby, F. (2013). *Speculative Everything: Design, Fiction, and Social Dreaming*. MIT Press.
Fast Company (2018, Nov 21). Inside Nike's new futuristic store. *Fast Company YouTube*. Retrieved from: https://www.youtube.com/watch?v=52nLywJeMRU
Frith, J. (2015). *Smartphones as Locative Media*. John Wiley & Sons.
Frith, J. (2017). Invisibility through the interface: The social consequences of spatial search. *Media, Culture & Society*, 39(4), 536–551.
Gaver, W. W. (1991). Technology affordances. In *Proceedings of the SIGCHI conference on human factors in computing systems* (pp. 79–84). https://dl.acm.org/doi/pdf/10.1145/108844.108856
Gillespie, T. (2010). The politics of 'platforms'. *New Media & Society*, 12(3), 347–364.
Gillespie, T. (2018). *Custodians of the Internet: Platforms, Content Moderation, and the Hidden Decisions that Shape Social Media*. Yale University Press.
Graham, M., Zook, M., & Boulton, A. (2013). Augmented reality in urban places: Contested content and the duplicity of code. *Transactions of the Institute of British Geographers*, 38(3), 464–479. doi:10.1111/j.1475-5661.2012.00539.x
Harper, S., Mehrnezhad, M., & Mace, J. C. (2021, September). User privacy concerns and preferences in smart buildings. In *International Workshop on Socio-Technical Aspects in Security and Trust* (pp. 85–106). Springer.
Hosey, L. (2019, February 6). Going beyond the punchlist: Why architects should embrace post-occupancy evaluations. *Metropolis*. Retrieved from https://www.metropolismag.com/architecture/architecture-post-occupancy-evaluations/
Kitchin, R., & Dodge, M. (2014). *Code/space: Software and Everyday Life*. MIT Press.
Levy, K., & Barocas, S. (2018). Privacy at the margins | refractive surveillance: Monitoring customers to manage workers. *International Journal of Communication*, 12, 23.
Liao, T. (2019). Future directions for mobile augmented reality research: Understanding relationships between augmented reality users, nonusers, content, devices, and industry. *Mobile Media & Communication*, 7(1), 131–149.
Liao, T., & Humphreys, L. (2015). Layar-ed places: Using mobile augmented reality to tactically reengage, reproduce, and reappropriate public space. *New Media & Society*, 17(9), 1418–1435.
Matterport (2024). https://matterport.com/
Neubert, H. (2019,Issue 32). Placemaking | The digital converges with the physical. *Gensler Dialogue*.
Nissenbaum, H. (2009). *Privacy in Context: Technology, Policy, and the Integrity of Social Life*. Stanford University Press. https://doi.org/10.1515/9780804772891
Norris, P. (2001). *Digital Divide: Civic Engagement, Information Poverty, and the Internet Worldwide*. Cambridge University Press.
Novarini, D., & Mendez, Circe (2018). But first let me take a selfie: Designing shareable moments. *Gensler on Lifestyle*. Retrieved August 20, 2021 from: https://www.gensleron.com/lifestyle/2018/2/26/but-first-let-me-take-a-selfie-designing-sharable-moments.html
Pappachan, P., Degeling, M., Yus, R., Das, A., Bhagavatula, S., Melicher, W., & Venkatasubramanian, N. (2017, June). Towards privacy-aware smart buildings: Capturing, communicating, and enforcing privacy policies and preferences. In Aibek

Musaev, Joao E. Ferreira, Teruo Higashino (Eds.), *2017 IEEE 37th International Conference on Distributed Computing Systems Workshops (ICDCSW)* (pp. 193–198). IEEE.

Pathmabandu, C., Grundy, J., Chhetri, M. B., & Baig, Z. (2020, September). An informed consent model for managing the privacy paradox in smart buildings. In *Proceedings of the 35th IEEE/ACM International Conference on Automated Software Engineering Workshops* (pp. 19–26). IEEE.

Scolere, L., & Malinin, L. H. (2023). The building that teaches: Exploring augmented reality affordances in academic incubators. *Journal of Interior Design*, 48(1), 64–79. https://doi.org/10.1111/joid.12229

Scolere, L., Malinin, L. H., & Ortega, F. (2023). Co-designing augmented reality: Exploring the role of boundary negotiating artifacts. *CoDesign: International Journal of CoCreation in Design and the Arts.* (pp. 1–20). https://doi.org/10.1080/15710882.2023.2255169

Shepley, M. M. (2011). *Health Facility Evaluation for Design Professionals.* Asclepion.

Srnicek, N. (2017). *Platform Capitalism.* Polity Press.

Terry, L. (2019, May 31). Shopper tracking: reinventing and reimagining the store experience. *Retail Info Systems News.* Retrieved from: https://risnews.com/shopper-tracking-reinventing-and-reimagining-store-experience

Wiebenson, J. (1998). Buildings that teach. *Educational Leadership*, 55(7), 61–64.

Zhao, X., Lampe, C., & Ellison, N. B. (2016, May). The social media ecology: User perceptions, strategies and challenges. In Jofish Kaye (Ed.), *Proceedings of the 2016 CHI Conference on Human Factors in Computing Systems* (pp. 89–100). ACM. https://www.google.com/books/edition/Proceedings_of_the_2016_CHI_Conference_E/hbAznQAACAAJ?hl=en

Reflecting on Experiences

Designing place-based experiences requires careful consideration. Whether you are creating a personal space or a space for others, it is easy to get caught up in subjective beliefs about taste and worry about making the "right" decisions based on others' opinions of good and bad. Instead, when furnishing and finishing out a space, consider how your choices will influence occupants' perceptions and behaviors. Likewise, if you plan to lean into technology to enhance interactions and experiences, know that this requires imagination and caution. One ultimate question in placemaking is whether people will use a space as intended, especially if taking a new or innovative approach. These areas of concern are just a few of the many experiential factors to account for when designing built environments, which can be anxiety-provoking to even seasoned designers.

Designing spaces that cater to individuals' specific needs can be challenging in real-world contexts due to the unpredictability of people. However, overlooking the importance of design intent can result in missed opportunities to create transformative moments, such as designing for awe. Even small decisions, like the arrangement of seating, can significantly impact the overall experience. By tapping into the latent potential of spaces, it is possible to cultivate environments that facilitate self-expression, support emotions, and nurture relationships with ourselves and others.

The experts featured in this section provided invaluable insights into the power of place and the importance of person-centered environments. Each author imparted ways the built environment can profoundly affect individuals regardless of whether they are created with purpose or out of happenstance. To assist you in making informed decisions, the authors have equipped you with the knowledge to navigate potential pitfalls and seize some of the countless

DOI: 10.4324/9781003004622-17

opportunities inherent in creating spaces. However, with great power comes great responsibility. Ethical considerations must be integral to the design process if the priority is to center the person.

Ethics refers to the moral principles that guide human behavior when shaping experiences. A necessary aspect of discussing ethics is ensuring everyone has equitable and safe experiences that benefit society. Going beyond the individual level, addressing broader social impact and environmental sustainability is also critical. Access to viable, renewable, supportive, and enduring spaces should be available to everyone—not just a select few—and should not come at the cost of the planet. To learn more, we will now transition from discussing *Shaping Experiences* to the next section on *Considering Ethics.*

PART 3

Considering Ethics

Framing Ethics

So far, *People and Spaces* has explored individual experiences within the built environment. The upcoming section on *Considering Ethics* shifts focus to a critical reality: not everyone is afforded *comparable* experiences. Spatial experiences are not universal, nor are they equal. Every person and their community occupies a unique physical and societal position, but regardless of their differences, each is part of something greater—a network of interconnected, complex systems. These systems, which shape where most of us spend our lives, such as our homes, workplaces, hospitals, and schools are formed and governed by powerful political, economic, and social forces. Consequently, when reflecting upon these structures and their downstream impact on people and their surroundings, it is crucial to realize that systems-level decisions are encountered and experienced on a very real human level. For this reason, this section examines how the world's institutions can perpetuate disparities through the built environment, alongside discussing some of the many ethical considerations that surface when studying the dynamic between people and place.

The contributors to *Considering Ethics* are experts in various areas, such as inclusive design, community engagement, technology, and climate change. Each author demonstrates how built environments can safeguard or endanger the frameworks described above. Through their examples, you will begin to understand how a system's stability depends on the integrity, validity, and equality of each part. However, differences in power can lead to vulnerabilities that can negatively influence even the most resilient system. This section explores how these complexities manifest within the context of people and the built environment, resulting in a sense of inequality or uncertainty. Restoring balance in any system—and ultimately, its impact on people—may require

DOI: 10.4324/9781003004622-19

revamping ineffective or outdated political, economic, or social structures, or providing additional support to the vulnerable parts to ensure all are equally robust. Furthermore, achieving equilibrium may also involve understanding overall behavior patterns within a system and challenging the status quo.

The following chapters in this section discuss the responsibilities of those who work at the intersection of people and place, as well as the obligation members of the general public have to protect society's most at-risk individuals and communities. While the authors express different worldviews, they all challenge us to see our surroundings through an ethical lens. Some contributors reveal injustices that disproportionately affect a select few. For instance, you will learn how built environments can impact a person's opportunities in life, and, as a result, how spaces can affect public health, inclusivity, and diversity. You will also learn that with the advancement of technology, ethical concerns are no longer restricted to physical space. Personal data is now widely collected and analyzed within built environments. This new existence means building occupants need to anticipate and plan how they want their data used to augment their lives while protecting the precious commodity of their identities. Finally, the authors remind us of the importance of caring for the natural world—the most precious shared resources in the most complex of systems. The intentional and unintentional consequences of systems on the built environment, and above all on people, can have a significant ripple effect across communities and the planet. Regardless of where you are on your journey to understand people and spaces, *Considering Ethics* will spur you to move out of your comfort zone and reconsider many aspects of your work and life.

CONNECTING 7

Ethics have been central to studying human nature and civilizations throughout time. From early philosophers to contemporary scholars and entire professions, humans have always been interested in examining their role as individuals and jointly as a society in safeguarding and promoting the greater good. Today, fields like medicine and law have ethical codes in place to establish standards that guide behavior and uphold a set of values. These principles are essential for keeping professionals on track within their respective fields, but genuine accountability and change start within each of us. Personal ethics, and by extension, the systems we exist within, should be living, breathing entities, continuously evolving as we grow as individuals and collectively as a whole. However, we must each be grounded in ourselves to support the transition of these structures. It takes courage, honesty, and vulnerability to acknowledge when it is necessary to shift, adapt, or speak up for what is right.

Considering Ethics begins with an interview with George Aye, the Co-Founder and Director of Innovation at Greater Good Studio, a design firm dedicated to serving the social sector. Aye discusses what motivated him to begin his practice, the uncomfortable realities he has encountered throughout his career, and the insights and values these experiences instilled. Aye offers practical guidance and wisdom for professionals at all stages of their careers, empowering them to have the resolve to do less harm now rather than correct mistakes downstream.

DOI: 10.4324/9781003004622-20

7

BYOE – BRING YOUR OWN ETHICS

An interview with George Aye
By Tamie Glass and Lindsay T. Graham

When searching for a voice on ethics in the design world, we reached out to designer and self-proclaimed "pissed-off optimist" George Aye. George created a ripple in the field when he wrote an open letter calling into question the ethics of a former employer who happens to be one of the world's most well-known innovation firms. In response to his experience as an emerging designer, George co-founded Greater Good Studio, a design firm that focuses exclusively on the social sector.

Whether the firm is generating a set of Artificial Intelligence standards for the Gates Foundation to make future essay writing software inclusive of all students, exploring health equity zoning in communities across Rhode Island, or working with the Chicago Department of Transportation to develop community-vetted recommendations on road interventions, Greater Good Studio is focused on people. It isn't usually hired for having content expertise in these subject areas, but rather for their expertise in engaging and amplifying the voices of historically and systematically marginalized communities. In our interview, George shares his career journey with a frankness that we hope will inspire readers to listen to their own inner voices when considering ethics.

Tell us about the role you see Greater Good Studio playing in the work that you do?

Our role is to elevate marginalized voices to those who have the power to drive change. This is often the funders or clients who are already advocates for these communities. Our goal is to bridge the gap between what is currently

DOI: 10.4324/9781003004622-21

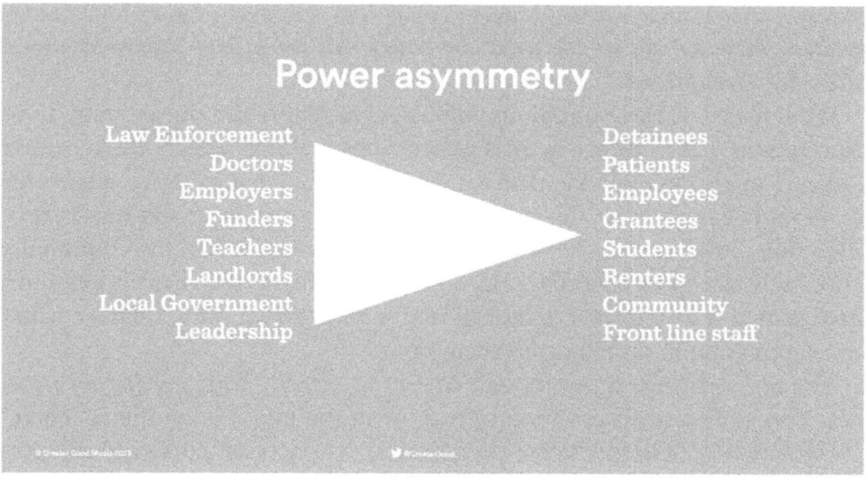

FIGURE 7.1 Power asymmetry graphic. George defines having Power as being able to change another person's reality, and he often talks about Power Asymmetry. The people most impacted by decisions are usually those with the least power, while those with the most power tend to be farthest from the real issues. Regardless of how aware we are, this proximity problem is where our ethics can be put to the test. Image provided by Greater Good Studio.

happening on the ground and a hope or vision for the future. We aim to understand the reasons behind the differences and design new products, systems, services, spaces, etc., that effectively address these gaps.

How do you address this imbalance in practice, especially given that so many individuals and groups are involved, including many who have already been working hard in this space?

So, the challenge is how to disrupt this power symmetry and create space for alternative approaches without disregarding or alienating those who have already been involved. It's crucial to honor those community members and grassroots organizations who have been doing the work but haven't received much attention. In our practice, we aim to be disruptive while elevating these marginalized voices. However, it often depends on whether our clients [on the powerful side of the triangle] are willing to confront uncomfortable truths. We have a track record of bringing forward uncomfortable findings, which might even implicate our client as having played a role in perpetuating power imbalances. This realization can be unsettling.

Making clients uncomfortable doesn't seem like your typical plan for securing projects. How do you set the stage for doing this work, how does your process allow for disruption?

We actually ask these questions upfront, even before the engagement, to set expectations—like, *are you sure*? If a client mostly wants somebody to execute a plan, I might jokingly say that we would be really annoying to work with. We would be really slow, find things they don't want to hear, and waste everyone's time—and actually burn a lot of trust with members in the community, who, sadly, are quite used to it. If, on the other hand, the client is genuinely interested in learning something new and is ready to act on it, then we would be religious about working with them on it.

The real challenge arises though when this actually happens *during* a project, after the contract has been signed, or in the midst of synthesis. There's this feeling like, "Oh that's cute rhetorical advice, George. He's not really serious, right?" It can be quite an ego killer for a client to have to confront that the work they have been doing hasn't registered even though they have shown up and made investments. We had a client who was upset when she discovered that something we shared directly contradicted what she had been doing for the past ten years. She was mad at us for not correcting the research participant, "Why didn't you tell him what we've been doing and set the record straight?" But it's not our job to speak for our clients, and it wouldn't have changed the situation. It's about the research participant's perception, and this is their reality.

What do you think is the magic sauce in a person or organization that allows them to have that ability to move forward, compared to someone who is not open to it or reacts by closing the door?

I don't know if I can tell you what the magic sauce is but we've seen some patterns. One can hope that folks are ready and have already done some internal work to understand their role and culpability in this work. However, there are some who think of themselves as, "one of the good guys. I'm so much better than all the other people I know who aren't even trying," or "Some of my best friends are the people in this community, so I can't be a racist." I think someone like this will have a harder time with some of these realities we find in our research. So, I can't exactly tell you what it takes, but those are red flags for us—where a client already sees themselves as mostly there, and they are hiring us to kind of like sweep up the edges.

When there's an openness to realize that what they've been doing for so many years and built their reputation and professional standing upon isn't working, they won't be threatened by new information. Their egos won't be destroyed by it, but rather, informed by it—that's a sign of personal growth and a desire for transformation. However, I can't really include that as a qualifier or requirement in a proposal. If we were responding to a request for proposals (an RFP), we would want to know if the client is ready to be transformed by the work. Are they willing to allow themselves to be changed by the knowledge of what is happening to real people on the ground? Seeking that openness to transformation is powerful, but it's hard to put into words without sounding strange, and others might just say, "yeah," in agreement without really understanding the implications.

It may seem absurd to realistically ask that question to a client, but there is a transformative nature to it. You can suddenly realize, "Wow, all this work I've been doing, perhaps my whole career, has missed the mark. So, what do I do now?" And it's not like we hold the key to a fountain of knowledge. It's about going out and being with people. Then, rather than assuming we know what they need, hearing what they have to say and taking it at face value as a genuine request for something real.

Can you say more about this part of your process?

The unique aspect of our approach is that we don't simply send our team off on a day of interviews to find out what we need to know. That wouldn't be very helpful. Instead, we conduct interviews across multiple individuals' lived experiences, looking for patterns that emerge from these conversations. By identifying patterns across multiple interviews and sessions, we can provide a slightly scaled view that is built on a deep understanding of individuals. This is what sets our work apart and I believe that's true for a lot of high-quality ethnographic research. But still even we can't guarantee high-quality outcomes on our end, a lot of it would still rely on the client's readiness for change.

What are your thoughts on the strategy of the person doing the work and wanting to bring about change and using discernment in selecting clients? Where do you see the power in that, and what value do you think there is in saying "no" to clients who aren't ready for that kind of change?

I should back up and say that discernment is something that wasn't inherent in me. It has taken a lot of time to become comfortable with everything you described, such as saying no. While it may sound incredibly sage, it felt very foreign to me because, as an immigrant, I grew up with a scarcity mindset. It wasn't natural for me to adopt an abundance mindset where I could easily say no. I never thought it was something I could do or had experienced before. On the other hand, my co-founder had a different upbringing where abundance seemed more natural to her. She was able to exude it in a way that was unfamiliar to me. Over time, I have practiced abundance enough to adopt that mindset, even if it initially feels fake—I can do a pretty good impression of someone who has it now! But, if you can really commit to that position, you will find yourself asking different questions than you would if you're working from a scarcity mindset.

You have been known to describe your approach to business development as an "energy conservation strategy". What do you mean by that?

The most counterintuitive aspect of discernment and turning things down is that when you become pickier, you actually have more capacity and energy. When you practice "no" for years, you become less distracted by energy-sucking projects and more available for the projects that align with your goals.

We find ourselves with more opportunities because we have developed strategies to deflect nonsense. We've sent 50+ breakup emails since 2011 and I just recently sent another one. Initially, it was challenging to know why we were saying no, but after discussions with the team and listing the bullet points of why, it became clear. Having that discussion makes it easier to say no because you understand what you're committing to. When people struggle with turning things down, it's often because they haven't explored and identified the specific reasons for declining a project. By writing down the bullet points that explain why you can't take on a project, you become better equipped to handle similar situations in the future. You can be more efficient, waste less time, and move on to the next opportunity.

By getting rid of projects that won't go anywhere, you are promoting the end goal of your team, which is making a real change in the world. Is that because the user base allows you to do that?

This is where it becomes a nightmare. Saying no requires knowing what your business is really about. If the primary purpose of your business is to make as much money as possible and coincidentally make some social change—cool, just say that out loud. If your goal is to make social change and you coincidentally make some money to be sustainable, say that bit out loud. But I think it's often the former, not the latter. It's like saying, "We want to make as much money as possible, and if we happen to make an impact, that's great." However, businesses escape by using a lot of inclusive language on their websites about their beliefs and values.

But when it comes down to it, they don't care about any of that because they keep taking on high-risk projects. The real motivation is to make money. It would be fine if they were straightforward about it, and people would probably appreciate the honesty. Employees would then understand that they won't have a long-term career there, they will make money, and then leave. But when companies promote one type of value over profit-based judgment, it becomes confusing for employees. They keep receiving mixed messages because their actions are incongruent with what they claim to value. I know we struggle with this as much as anyone.

This reminds us of the common model where you hear a firm or business say, "We'll do this work for profit and make as much as we can, because we also

want to do these important pro bono projects." There's a sense of "we need to do this – to support that."

There's a really good book titled *Winners Take All: The Elite Charade of Changing the World* by Anand Giridharadas that I found very helpful. It explains that there are a lot of really good narratives that exist in the world of profit-driven philanthropy. The author cites a piece from, I think, Andrew Carnegie that simply says, the reason for profit is to make amends, to give back. One interpretation is that this gives every capitalist a pass. That says, it's your duty to make as much money through exploitation as possible because eventually you'll give it back. To which one could say hold on a second, maybe we don't have to do so much repair work if we weren't so harmful in the first place.

Anand makes the analogy that this is like being at a firefighting convention hearing someone talk about ways to be better stewards of the safety protocols in your house, when everything they sell sets it alight. I find the narrative of having to make as much money as possible in order to do good very problematic. And I would rather that we did less harm in the first place, as opposed to being really good at repair work later. But that seems to be the common narrative because that's what we've been told: One gives back…when you're tired of destroying the earth.

But that's the mentality of the contemporary workforce. If we look at the spirit of most students though, they really want to make a difference. Maybe everyone else did, too, when they started their careers. However, as students enter the working world, they start to realize that certain ways of working don't align with that goal. What would you say to those individuals who are just beginning their careers?

I hope they maintain a connection with their inner voice, which tends to fade away by the time they become senior managers. They see everyone around them prioritizing their own interests, but no one talks about it openly. They start thinking they're strange because they don't see anyone else addressing it. The collective apathy of their team makes them think, "I must not somehow fit into this culture." So, then you suppress it. You start to ignore the signs that your body's telling you that something's up. And that's really concerning, and that's basically what most of my professional design career has been. Finally, I couldn't do it anymore, and I left.

What advice would you give educators on how to help students become more resilient and prepared to face reality?

Yeah, I think it's important to expose students to scenarios that highlight the ethical compromises they are likely to face. I've been giving talks at universities specifically about this topic and highlighting the kinds of stuff I wasn't aware was even a thing, until I realized, "Oh shit, I've been doing this for 10 plus years."

I am recognizing that the industry is essentially "BYOE", a bring your own ethics game. There's nothing industry-wide and there's no general guidance. It's all completely made up. Which means that you will be on your own when it comes to trying to develop a sense of what is right or wrong because you can't rely on your team to do it for you. We have to be mindful that if nobody is keeping an eye on things, it's like there's no designated driver in the relationship. Imagine if the 22-year-old coming out of undergrad might have the best ethical framework of anybody on this team. What a position to be put it.

So, it's important for students not to be scared of speaking up. I want them to know that their peers likely have the same questions, and maybe even some of their professors. It's crucial to ask, "Am I reading this correctly? Are these just first-time nerves, or am I onto something?" We shouldn't dismiss everything as nerves though because there might be cases where what they're experiencing is actually abuse or ethically harmful behavior within the team. That's concerning, and it should be flagged. Just like we have Title IX for state-funded or federally funded institutions, where there are obligations to report abuse, there's nothing like that in design for ethical behavior. I might not fully understand all the details, but there should be some form of due diligence, a designated reporter role that says if you hear about abuse, you are obligated to report it. Unfortunately, such standards don't exist in the design field.

How did you access your intuition and maintain your center? What helped you stay grounded as you started your own practice?

So, I didn't do anything, and I buried it for most of my commercial design career. I couldn't stand how I felt about myself in those situations, so I just left without any sophisticated plan. I moved to another studio, but it turned out to be even worse and more corrupt. It made me realize that the industry as a whole was broken and made me want to leave design. I spent a year working in public transit just to get away from it all.

When we started Greater Good Studio, we decided to do the opposite of all the terrible things we had experienced. You'd be surprised how far you can get as a studio starting really from a vision of something you don't want. That strategy guided us for the first five years. But now, in the last five years, and moving forward for the next ten years, we are focusing on what we actually want to achieve rather than simply running away. It's incredibly challenging to know what that is.

What is the latest evolution in this process for you?

In the past couple of years, I have been reminded of the struggles I faced. I was in a place where I was hearing stories from alumni of my first employer and coincidentally teaching a class on ethics. This made me confront the question of whether I should take action.

As I read the final essays from my students about how they responded to my class, I realized that I couldn't be their teacher if I didn't take the next logical, ethical step. I couldn't stall on my own ethical decision. So, I made the choice to write a letter that told all the stories I had heard and committed to dealing with the fallout. It was terrifying, but I couldn't stand not doing it.

And was the fallout as bad as you thought it would be?

That's a great question. So, this is the thing. We tend to magnify the worst possible outcomes and discount the damage caused by not speaking up. I thought it would be catastrophic, but it didn't happen. I also realized how much it had been burdening me to not say anything all that time. So, now that it's done, I'm in a stage of healing. I didn't think I could get there.

And, how did your students respond?

I don't know about most of them, even now. But I owe a lot to my students because if it hadn't been for them, everything might not have come together in that moment.

Yes, we all owe a lot to students. They teach us so much. It's impressive what working with students can spur us on to do. We've seen George in action in the classroom, and students are hungry to hear what he has to say. But so are all the rest of us. Making ethical decisions is something we all face every step of the way. We are grateful to George for being vulnerable and sharing his journey with us so we can all learn from it.

CONNECTING 8

As Aye pointed out in the previous chapter, without an overarching guidance system providing a roadmap between right and wrong, navigating where to invest, where to devest, and what to preserve when considering the relationship between people and spaces can be challenging. However, if we can all agree on three fundamental principles—that spaces should support the human experience, spaces should not harm people, and spaces are essential for humans to flourish—then we can use these principles as ethical guideposts. For instance, if a space is intended to positively support people and their experiences, it must support *all* people. Similarly, if a space should do no harm, it must be safe and healthy for *all*. Those who construct built environments have a responsibility to anticipate and avoid potential negative consequences for current and future generations. In this next chapter, interior designer Kia Weatherspoon emphasizes the power spaces have in bolstering the lives of minority populations. She also showcases the significant ramifications that occur when people fail to address racial and socioeconomic inequality in the way they approach designing and constructing built environments.

DOI: 10.4324/9781003004622-22

8

DESIGN IS SERVICE TO THE PEOPLE

Kia Weatherspoon

Do you know **you are defined by more than just a title?** Or, more importantly, your title doesn't limit how much or how far you can go in the pursuit of ensuring equity. Yes, I said it right off the bat—equity—the buzzword of current times. In being more than just our title(s), we all have influence and power if we choose to be relentless in our pursuit of equity for all.

Now, I did not grow up knowing the power of interior spaces. I did, however, experience the effects of interior spaces at two pivotal points in my life. First, at the age of 16, I began visiting by brother in prisons, which would span 15 years. The visceral way these spaces touched my being and emotions stays with me to this day. It's also where I developed concern for how others experienced this type of space. The second experience was at the age of 19 while I served in the United States Air Force during wartime after September 11. I sought emotional and physical solace in a sparse military base in the Middle East. I found it by hanging three sheet walls around my cot to create a space for myself. The emotions each of those interior experiences evoked is a visceral reminder of why Interior Design(ers) matters.

> "We have to secure these spaces."
> "We can't have any soft seating for them to hangout."
> "Our funding doesn't allow us to make it look this nice."
> "They all need to be watched."

You may think these statements allude to descriptors for the prisons, or the bare military base referenced above. However, they are not, these statements are in reference to someone's home. Let's pause…think of *your* home. Think of the homes of *your* loved ones—your mother, brother, father, sister, children,

DOI: 10.4324/9781003004622-23

or a grandparent. Think of *their* interior spaces. Don't think about what they look like, but about the feelings you want for yourself or those you care about. Are any of the above statements applicable? This is a serious question. Are any of the above what you'd want to experience in your home, in their home? Imagine a home described as a prison, a home devoid of soft furnishings, or a governmental entity regulating how "nice" their home could be. Between 2012 and now, these types of explicit biases are ever-present during the process of developing, constructing, and designing affordable housing. My team and I have heard variations of these phrases from every constituent required to build housing; real estate developers, housing authorities, architects, general contractors, and property managers—which leads us to my title and craft.

I am *just* an Interior Designer. My **creative craft requires serving people through design.**

The first time I heard one of the blatantly biased statements for low-income families was around 2013. A real estate developer casually remarked that the chair my design firm had specified for the space was "too nice for these people." For a moment, I was perplexed, and I paused as briefly as I could during a client presentation. An important detail to mention is this was the first significant client my company had ever had. All that pressure aside, when my perplexity subsided, I was left thinking, "well, that's just WRONG." But now, here is where I leaned in and instead of exclaiming that, I simply asked, "Why?".

It wasn't a rhetorical question—it was about seeking understanding. **Asking WHY is a creative professional's number one responsibility**. It was apparent the above statement and all the variations I would hear over the next ten years were rooted in explicit biases and inequity—and truly are just wrong. As *just* an Interior Designer who's trained to understand aesthetic, function, safety, decoration, codes, style, and welfare, it's never *just* about "the chair." It's about ensuring no person is deprived of an elevated, healing, safe, and beautiful space regardless of their ethnicity or socioeconomic status. Remember, our training and titles do not limit us in how much or how far we can go in the pursuit of ensuring equity.

However, **empathy strengthens equity** and allows you to create beyond what is just asked of you.

Empathy also requires **leaning into one's own ignorance in the pursuit of understanding**. For instance, do you know low-income Black, Indigenous, Hispanic, Latinx, Asian, and all minority groups of color are subject to inadequate and, at times, deplorably designed spaces? Has the idea that people could live in conditions that are less than something you've ever even had to think about? This question is not dependent on whether or not you are an Interior Designer, and it is not judgment-based. This question is about identifying the prerequisites of empathy are understanding and education. If you

FIGURE 8.1 Project Girard St. Apartments. Image copyright Determined by Design.

have never been to or lived in the projects, ghetto, affordable housing, or the new, more acceptable identifier, "workforce housing," how would you know these inequities have existed. Now, more importantly, how can you actively become an advocate within your creative space?

The lack of empathy is why I trademarked our Design Equity® services. Our Design Equity® services are a creative, empathic, and concept-based design approach to provide equitable design outcomes for disenfranchised people and communities. This creative practice is rooted in service and elevated interior design specifically to Black, Indigenous, Hispanic, Latinx, and other minority groups.

FIGURE 8.2 Project Archer Park. Image copyright Determined by Design.

I started this journey by identifying that Real Estate Developers, Housing Authorities, Architects, General Contractors, and Interior Designers (like myself) all have a responsibility. We all need to work as staunch advocates of elevated design for all, and actively speak up against every inequitable practice and bias we and our clients face. It's important to ask yourself how your professional and personal roles—as a mother, father, sister, brother, grandparent and community member—hold responsibility here too.

There is a complexity to how communities are developed and planned. The goal is not for you to become a housing expert, but rather to offer a *glimpse* into how your own biases may show up. The US Department of Housing and Urban Development (HUD) defines Affordable Housing as dwellings in which the occupants spend no more than 30% of their gross income on total housing costs. Three factors to consider are:

1 Affordable Housing is predominately predicated on the cost of housing based on the income of one family in comparison to the families around them.
2 The families who can apply to live in an affordable housing project are categorized based on the percentage of which their income falls below the average of families around them.
3 Affordable housing is historically concentrated to neighborhoods with like income ranges.

For our exploration, we will focus on the nation's capital Washington, DC. The average median income (AMI) in Washington, DC for a family of four is $129,000.[1] A family of 4 can apply to live in an affordable housing building if their income is 30% to 60% of $129,000. Which means a family of 4's income would fall between $38,700 and $64,500. This average income range predominantly represents African American and minority families in DC.[2] Additionally, this average income range is concentrated to two wards in the Nation's capital.

It was important to provide the above context before I posed my next questions. How can you actively counteract inequitable practice and bias as a community member? Step one is to answer this next question. Suppose a 60-unit affordable housing building was being proposed in your neighborhood. The building would be comprised of Black and minority families of 4 who make 30% AMI, or $38,7000 annually. Would you actively encourage this type of housing development in your neighborhood?

If your answer was "No.", this is the definition of NIMBYism.[3] This systemic explicit bias construct plagues the development of affordable housing in every major metropolitan area. It can delay the creation of housing for families in need for upwards of 18 months to even years. No one wants transitional housing, a homeless shelter, or an affordable housing project in their community. Yet, we often hear the sympathy expressed for these types of at-risk populations, from afar, in the comfort of an affluent community. But this is not the empathy required to activate assistance, acceptance, and aid in developing homes and buildings for these families in your community.

This reality of these inequities has become even more apparent during the height of the COVID-19 global pandemic—a time that shuttered the doors of nearly every business, workplace, restaurant, hotel, and more. It forced us all into our homes, and it also created a narrative of "heroes," mainly front-line medical workers. In contrast, the overlooked "heroes" were the maintenance crews at medical facilities and the familiar faces of your local grocery store cashiers. Did you know grocery store cashiers makes an average income of $25,712[4]? Unfortunately, this unsung hero makes 35% less than the AMI for our 60-unit 100% affordable housing project. The one that many do not want in their backyard. Meaning their prospect of living within the community where they work is still unattainable without assistance.

Let's go back to the beginning of the essay. How did you respond when you learned the systemic explicit bias of Real Estate Developers, General Contractors, and Housing Agencies results in homes referenced as if they were a prison, devoid of softness? Now, how did you feel about 60 "poor" families whose income was $38,700 in your backyard? Your response has made your implicit bias an explicit basis.

With my specific title, trained responsibility, and power as an Interior Designer, I can offer understanding to one justifiable reproach. Historically, affordable housing and their interiors were ugly, undignified, and inadequate. Why? Because many creative professionals in the space of Architecture and Interior Design did not challenge or ask why. At the start of our journey, I talked about "the chair" that was too nice for "that demographic." In the end, we used "that chair" because I would not settle for less than what I would want for my own loved one. That's empathy in practice. Interior Design is equitable when rooted in empathy. Equitable design requires us to put ourselves in a space where we do for others what we would do for ourselves, we must check those places where our own lived experiences can cause gaps in our empathy and understanding. For instance, when 89% of architects are White, we need to be hypercritical of the spaces designed for Black, Indigenous, Hispanic, Latinx, and other minority groups.[5] As one can/should question have our White architectural counterparts done less than because the demographic of the building is not one they can see themselves in. This puts their design decision into question.

The socioeconomic status of a family should not limit their access to elevated design.

On numerous occasions, colleagues have asked, "How did you get that developer to spend all that money?" or stated, "We can't bite the hand that feeds us." My firm's response is always the same, "We lead with a concept that focuses on the people."

It's very telling and often reveals that their focus and approach is instead profit-driven. This critique comes when poorly designed spaces and subpar building materials leave minority communities depressed. For example, "This community does not need two million dollars' worth of brick facade" was a statement made by a major stakeholder of a redevelopment project we worked on in a historic designated retail corridor of a Black community. A comment one could easily assume was made in response to exceeding overall project cost. Yes, the exterior facades of buildings often necessitate value engineering, or reducing cost. However, when located in an affluent, white neighborhood where historic guidelines must take precedent, the worthiness of a facade isn't correlated to the overall residents' perceived value and needs. This is when the **project team(s) must lean into their responsibility, not the bottom line**.

Bottom-line thinking results in bottom-line design—especially for those who are below the poverty line. Which depending on where you are in the country, are historically minority communities. What I am now steadfast in is our success—my practice has, and will continue to thrive as we prioritize people. The profit comes to any community, business, and entity **rooted in service to the people. Design is for the good of all people.** My architectural counterparts' partners do not often see themselves in the communities they design for. However, they must begin to acknowledge the lasting effects

FIGURE 8.3 Project Capitol Vista. Image copyright Determined by Design.

of oppression caused by the field's brutalist designs plaguing and devaluing generations of families.

Dough Boy from the movie *Boyz n the Hood* said, "Either they don't know, don't show, or don't care about what's going on in the hood." Now, you are in the know. You are now a voice that knows **empathy and equity are required to create just(ice) and beauty** within communities for all families. Now the necessity and possibility of elevated design falls on the shoulders and collective power of us all—no matter what our title is.

We are all immersed in problems, challenges, and various systems of oppression that plague us as a society. The choice of not knowing no longer exist. Sympathy without action toward change makes us complicit. My team of Interior Designers and I have and will continue to make sure the next generations grow up knowing the power of interior spaces. We will be steadfast in asking why. We will design and create stories that evoke a feeling and reminder of value not predicated on ethnicity or socioeconomics.

What is your title? What is your superpower? How far will you go in the pursuit of ensuring equity?

You are defined by more than just a title.
Creative craft requires serving people through design.
Asking WHY is a creative professional's number one responsibility.
Empathy strengthens equity.
Leaning into one another's ignorance is the pursuit of understanding.
The socioeconomic status of a family should not limit their access to good design.
Project team(s) must lean into their responsibility, not the bottom line.
Empathy and equity are required to create just(ice) and beauty within communities.
Rooted in service to the people. Design is for the good of all people.

Notes

1 (Loria, 2021)
2 (Median Household Income: Black/African American, 2021)
3 (Not in My Backyard Phenomenon, 2021)
4 (Salary.com, 2021)
5 (2021 Demographics, 2021)

References

Loria, K. (2021, July 14). HUD's 2021 income data bumps DC's median family income by 2.4%. Commercial Observer. Retrieved from Commercial Observer.

National Organization of Minority Architects. (n.d.). Research. NOMA. https://www.noma.net/research/

Neilsberg. (2024). *District of Columbia, DC median household income breakdown by race between 2012 and 2022.* Neilsberg, https://www.neilsberg.com/research/datasets/cda4121a-8924-11ee-9302-3860777c1fe6/

Preliminary Zoning Analysis. (n.d.). Not in my backyard: NIMBY. Preliminary Zoning Analysis. https://preliminaryzoninganalysis.com/blog/not-in-my-backyard-nimby/

Salary.com. (2021). Grocery Store Cashier Salary. Retrieved from Salary.com.

CONNECTING 9

As Weatherspoon highlighted, if spaces should help individuals flourish, then spaces must provide equal opportunities and existence for all, regardless of ethnicity, gender, nationality, sexuality, identity, ability, background, or socioeconomic status. Like Weatherspoon, architectural designer and advocate Ileana Rodriguez shares insights gained through her professional practice and personal lived experience in supporting all occupants. In the following chapter, she discusses the importance of paying extra attention to vulnerable populations. Specifically, Rodriguez illustrates the benefits of creating spaces that promote universal experiences for individuals of all physical abilities, and what can happen when clients, industry, and government go beyond basic building codes and accessibility guidelines. She emphasizes and illuminates the power in challenging standards and deficit thinking when considering disabilities.

DOI: 10.4324/9781003004622-24

9

SOCIAL JUSTICE THROUGH INCLUSIVE DESIGN IN THE BUILT ENVIRONMENT

Ileana Rodriguez

Embracing Variation in the Human Body

Architectural styles relate to human needs. They historically respond to various political, social, and religious aspirations to inform design solutions from decisions of scale, geometry, symmetry, and many other qualities. Even today, the architecture and design industries continue to be in a state of constant evolution. But, with social justice at the forefront of global discourse, the field still has lots of work ahead of it to fulfill its due diligence to understand what it means to design in today's world. Inclusion and access go hand in hand with the view that "everyone deserves equal economic, political, and social rights and opportunities."[1]

It would be impossible to cover all the interpretations of inclusion in this essay, so we will instead focus on accessibility and design for people with disabilities. The question is ever-present: How can designers have a meaningful impact in this area? Will industry fail to make progress if it continues to think of the human body as Michelangelo's "perfect machine" or even as the modern theories of Le Corbusier?

We must move to a more accurate representation that includes *all* bodies—the tall, the short, the aging, the infant, the wheelchair user, the visually impaired—and the variations the human body anyone can evolve to at any given point during their lifetime.

Navigating Inclusive Approaches and Universal Design

Several books, guides, manuals, and organizations have started exploring designing for inclusivity with disabilities in mind. There has also been an emergence of terms used to try to define and quantify this type of design.

DOI: 10.4324/9781003004622-25

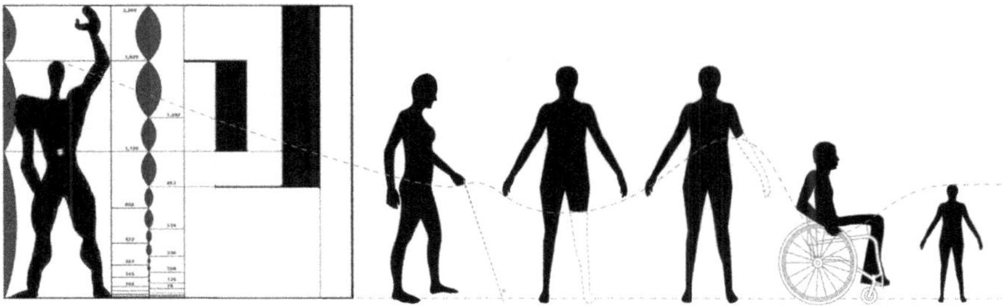

FIGURE 9.1 A representation of the ideal Le Corbusier Modulor Man and what inclusion would look within this context. Image by Flickr user eager, https://www.flickr.com/photos/eager/5031911411, used under a Creative Commons Attribution 2.0 Generic license, https://creativecommons.org/licenses/by/2.0/, changes were made.

For instance, the term "universal design" has entered into the vernacular. At the Center for Universal Design at North Carolina State University, *universal design* is defined as "the design of products and environments to be usable by all people, to the greatest extent possible, without the need for adaptation or specialized design" [2] (Connell et al., 1997). However, there are multiple names for and definitions of universal design. Some are broader, others are narrower, and specific emphasis varies. But reaching consensus is unnecessary; differing terminology signifies healthy engagement with the concept and is useful for practitioners who are seeking helpful wording for many different applications. Regardless of the terms used, the goal is profound: we can and should make our human-made world as accessible and usable as possible for as diverse a user population as possible.

Since its conception, to great benefit, the Center for Universal Design has generated much conversation. Along with the definition of universal design, it has produced a manual with a set of widely used principles. However, the overall approach focuses primarily on the end product having functionality for many. But what happens if we challenge these principles by rethinking the early stages of the design process and, ultimately, its impact on the final design solution? Further, what if designers use these guides as a filter, embracing an inclusive design approach for architecture and products that explore *opportunities* rather than focusing on the challenges presented by a person's inability to perform an activity in a certain way? This strategy shifts designers' attention away from individuals' *perceived deficits* currently embedded into design decisions and provides a new way of thinking by focusing on what can be enhanced and supported.

It is essential to understand different users, their body types, and what having a disability means to them in terms of disadvantages *and* advantages. Discovering the weaknesses of a body has been the standard in the writing of many of today's accessibility design guidelines. Yet, it is equally important to recognize a body's strengths. This understanding allows designers to enhance those as opportunities in their designs, rather than merely account for what an individual doesn't have. However, the diagram below looks at three crucial

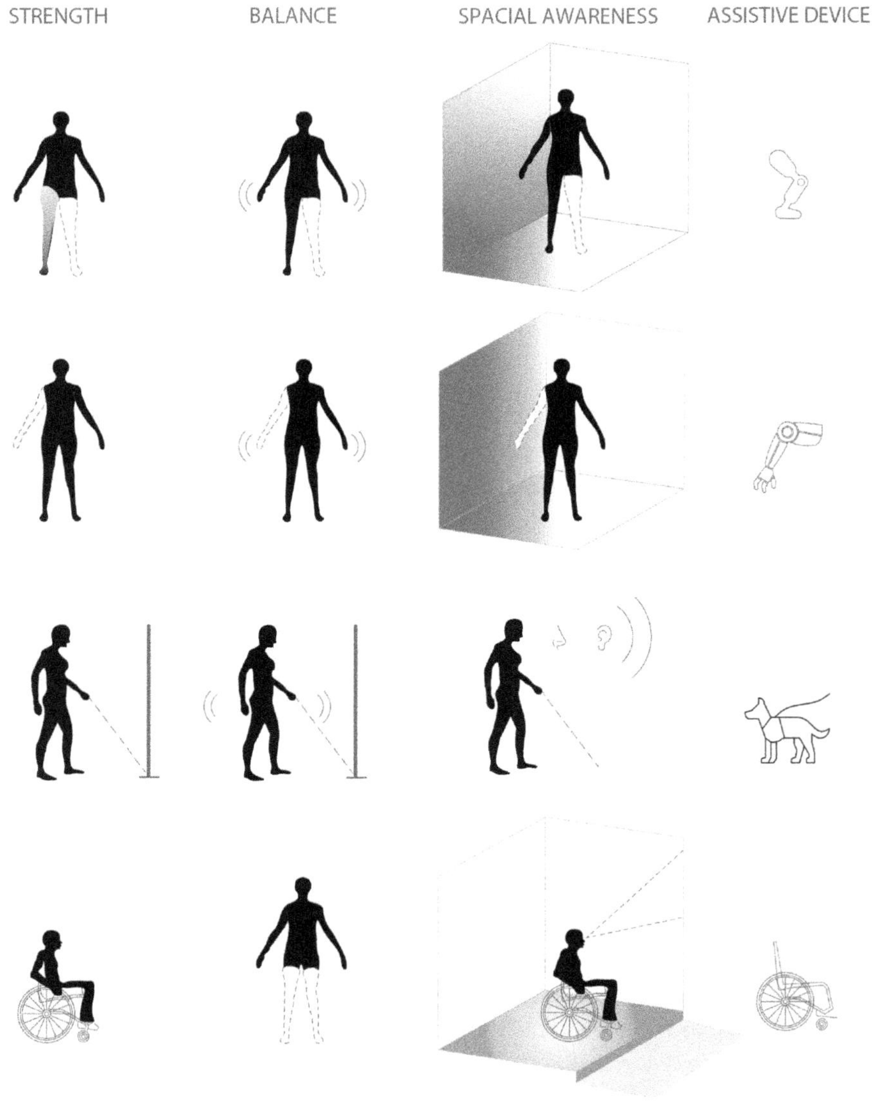

FIGURE 9.2 This is a representation of a section of disabilities and their relationship to spatial experience. In each example, an individual's bodily strengths are highlighted rather than focusing on any perceived deficiencies. The image identifies the devices each person may use to enhance their spatial experience. Diagram created by Ileana Rodriguez.

aspects of a bodily disability: strength, balance, and awareness. Consider how these may present possibilities, rather than merely limitations.

Social Impact

Unfortunately, it is common to assume that someone with a disability can adapt to their environment. But with this assumption that they can adapt, comes the *expectation* that they *should* adapt. Indeed, people with disabilities have a remarkable ability to adapt to both the built environment and people's attitudes toward them, as well as disabilities more broadly. The constant interaction with these barriers often challenges individuals to build the necessary resilience to navigate daily life activities. Unfortunately, this conditioning and the lack of an inclusive approach to spaces, services, and society has become the norm—hindering a large segment of the population from having a fully independent life with access to all, equal opportunities, and a sense of social belonging.

The current approach to design and accessibility has also created a negative connotation that places the need for access as a requirement of law, rather than an opportunity for better design practice. Progress on this topic tends to come from the implementation of policy. These developments should not be left out when discussing the issue and how this group is represented. The laws, as well as the design, should look at the differences found in the diversity of people as an *opportunity*. Understanding the impact of regulation from both an individual and holistic perspective affords the benefits of creating more accessible environments that go beyond the 15% of the population with a disability—often a common reference point when discussing these impacts.

According to statistics presented by the United Nations, 1.5 billion people in the world live with some form of disability. Further, as indicated by the census bureau in the United States, at least one in every American family experience a disability. This means even if a person is not experiencing a disability as a part of their direct lived experience, they are indirectly impacted by disability at some point in time. The following graphics, represent the population of the United States and the World—drawing a comparison between the two to understand the size of the number of people with disabilities.

In 2020, the US Department of Labor reported that 19.3% of people with disabilities between the ages of 16 and 64 are employed compared to 66.3% of people without disabilities.[3] The gap is evident, and we can argue that having a disability is challenging and can hinder a person's ability to work. However, these challenges are perpetuated and inflamed by the lack of opportunities offered in the environmental infrastructure and the flexibility of the workplace, alongside common inaccurate prejudices and lack of education and knowledge from the employer.

Let's look at the 61 million people in the United States who live with a form of disability and multiply it by 4. Based on this simple calculation, we can

FIGURE 9.3 This map shows the consolidation of all individuals with some form of a disability across the entire globe (i.e., 1 billon people). In other words, those 1 billion individuals would equal the entire population of both North and South America. Diagram created by Ileana Rodriguez. Map by Vemaps.com.

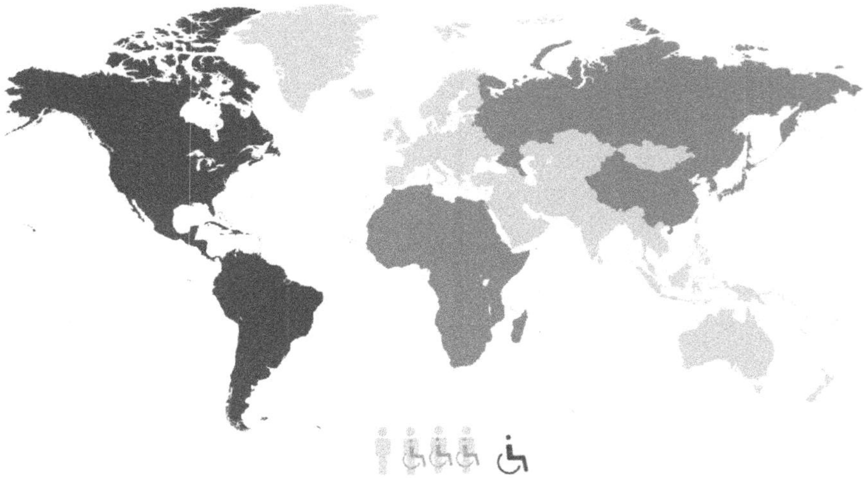

FIGURE 9.4 This map shows the consolidation of all individuals with some form of a disability, and those individuals connected to someone with a disability. It also shows those who are not directly or indirectly affected by disability across the entire globe. Diagram created by Ileana Rodriguez. Map by Vemaps.com.

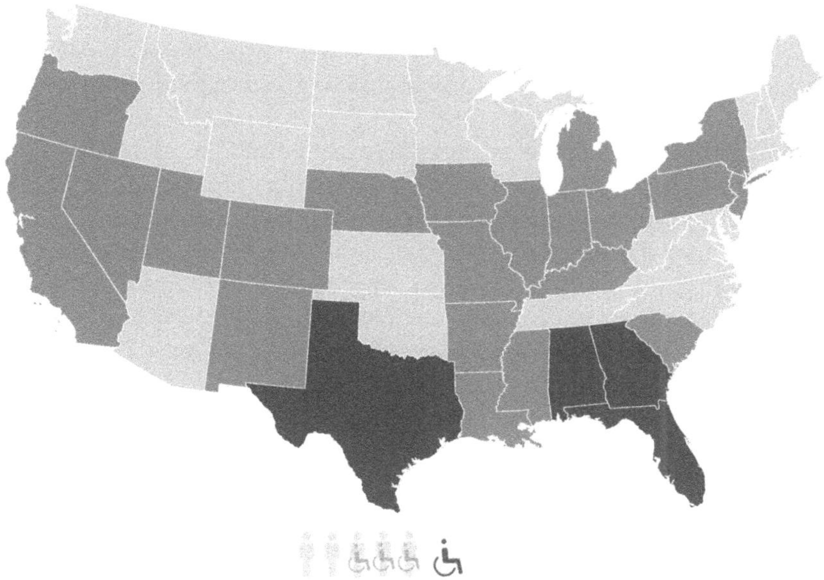

FIGURE 9.5 This map shows the consolidation of all individuals with some form of a disability, and those individuals connected to someone with a disability in the United States. It also shows those who are not directly or indirectly affected by disability. Diagram created by Ileana Rodriguez. Map by Vemaps.com.

assume that more than 60% of the American population at some point in their life is affected by a disability, either directly or by a close personal connection. It is thus safe to conclude that every American household has a relationship with a person with a disability. Therefore, this presents a moral, social, and strong business case for universal design, and designers should understand the opportunities found in design to better serve *all* users.

During the United Nations Convention in 2010 on the Rights of Persons with Disabilities, delegates identified eight principles, all of which would be negatively impacted by the built environment.

The Eight Guiding Principles:[4]

1 Respect for inherent dignity, individual autonomy, including the freedom to make one's own choices, and independence of persons.
2 Non-discrimination.
3 Full and effective participation and inclusion in society.
4 Respect for difference and acceptance of persons with disabilities as part of human diversity and humanity.
5 Equality of opportunity.
6 Accessibility.

7 Equality between men and women.
8 Respect for the evolving capacities of children with disabilities, and respect for the right of children with disabilities to preserve their identities.

The diagram in Figure 9.6 analyzes an existing building that complies with all the regulations and is considered accessible. The design solutions are examined in detail to understand where the Convention's principles have not been met due to the building design focusing on compliance, rather than accessibility with an inclusive approach. Furthermore, a genuinely inclusive built environment ***must co-exist alongside occupants with a supportive attitude to accomplish the eight guiding principles.*** One system can't operate without the other.

Technical Competency vs. Quality of Life

The purpose of having guidelines and codes is essential. Design requirements or regulations are there to protect the welfare of people and help designers understand the minimum requirements to accomplish a safe building. In the case of guidelines like the Americans with Disabilities Act Accessibility Guidelines (ADAAG), they were created to protect the rights of people with disabilities to have equal access to the built environment. The impact of policy, in this case, has brought tremendous improvement in the lives of people with disabilities. Still, the question remains—has the Americans with Disabilities Act (ADA) or ADAAG responded to the previously presented principles? In terms of policy and standards, there are undoubtedly many improvements still needed in built spaces.

These guidelines have proven to provide technical solutions in making spaces accessible. However, the many architects and designers who apply these guidelines tend to limit their decisions to mandated regulation. Architect and writer Diana Agrest discusses this topic in her paper "Design vs. Non-Design." She discusses the lack of good design found in regulations. If this concept is applied to accessibility, we find that by focusing on the code and the regulations, we are neglecting the opportunities found when we are creative when our focus is on the relationship between the space and the user regardless of abilities.

Exasperating this concept that purely focuses on the minimum requirement, design schools often resort to reference books and codes as primary resources when teaching students about accessibility; and sadly, that pattern continues into professional practice. Accessibility is directly related to an order or a mandate, not a design opportunity. Unfortunately, there is not a strong push for design-driven solutions to complex problems related to accessibility. Codes and regulations are intended to be referenced as the baseline, not as creative, quality design solutions. If all buildings were derived solely from codes and regulations, it would be unnecessary to have an architect or designer. Many people can open a book and follow instructions; however, this leaves little room for creative, experiential, and designed solutions.

While little research exists on the impact that design and architecture have on people's quality of life with a disability, my lived experience underscores the undeniably strong relationship between the environment and my wellbeing. Put simply, fewer barriers equal more access and significantly better quality of life for myself and those around me. The diagram in Figure 9.6 illustrates the limited reach of designing to code. However, access significantly increases when a design is not based solely on a code solution, but rather incorporates an inclusive design approach.

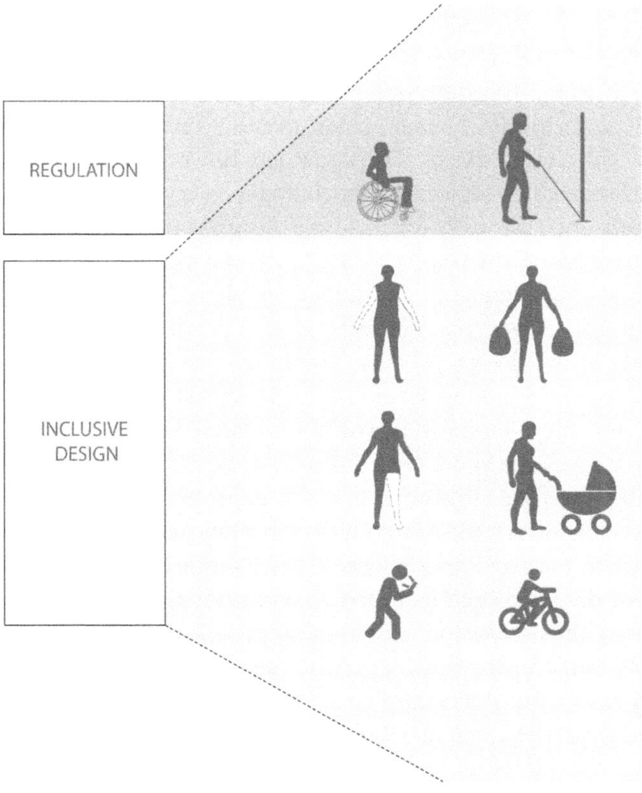

FIGURE 9.6 This diagram shows the impact of accessibility when regulatory codes guide a design versus the impact when an inclusive design approach is used. Diagram created by Ileana Rodriguez.

The Business Case for Inclusive Design

It is certainly not true that all architects or designers approach design from a technical or purely functional point of view—this is only one side of the coin. Some also focus on designing for the human experience. However, all architectural design—whether technical or experiential—follows the same professionally recognized design process that includes set phases including schematic design, design development, construction documents, and construction administration. Each phase is responsible for a different aspect of the project's design. The overall process is based on refinements that happen at each stage until the outcome is realized.

Designing for people is a huge responsibility and during each of the design phases coordination of each specialty of design such as mechanical, structural, or any other areas is closely studied. However, suppose the design process embraced inclusion as a top priority along with all the other specialties. In that case, the short-term impact would be significant, but the impact of this approach would only increase over time as more diverse individuals experience and use the space. The unique relationship between space and different types of disability, proposes adding another layer of refinement within each design phase as a tool to embrace inclusion based on potential occupants and their abilities to experience life. It can help inform scale, color, material textures, and other decisions that are part of creating spaces. This approach, however, must be present in the conceptualization of all projects and included in every design phase.

One important case study for inclusive design is the venues in Lima for the 2019 Parapan American Games. Here both the client and the design team identified that following only the guidelines offered by the legislation would not be sufficient. This project reflects what is possible when inclusion is prioritized early in the design process, becoming the main driver for the event. The guidelines were lacking by not considering all people who would be at the games, and these limitations would ultimately hinder the usability of the space. In that case, the short-term impact would be significant, and it would only increase over time as more individuals experience and use the space.

To achieve inclusion, the design team continuously revised the design process to enhance the self-imposed accessibility requirements of the event. The interventions the team used included an educational component, followed by reviews during the design and construction phases, resulting in more than just an accessible building for the Games, but also a new facility available for the community afterward. According to Pedro Indacochea, Architect and Accessibility Lead from the Lima 2019 team, accessibility was essential. Even when the building was valued engineered, cost cuts came from other areas of the project. Therefore, accessibility wasn't an area to be compromised and was considered a valuable component with a return on investment. In addition, the building is more sustainable and has left a strong legacy after the Games. The team questioned many decisions during the design process, implementing novel practices that even pushed for new legislation and better rights for people with disabilities in Peru.

According to Lucha Villa Gálvez, president of the National Paralympic Association of Peru, the project mentioned above has continued to support all athletes who now have access to training facilities. Both Olympic and Paralympic athletes can use the same facilities effectively and side by side. In the past, the Paralympic Athletes in Lima were segregated and trained in different facilities around the city, lacking optimal training conditions and breaking down the possibility for community. But now, the new venues have brought more equal opportunities to all athletes. The inclusive approach in the design of these venues extends way beyond the infrastructure. Architects, builders, maintenance staff, coaches, spectators, and anyone who occupies any part of the building can see the athletes for their abilities in the sport, not their disability. The venue has also become an education tool by exemplifying an environment that promotes inclusion. It has also created a precedent for future facilities in other parts of Peru, and a reference for other countries in the region.

To sum up, design has the power to change perception and open opportunities for people to thrive and accomplish great things. The built

FIGURE 9.7 This is a photo of a pool built for the Lima 2019 Parapan American Games. This is an example of an inclusive space in which both athletes with and without a disability can seamlessly and fully inhabit and train together. Photograph by Ileana Rodriguez.

environment is home to all our activities. Architecture and design should consider inclusive design an essential part of its approach to social justice, and inclusion should not be an isolated topic. It should be intrinsically present at every design decision to accomplish justice and opportunity for all individuals equally.

Notes

1 https://www.sdfoundation.org/news-events/sdf-news/what-is-social-justice/.
2 The Center for Universal Design (1997). *The Principles of Universal Design, Version 2.0*. Raleigh, NC: North Carolina State University.
3 https://www.dol.gov/general/topic/disability/statistics.
4 https://www.un.org/development/desa/disabilities/convention-on-the-rights-of-persons-with-disabilities/article-3-general-principles.html.

Reference

Connell, B. R., Jones, M. L., Mace, R. L., Mueller, J., Mullick, A., Ostroff, E., & Sanford, J. (1997). The principles of universal design. In M. J. Ostroff (Ed.), *Universal Design Handbook* (pp. 1–10). New York: McGraw-Hill.

CONNECTING 10

The built environment has become emblematic of the many ethical tensions in communities throughout history. Although people may claim they believe in treating everyone with dignity and offering equal opportunities, considerable division remains. Unfortunately, some spaces, for example, restrooms in public schools, are a barometer for what is happening in society. From civil rights movements and racial segregation in the 1960s to "bathroom bills" and sex segregation issues that have arisen in the 2020s, there is ample evidence to demonstrate how people's moral principles manifest in a brick-and-mortar world.

But in contemporary times, there is not just one, but two, types of spaces—the physical and the virtual. Today, people tend to experience more and more of their lives within virtual or blended realms. Not surprisingly, age-old spatial questions are emerging here, too, but with new complexities. There are concerns about establishing boundaries and creating a sense of safety in this more recent spatial dimension. Also, how should individuals' privacy be preserved while protecting and advancing the broader ecosystem?

Next, you will hear from interior designer David Euscher, who pulls these concepts to the forefront of our minds. As he does, Euscher draws upon a systems perspective. Indeed, when people speak about the intricacies of personal data, virtual networks, and smart environments, they are undoubtedly examining broad, complex systems that require a keen eye toward knowing how each piece fits together and influences one another. The same is true when considering individual people existing within environments—regardless of whether the environments are virtual, physical, or hybrid spaces. As living organisms, humans influence and are influenced by one another. Therefore, as you think of how to ethically craft and maintain various spaces, you must approach the more extensive system of potential occupants by considering the individual and the overall experience within a space.

DOI: 10.4324/9781003004622-26

10

BIG DATA, BIG INSIGHTS

Data-Driven Design for Desired Outcomes

David Euscher

Innovative Technology Leads to Insight

My teenage son is a major sports fan. I see him in the living room, thinking he's found a game to watch while taking a break from his homework. There's action on the screen, cheering from the crowd, announcers calling the game—and then I realize my son is playing a video game. The fluid and natural motion of the players adds an impressive realism, including signature moves from the star players represented in the game. The motion capture technology that enables game designers to create these rich gaming experiences, also helps real-world trainers analyze an athlete's movements. With the ability to study the movements, trainers can recommend modifications that increase effectiveness and reduce risk of injury. The information gathered not only contributes to understanding how humans move through space but enables objective study and analysis of the motion. This analysis yields scientific recommendations for optimizing performance, and propelling thought forward into new areas of inquiry and deeper understanding. This is not a new concept. Over a century ago, Eadweard Muybridge used the (then) new technology of photography for "time and motion studies." Lilian and Frank Gilbreth, along with Fredrick Winslow Taylor harnessed these techniques, and through objective measurement and observation, developed a scientific method of management, which transformed the design of workflows and processes, as well as the space they occupied by measuring, analyzing, and optimizing the movements a laborer made in a particular workflow. Similar to the advanced motion capture technology of today, this early work also enhanced understanding of the ways humans occupy and move through space.

DOI: 10.4324/9781003004622-27

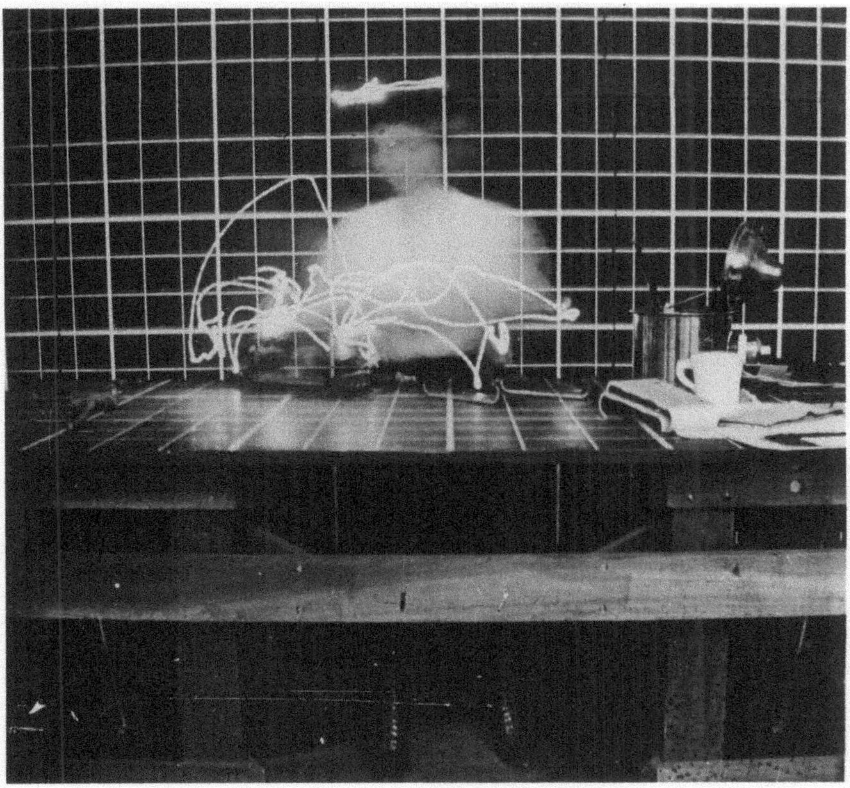

FIGURE 10.1 Motion efficiency study, by Frank Gilbreth, circa 1914. Courtesy of the Frank and Lillian Gilbreth Collection, Archives Center, National Museum of American History, Smithsonian Institution, Kenneth E. Behring Center, Division of Work and Industry.

Rules-Based Architecture

In 1941, the 3rd edition of *Architectural Graphic Standards* introduced reference material on anthropometrics, providing architects with rules for design based on human dimensions, including such Taylorist[1] ideas as the kitchen work triangle. *Architectural Graphic Standards* as well as other published design guidelines, still inform the design of spaces relative to average human dimensions and motion; whether it be a residential kitchen, a hospital's surgery suite, or the layout of a city.

Whether to define rules for a functionally optimized space, or even for architectural beauty, the effort to write "rules" for architectural design is as distant as the *Ten Books on Architecture* by the Roman architect and author Vitruvius and as proximate as the data-driven parametric design software employed in

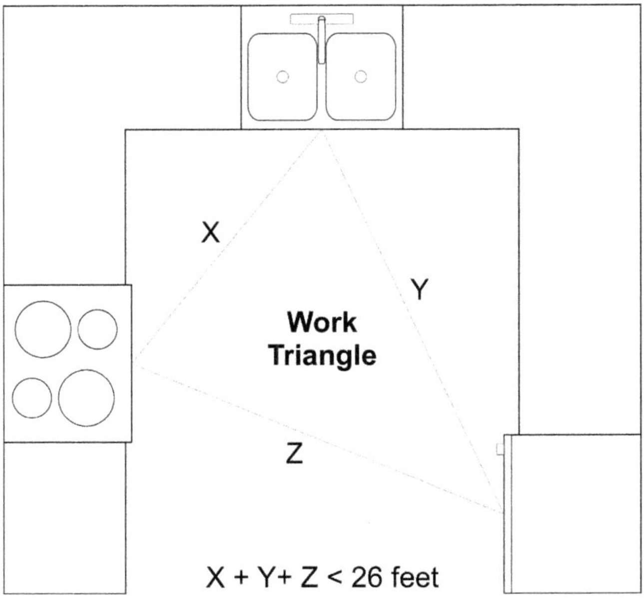

FIGURE 10.2 Kitchen work triangle. This diagram, created by the author, is based on the concept of the kitchen work triangle developed by others.

contemporary architectural and design practice. Objective rules and standards for design support the designer's authority, while providing impartial validation of design solutions and reliable decision support to those who assume the financial risk of funding architecture and design projects.

No matter how well-intentioned they are, standards, rules, and guidelines, are criticized as having a limiting effect on innovation in design. The resulting "program-driven" projects are derided as lacking creativity—serving function first and aesthetic value second. Critics of architectural programming argue that focusing only on function does not yield great architecture. Others argue that the functional program of a space does not drive the behavior of the people in that space, and so, should not be the primary goal for design. For anyone who has slept in a lecture hall, eaten in bed, or worked from home on the couch, this argument is easily understood. However, developments in data-driven design software enable architects and designers to not only explore more complex forms and spaces, but to effectively manage diverse programmatic priorities (e.g., a project's function, its site conditions, the budget, relevant building codes, and sustainability goals) as equally important design parameters. These tools challenge conventional thinking about design and provide an opportunity to explore even further than before.

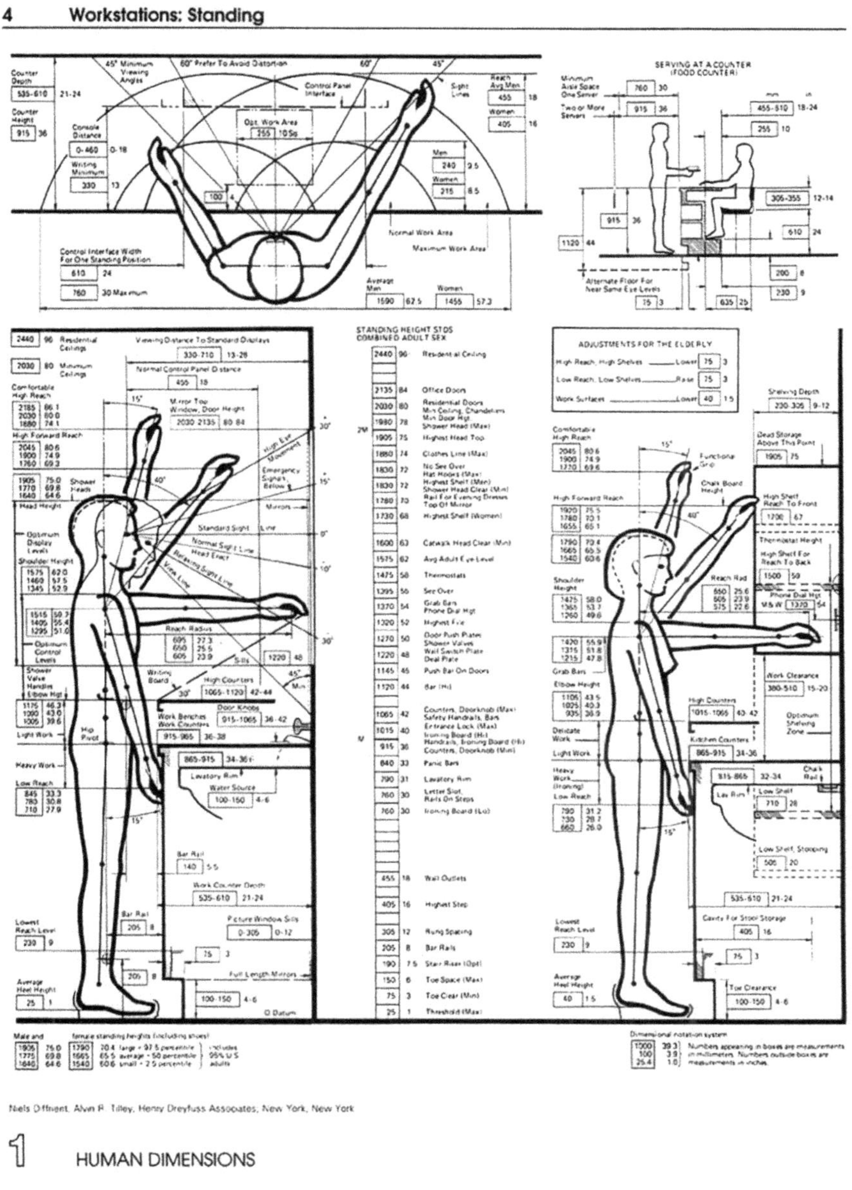

FIGURE 10.3 Anthropometrics diagrams from *Architectural Graphic Standards.* Originally created by Henry Dreyfuss Associates. Permission to use granted by Judy Crookes, previous owner.

Note: Edition unknown.

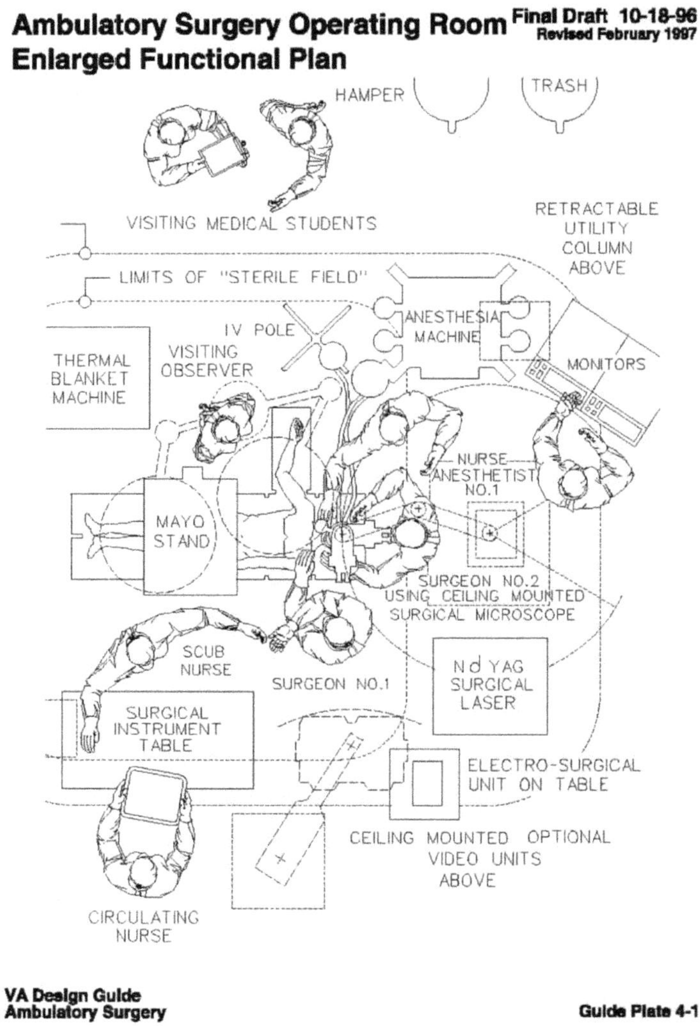

FIGURE 10.4 VA design guide ambulatory surgery operating room functional plan. Retrieved from https://vacriteria.tpub.com/ambsg/ambsg0027.htm. Note: Attempts to contact the site owner for further permissions were unsuccessful.

New Tools, New Thinking

Just as photography enabled new ways to study human movement in space, developments in computation have helped researchers uncover insights into the complexities of our physical world, thus propelling thought forward in new directions. For instance, innovations in computer technology accelerated through the second world war as engineers were faced with solving complex

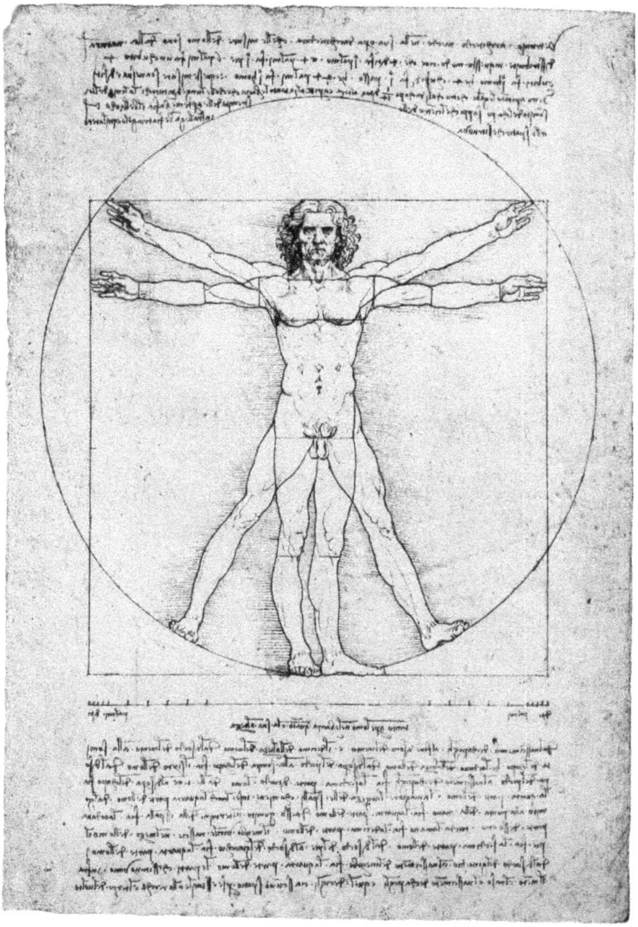

FIGURE 10.5 Vitruvian orders and human proportions or Vitruvian Man by Leonardo da Vinci.

Source: sqback, Pond5. Licensed image.

communications and control problems. Although Systems Theory was established decades before, its emergence in the 1950s and 1960s parallels advancements in computational power, which increased the ability to process large amounts of information, enabling simulation and analysis to take place at the system level.

The Problem Seeking method of architectural programming published in 1969 by William Pena and John Focke of architecture firm Caudill Rowlett Scott, reflects the influence of Systems Thinking on design, and reimagines architectural programming as a complex open system of interrelated problems. The Problem Seeking method's participatory and inclusive structure is

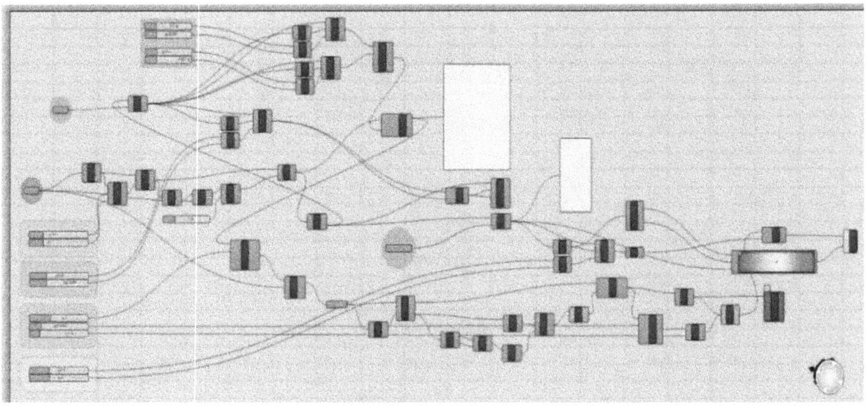

FIGURE 10.6 Grasshopper script flow diagram. Image created and provided by Corgan.

exploratory. It seeks to collect input from multiple sources to understand how people in an organization interact, the external influences on that behavior, and how the interactions and behaviors should define the problem—which in turn is to be solved through the architectural design process. Collected information prompts further questions, which leads to deeper insights and understanding of the quantitative, qualitative, and aspirational goals of a project. Understanding the problem across multiple dimensions, the designer can then respond to the parameters defined by the process.

What Does the Data Tell Us?

The automated systems that operate and monitor the use of buildings also collect a vast amount of information about buildings and the people who inhabit them. Companies offering measurement tools and assessments of space tend to focus on utilization. Their value proposition for clients is that in proving underutilization, they provide justification for reducing real estate—optimizing space and reducing cost. However, if more of the available data were studied, and more questions asked, as in Post Occupancy Evaluations, a deeper understanding might be gained about why one space is used, and another is less favored.

Access control systems can show us patterns of arrival and total numbers of people in a facility. Meanwhile, room occupancy sensors can measure the quantity of people in a room and the duration of the gathering. Alone, these measurements only count occupant density. Taken together, patterns of arrival coupled with time and duration of room occupancy begins to give a picture of group behavior in a space. Advanced radio frequency identification (RFID)

FIGURE 10.7 Eating in bed.

Source: Jesse Morrow, Stocksy. Licensed image.

sensor technologies and Real-time Locating Systems can add a further layer of specificity, monitoring not only the number of people or tagged objects in a space, but also their location, and perhaps most importantly, who is in the environment.

This capability already enables medical personnel to track equipment and patients and helps caregivers to deliver timely responses to medical care. It is being tested in airports to pair wheelchairs and attendants with passengers needing wheelchair assistance. While this information has its intended purposes and benefits, a byproduct of the information collected illustrates real-time

FIGURE 10.8 Working on couch.

Source: Prostock-studio, Envato Elements. Licensed image.

FIGURE 10.9 Sleeping in lecture hall.

Source: drazenphoto, Envato Elements. Licensed image.

movement of people and objects through a specific space, in a specific configuration. Further analysis of this data can reveal the efficacy of spatial layouts and patterns of movement for efficiencies in workflows and processes or drive the location of new features. As an input to simulation software, the designer can simulate activities in the design of an environment and run iterative configurations to find the optimal solution. This simulation and analysis enable predictive analytics processes to run for scenarios with regular and repeated

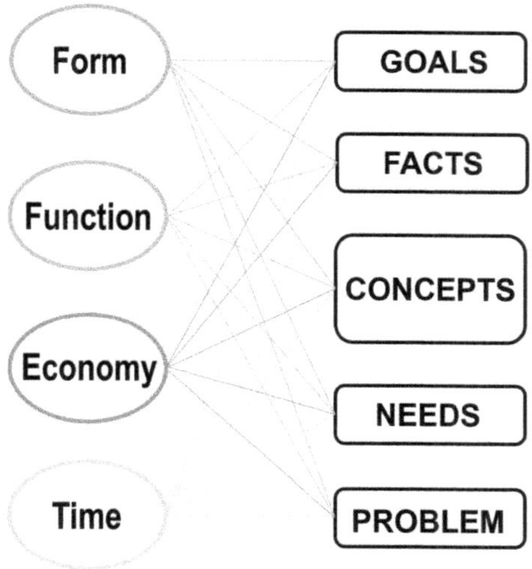

FIGURE 10.10 Problem seeking diagram, from *Problem Seeking* by William M. Pena and John W. Focke (1969), published by Caudill, Rowlett, Scott, p. 18. Redrawn by David Euscher.

functions. Fulfillment center operations and hospitals use such simulations to study and improve processes, much like Taylor and Gilbreth's studies and process management. However, these simulations do not currently account for the variability of effects of space on an individual's behavior or perceptions, or how the configuration of a space may impact the interactions between people who inhabit the space.

However, researchers at MIT have developed sociometric badges that not only measure the location of individuals, but also the distance between them and their interactions. Individuals get specific feedback on their behavior, and the organization receives anonymized aggregate data about the occupants. This data highlights patterns of behavior across an organization and correlates it to performance indicators and the configuration of the space they occupy; clearly drawing a strong connection between the design of space and the dynamics of group and interpersonal interaction.

Even without RFID or sociometric badges, the devices we interact with regularly measure our interpersonal behavior, give us health metrics, and record our preferences in everything from politics to shopping and entertainment. This information, which we give away freely, is used to curate convenient and personalized experiences online and in the real world. Moving beyond the algorithms used to drive online content to our attention, designers can begin to use data collected from the built environment and its users to create more responsive spaces. By examining the vast amount of data collected about built environments and the people who use them, we may gain a deeper understanding of the experience of space, and how that shapes individual or group behavior.

Present state predictive analytics models simulate and analyze regular and repeated activities, relative to spatial arrangements, to optimize both these repeated processes and space utilization. If predictive analytics modeling could add more inputs to the simulation, and draw on the information being collected from both environments and occupants, a more robust and complex interrelationship between environment and occupant could emerge. Suppose more complex and variable behaviors could be modeled and simulated. In that case, the interactions between humans and the built environment could be examined as an open self-organizing system, from which emerges a higher level of order.

Complex Systems

In flocks of birds and schools of fish, each "agent" (bird or fish) is part of an open system (flock or school) that behaves as an individual, while also responding to both the movements and behaviors of the surrounding agents and stimuli from the environment. By engaging in this network of actions, the movements and behaviors of each agent simultaneously affect that of the other surrounding agents. Up close, one sees individual birds moving, but cannot understand the flock's behavior as a whole. When observed from a distance, the flock exhibits dynamic behavior as a system that is continuously moving and changing form.

Similarly, drivers maneuver their vehicles, accelerate and brake in response to road conditions, weather, and the surrounding vehicles in an open, complex system we call "traffic." To examine the behavior of an individual driver would give an incomplete picture of the phenomenon of traffic. For drivers *in* traffic, the ability to understand what is happening in the system overall is even more confounding. One must get outside the system in order to study its structure and see relationships between the agent and the environment, and the collective behaviors that emerge from the system.

Consider human behavior and places where people gather, and the phenomenon is similar. Whether in a shopping mall or a museum, a busy office floor, or an airport terminal, people move through space in response to environmental cues and the people around them in a fluid manner that can be viewed as a system. As agents in the system, we may not be fully aware of the influence we have on others' behavior, or the behavioral influence that others and the environment exert on each of us. By gaining an outside view of the system, we can begin to understand its critical dynamics.

As early as the 1980s, computer models have been able to simulate flock behaviors, though not with the sophistication of the majestic computer-generated imagery (CGI) scenes of flocks of birds we see in the movies today. The phenomenon we see on screen is a result of computer programming that doesn't model the individual movement of each bird, but rather establishes rules of behavior and interaction between "agents" and their virtual environment to create realistic movements. Similarly, traffic engineers employ complex system simulation and modeling software to design highways, including the interchanges and intersections of surface roads. By simulating the complex behaviors of traffic, the geometry of the roadways, and variables such as pedestrians and bicycles at intersections, traffic engineers learn about the relationship between the design solution and predictable resulting outcomes. Considering groups of people in architectural space as an open system, it follows that simulation of complex human behavior in an architectural space is within reach.

Autodesk's research studio, The Living, has demonstrated how generative design tools can gather multiple qualitative inputs and use those rules to generate and evolve thousands of plan iterations—while simultaneously satisfying end user preferences, functional requirements, and physical constraints. Such tools, if coupled with complex systems simulation and predictive analytics tools, could rapidly iterate architectural design solutions and predict the behavior of the humans that would occupy them. With the ability to correlate spatial design and system behavior, generative design systems could enable designers to create environments that orchestrate predictable behavioral outcomes. With the addition of real-time data collection and sensory feedback technologies, augmented reality, and applied sensory stimulation technologies, designers could create spaces to provide immersive experiences ranging from adrenaline-fueled adventures to soothing therapeutic healing. The more data collected about an individual and the spaces they have encountered, the more personalized the curated experience could be. As with any data collection proposition, the concern over privacy, and fear of the information being misused for unintended purposes, is ever-present. However, just as accepting cookies allows users to opt-in with the promise of an enhanced online experience, many would just as willingly give up their data in exchange for an improved and personalized real-world experience.

While this concept of a personalized, data-driven space is conceivable, it would be challenging to execute more broadly at the scale of architecture. Moreover, when data is collected by an employer, government agency, or other entity where the benefit to the individual is less clear, suspicion and privacy concerns arise. However, designing spaces for the desired behavior of *groups* of people, conceived as a system, may be within reach through technologies available today. Further, when data collection yields a direct individual benefit to the user, the concern over privacy versus benefit is relatively low.

To mitigate these struggles of privacy and benefit, much of the information collected that would be useful for design simulation and analysis could be aggregated to study the behaviors of a group, rather than the individuals in the group independently. As is the case with sociometric badges and other

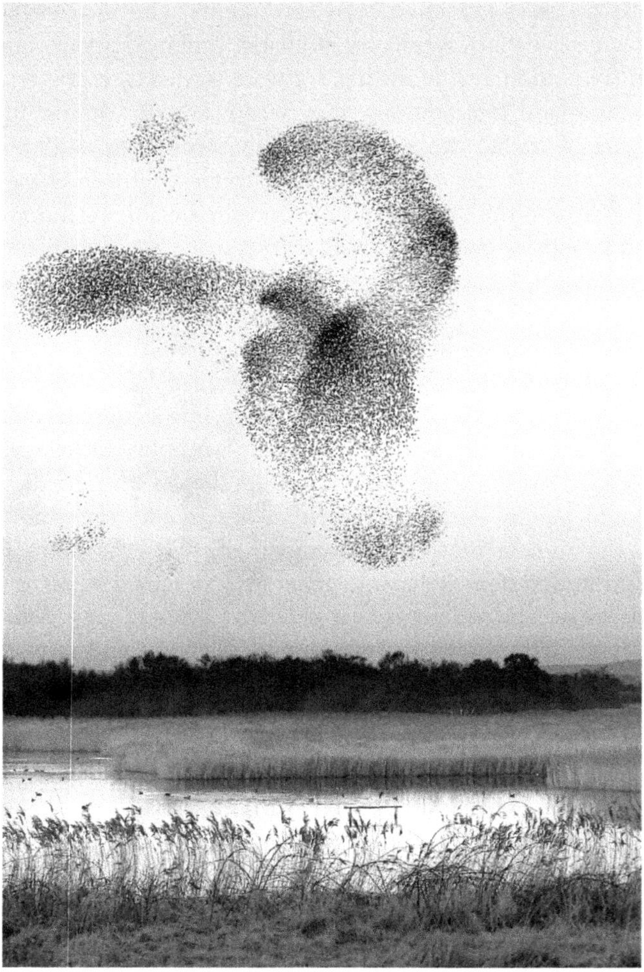

FIGURE 10.11 Starling murmuration. Photo by Tony Armstrong-Sly, available under a Creative Commons Attribution-NoDerivatives (CC BY-ND 2.0) license.

measurement tools, the data collected is anonymized and aggregated to protect privacy, but also to examine the system rather than the individuals. This aggregation of data used as inputs into a simulation may yield a design that produces an anonymized, un-personalized experience based on the behavior of the system. In other words, the data could lead to a designed environment that responds to the system's aggregate behavior, rather than the individual behaviors of those within the system. This is not to say that every person in a space designed through this method would experience the space in the same way. Each person would have a different and localized experience, that also

FIGURE 10.12 Image from driver's seat in traffic.

Source: WildMediaSK, Envato Elements. Licensed image.

FIGURE 10.13 Aerial view of complex traffic interchange.

Source: oneinchpunchphotos, Envato Elements. Licensed image.

contributes to the experience of other individuals in the group; like a bird in the flock, moving independently, yet influenced by the immediate neighboring agents and the environment they share.

Designing space to achieve a predetermined behavioral outcome is an exciting opportunity to orchestrate human experiences in the built environment to positive effect. Architectural programming has traditionally been a process to guide the design of spaces that support specific near term and anticipated future functional requirements by defining their functional and aesthetic requirements with predefined metrics. This new process defines desired outcomes and the behaviors that produce those outcomes with correlated space typologies that enable or encourage the desired behavior. However, concerns surround the potential harm that may arise from manipulating unwitting users of a space into behaving in a manner they may not be consciously aware of.

Even if this speculative ability to design space for desired behavioral outcomes does not find its way into contemporary practice, the potential value remains in the pursuit of a deeper understanding of the relationship between human behavior and the built environment. As data collection increases, there will be a heightened obligation to learn from the information collected and seek out the patterns that may not be immediately apparent. As we learn more, we must ask more questions and seek a deeper understanding. Big data leads to big insights and enables designers to be more responsive to the people they serve and be responsible for the predictable outcomes resulting from their work. If such data-driven simulation and predictive behavioral analytics processes become integrated into contemporary practice, it does not relieve the designer of authorship or accountability. With staggering amounts of information to consider and process, big data analytics and artificial intelligence (A.I.) systems will become more commonly available, and quite possibly in ways that escape our notice. Even so, A.I. can be considered as ***augmented intelligence,*** expanding human thinking and exploration beyond the limits of our collective knowledge and creativity. While the most sophisticated data-driven generative design systems can create thousands of options faster than human minds can, the final design choice is subject to and dependent on human discernment. Ultimately, humans are making choices informed by data and responding with empathy, creating enhanced human experiences through the design of space.

Note

1 Taylorism – late 19th century concept by Fred W. Taylor who studies human motion and sought efficiency in movement as a part of "Scientific Management", In Taylor's view, the task of factory management was to determine the best way for the worker to do the job, to provide the proper tools and training, and to provide incentives for good performance. Taylor broke each job down into its individual motions, analyzed these to determine which were essential, and timed the workers with a stopwatch. With unnecessary motion eliminated, the worker, following a machinelike routine, became far more productive.

Bibliography

AB Staff. (2019, March 28). The present and future of motion tracking in sports. *Athletic Business*. Retrieved September 20, 2020, from https://www.athleticbusiness.com/operations/media-technology/article/15156975/the-present-and-future-of-motion-tracking-in-sports

Anylogic. (2020, December 10). Material handling simulation [White paper]. Retrieved January 21, 2024, from https://www.anylogic.com/resources/white-papers/material-handling-simulation/

Arnold, R. D., & Wade, J. P. (2015). A definition of systems thinking: A systems approach. *Procedia Computer Science, 44*, 669–678. https://doi.org/10.1016/j.procs.2015.03.050

Hildenbrandt, H., Hemelrijk, C. K., & Carere, C. (2010). Self-organized aerial displays of thousands of starlings: A model. *Behavioral Ecology, 21*(6), 1349–1359. https://academic.oup.com/beheco/article/21/6/1349/333856?login=false

Kamel Boulos, M. N., & Berry, G. (2012). Real-time locating systems (RTLS) in healthcare: A condensed primer. *International Journal of Health Geographics, 11*, Article number: 25. https://doi.org/10.1186/1476-072X-11-25

Ladyman, J., Lambert, J., & Wiesner, K. (2013). What is a complex system? *European Journal for Philosophy of Science, 3*, 33–50. https://doi.org/10.1007/s13194-012-0056-8

Leung, C. S. K., & Lau, H. Y. K. (2020). Simulation-based optimization for material handling systems in manufacturing and distribution industries. *Wireless Networks, 26*(7), 4839–4860. https://doi.org/10.1007/s11276-018-1894-x

Merriam-Webster. (n.d.). Taylorism. *Merriam-Webster.com Dictionary*. Retrieved January 20, 2024, from https://www.merriam-webster.com/dictionary/Taylorism

Rostami-Shahrbabaki, M., Weikl, S., Niels, T., & Bogenberger, K. (2023). Modeling vehicle flocking in lane-free automated traffic. *Transportation Research Record: Journal of the Transportation Research Board, 2677*. https://doi.org/10.1177/03611981231159405

Sar, G., & Ghosh, D. (2023). Flocking and swarming in a multi-agent dynamical system. *Chaos: An Interdisciplinary Journal of Nonlinear Science, 33*. https://doi.org/10.1063/5.0168050

Stuart, K. (2010, June 12). Sports sims: How they became the real deal. *The Guardian*. Retrieved September 20, 2020, from https://www.theguardian.com/technology/2010/jun/13/sports-sims-motion-capture-technology

Takahashi, D. (2020, August 27). Move.ai enables AI motion capture without the hassle for video game production. *VentureBeat*. Retrieved September 20, 2020, from https://venturebeat.com/business/move-ai-enables-motion-capture-without-the-hassle-for-video-game-production/

Van der Kruk, E., & Reijne, M. M. (2018). Accuracy of human motion capture systems for sport applications: State-of-the-art review. *European Journal of Sport Science, 18*(6), 806–819. https://doi.org/10.1080/17461391.2018.1463397

Waber, B. N., & Pentland, A. (Eds.). (n.d.). Understanding organizational behavior with wearable sensing technology. In *Academy of Management Annual Meeting Proceedings*. Retrieved January 21, 2024, https://hd.media.mit.edu/tech-reports/TR-618.pdf

Walmsley, K., & Villaggi, L. (2019, January 4). Generative urban design: A collaboration between Autodesk Research and Van Wijnen. *Autodesk University*. Retrieved from https://medium.com/autodesk-university/generative-urban-design-43f4ea48039d

CONNECTING 11

Earlier in this section, Aye touched upon professional codes of ethics. In the next chapter, this topic is explicitly revisited for architects, and by extension, everyone responsible for designing the built environment. While Euscher expanded the realm of moral responsibility beyond the physical world, architect Janice Barnes brings us squarely back. She maintains a similar systems perspective but emphasizes the need to act decisively to protect the planet—our most valuable and irreplaceable shared resource. Without it, civilization could no longer live as we all do today.

Barnes acknowledges the diverse knowledge and skills design practitioners must possess. However, she also highlights, like Rodriguez, how professionals have become overly reliant on adhering to industry norms rather than advancing past them. Instead of futureproofing, the field remains committed to standards that may have been good enough in the past but need to be improved going forward. Environmental concerns have ebbed and waned over time, but when is it too late to care and take action? What are the architecture and design industry's ethical obligations to people today and future generations? Barnes raises these questions and warns all of us of the global risks of not addressing climate change, which will impact the economy, jeopardize human health, and ultimately threaten humanity's existence.

DOI: 10.4324/9781003004622-28

11

#WeCantUnknowThis

Design and Climate Change

Janice Barnes

Addressing climate change is one of the greatest of the "grand challenges" faced globally. While each country determines its commitment to the challenge, reflecting on ongoing work in the United States offers insights. According to the United States White House Office of Science and Technology Policy (2013), grand challenges are

> Ambitious but achievable goals that harness science, technology, and innovation to solve important national or global problems, and that have the potential to capture the public's imagination. Grand Challenges can: Help create the industries and the jobs of the future; expand the frontiers of human knowledge about ourselves and the world around us, help tackle important problems related to energy, health, education, the environment, national security and global development, and serve as a north star for collaboration between the public and private sectors.

Presenting climate change as a grand challenge is not new. Since the 1960s, Dr. James Hansen studied climate impacts, and in 1981 published the first global temperature analysis (Hansen et al., 1981). By 1988, with the most recent eight years of data demonstrating notable global warming, Hansen testified to the US Senate about the cause-and-effect relationship of the greenhouse effect and its impacts on extreme weather events (Hansen, 1988). And beyond these formative years, many have beckoned consideration of climate change—from globally recognized publications such as *The Lancet* (2017, 2018, 2019), organizing bodies such as the G20 (i.e., "Group of 20"; GCIT, 2016), professional associations such as the American Institute of Architects (AIA, 2019), to business leaders such as the World Economic Forum (2020).

DOI: 10.4324/9781003004622-29

The Lancet notes the correlated relationship between climate change and health. The projected climate changes for the latter part of this century will have wide-ranging deleterious effects on locational habitability and population health if significant adjustments are not made. *The Lancet* (2020) advocates for increased awareness of extreme heat risks to vulnerable populations, and it fosters increased commitment to assure that children born in 2020 do not have their future health defined by the climates they will inhabit.

Climate change will hurt our health

Note: The symbol used throughout is a CODA mark, used in music to conclude a musical section. It is employed here to emphasize and summarize the main points.

Similarly, the G20 (2016) recognizes the disproportionate risks associated with climate change and global economic stability, offering 12 specific recommendations for risk reduction in their 2016 preparation for the Hangzhou, China summit. The prior year, the Financial Stability Board (FSB), a subset of the G20, announced the Task Force on Climate-Related Financial Disclosures. The TCFD "seeks to develop recommendations for voluntary climate-related financial disclosures that are consistent, comparable, reliable, clear and efficient, and provide decision-useful information to lenders, insurers, and investors."

Climate change will imperil our economic systems

In this same year, with a presidential administration change, the new White House occupant decreed withdrawal from the Paris Accord: the substantial agreement for a global drawdown of emissions to reduce the worst of the coming impacts of climate change. This same administration also politicized climate change as a party perspective instead of the bipartisan, can't-opt-out-however-much-one-tries, global risk that it is. While regressive, it is also counter to our early political history wherein republicans and democrats worked toward resolutions (Dunlap and McCright, 2010). These authors reference Theodore Roosevelt's conservation work via the National Parks Service, Franklin Delano Roosevelt's work in the New Deal's Soil Conservation Service, and Nixon for various pieces of environmental legislation. However, with the Reagan era, the language shifts to economic burdens wrought by environmental protections—followed by Gingrich's time in Congress and George W. Bush's refusal to sign the Kyoto protocol. And so, the partisan divide that

"As a profession, we have the responsibility to prioritize and support effective actions to exponentially decelerate the production of greenhouse gases contributing to climate change. Our goal, as set forward by AIA and partners like Architecture 2030, is net-zero emissions in the building sector by 2050."

"It is our responsibility to work globally to help reduce operational and embodied greenhouse gas production with passive design techniques, employ energy efficiency measures, adapt existing buildings, and specify low-impact building materials that increase human health and productivity while withstanding the effects of a changing climate."

"It is our responsibility to make the business and financial case to clients to help them better understand and support the need to integrate renewable energy sources into all buildings, making them more sustainable, resilient, and economical."

FIGURE 11.1 American Institute of Architects Resolution for urgent and sustained climate action.

characterizes current discourse drags climate change, a decidedly nonpartisan risk, into its maw. However, with the Biden/Harris administration's actions in early 2021, including multiple executive orders for a more integrated approach to tackling climate change, such as reentering the Paris Climate Accord, and their commitment to building unity across parties, there were reasons for optimism (White House Briefing Room, 2021). With the coming shift in leadership in January 2025, this is less so.

In 2019, the AIA made a public commitment to climate, ratifying the Resolution for Urgent and Sustained Climate Action. The AIA asked, "architects around the world to support humanity's collective call to climate action through an unrelenting commitment to sustainable and resilient design" (AIA, 2019). Yet, this same year in an oil-enriched city, AIA regional convention attendees warned against climate change discussions (Barnes, 2019).

Climate change is a collective responsibility for design practitioners (architects, interior designers, engineers, landscape architects), but partisanship and/or economic benefactors provide cover to opt out

The World Economic Forum (WEF) publishes its annual Global Risks Report to alert investors of risks to the global markets. In 2020, for the first time, WEF anchored climate change as the highest likelihood, and highest impact risk, facing global markets. Specifically, WEF highlights climate action failure, extreme weather, biodiversity loss, water crises, and natural disasters. These dire warnings underscore the scale and frequency of climate-related disasters impacting millions of lives. Headlines shout: Too much water. Too little water. Too much heat. Too strong winds. The consequences of these warnings have played out across the globe as well. For instance, to the point of climate action failure, evidence of mass migrations and mass immigrations link the civil war in Syria and compounded water stress for farmers (Friedman, 2013). Quoting Syrian economist Samir Aita, "the drought did not cause Syria's civil war, but the failure of the government to respond to the drought played a huge role in fueling the uprising." Lustgarten (2020) writes about the loss of habitable places and projected areas where one cannot live if one steps outside. With temperatures of 130 F in Death Valley, as well as in more inhabited parts of California in August of 2020, it is not unreasonable to imagine these risks. With the scale of events coinciding with population and investment growth, compounded losses increase, investors and municipalities retract (Valmeyer, Illinois, Knobloch, 2005 and Fairbourne, Wales, a to-be-decommissioned town, Wall, 2019), and insurers and bond raters demand risk assessments and adaptation plans (Freitas et al, 2019, Freitas and Zhang, 2019).

Climate change and our inability to act on it promptly warrants its ranking as the highest global risk

In summary, these respected voices believe that climate change will hurt our health and our economies. It stultifies our environment—impacting our water and biodiversity and increasing our exposures to natural disasters brought about by extreme weather. Design practitioners owe a professional responsibility to help address this grand challenge. With responsibility, one is expected to be answerable for one's actions, accountable to others, and cognizant of decisions within larger contexts. To act ethically, one must honor those responsibilities, or take ethical responsibility. To assume ethical responsibility in medicine is to exemplify the Hippocratic Oath, or to "do no harm." To assume ethical responsibility in design is to protect the health, safety, and welfare of occupants, or to "do no harm."

The AIA Code of Ethics describes the expectation for designers to protect the health, safety, and welfare of the public; addresses environmental equity and justice; and reaffirms obligations to the environment. Ethical

Standard 1.5 Design for Human Dignity and the Health, Safety, and Welfare of the Public notes that "Members should employ their professional knowledge and skill to design buildings and spaces that will enhance and facilitate human dignity and the health, safety, and welfare of the individual and the public." Ethical Standard 6.5 Climate Change notes that "Members should incorporate adaptation strategies with their clients to anticipate extreme weather events and minimize adverse effects on the environment, economy, and public health" (AIA, 2020).

Considering such responsibility, designers must also recognize that climate change is but one part of resilience, or the ability of a place to manage its risks and threat multipliers. A threat multiplier is a chronic issue, like a dull ache, that amplifies a climate event's impact. The racist practice of "redlining," for example, signaled systemic disinvestment in communities of color. With that disinvestment came fewer parks, fewer trees providing canopy cover, more pavement, and a much greater vulnerability to heat exposure as temperatures rise (Cusick, 2020). In Ferguson, Missouri, the threat multipliers of poverty, systemic racism, and municipal debt combined to make the tornadoes that warranted a national disaster declaration fall to the back burner of the national debate. While those storms destroyed homes and displaced families, the greater social justice issues were far more traumatic. Ferguson's poverty-imperiled black families bore the brunt, not only of historic systemic racism, but they were also targeted by a police force that was struggling with significant municipal debt. As a result, the mostly white police department, mined the black community for funds through increased traffic ticketing to refill municipal coffers while recognizing that those same impoverished families had no way to pay (Friedersdorf, 2015, Eligon, 2019).

While designers may argue that broader societal issues are too wide-ranging to tackle, the climate remains an indisputable criterion to consider. Architects are expected to understand the climate of the places they are designing and to integrate that knowledge into design decision-making to protect the health, safety, and welfare of *all* occupants of those environments (AIA, 2017, AIA, 2020). Unfortunately, the Standard of Care rests on industry norms, which in turn rests on climate history—looking at where a place has been to understand where a place is going. Building codes, design guidelines, engineering calculations, and even client expectations are frequently backward-looking, at least historically. However, looking forward to probable climate scenarios is new-ish.

The National Climate Assessment (NCA) is a quadrennially-mandated nation-wide climate assessment convened by the U.S. Global Change Research Program (USGCRP). The USGCRP "is legally mandated to conduct a state of the science synthesis of climate impacts and trends across U.S. regions and sectors every four years." Formed in 1989 by Presidential Initiative and mandated by Congress in 1990, the USGCRP completed five quadrennial assessments and is developing the sixth, the NCA6 (Global Change, 2020). For many designers, that means that an entire professional career is shored up by USGCRP research. So not so new. With such resources embedded in national governance for the last 30 years, and in organizations such as *The Lancet*, WEF, AIA, and others conveying the importance of the issue, is climate change in the mix as designers make daily decisions? Unfortunately, no (Stamp, 2020, UNEP, 2019).

In 2016 as the AIA ramped up its focus from sustainability to resilience, a leading Federal expert shared climate-related expertise with a caveat: in guiding the audience on how to think through climate-related risk issues, it became the participants' responsibility to take action. The message was, "You can't unknow what I tell you. You need to act on it (Barnes, 2016)." Reflecting on those wise words and thinking about how the resonance warranted personal action—responsibility for decisions growing exponentially with that simple phrase, and the memory still ringing with the aural and visual cues delivered that day—a hashtag that describes a professional mission was born: **#WeCantUnknowThis** (Barnes, 2016). However, culture has inertial power (Hoffman, 2015). As recently as 2020, questions arose regarding whether it's possible to charge clients more for dealing with climate change, as the designer's plate is too frequently overloaded. This rationale is akin to asking a physician whether they charge extra for giving the best advice versus average advice.

While leading the Bank of England, Mark Carney (2015) spoke eloquently of the "Tragedy of the Horizon." Drawing from the tragedy of the commons, wherein self-interests trump the common good (Hardin, 1968 and Lloyd, 1833), the Tragedy of the Horizon argues that by the time the global economy recognizes the impending risk of climate change, it will be too late to avoid the most significant consequences. Carney defined three types of risks: physical risk, or what will happen to the environment; liability risk, or what will happen to those responsible; and transition risk, or what will happen during the transition to a low carbon economy. With too short of a horizon, decision-makers miss critical investment windows, exposing people and assets to greater risks.

Too often, designers cannot answer three basic questions connecting climate science to their daily work: (1) What are the climate projections where your project is located? (2) What are the vulnerabilities and their cascading consequences related to those projections? (3) And how does your design address those vulnerabilities? Without answering these basic questions, designers face the tragedy of the horizon, assuming their project, situation, or location doesn't need to address those issues yet. But all projects have service life assumptions. Those assumptions carry capital value, and as designers are responsible to their clients to bring fiduciary care to the design investment, that tragedy becomes an ethical question. Without a climate-forward, service-life-informed understanding, designers guide client investments with *average advice*—not the best advice possible—not the advice that supports the health, safety, and welfare of occupants.

Yet, designers have access to resources to answer those very questions. The National Climate Assessment (Global Change, 2020) sets the big picture of climate projections across regions and sectors in the United States. The Intergovernmental Panel on Climate Change (IPCC, 2020) anchors international perspectives. The U.S. Climate Resilience Toolkit (Global Change, 2020) provides, per zip code, temperature and precipitation projections, histories, and case studies on how to integrate these challenges in feasible ways. The AIA offers Resilience Training Certification, including a primer on vulnerabilities assessments (AIA, 2019). Enterprise Community Partners provides guidance for climate preparedness for homes (ECP, 2019). Municipal Climate Action Plans (such as Climate-Ready DC) identify the connections between climate probabilities, vulnerabilities, and adaptation strategies, explaining the risks in the context of downscaled climate assessments and state-required hazard mitigation plans (DoEE, 2016). And, the Urban Land Institute offers annual briefs on lessons learned.

As professional organizations test members' readiness for greater climate change integration, a range of challenges include:

1 Political alignment against dealing with climate change as fostered by the previous federal administration (Carter et al., 2017).
2 Fear of assuming responsibility for probabilistic projections and concerns about fee exposure given the work required to understand and act on climate data (AIA, 2020).
3 A lack of inculcated process from professional education programs and continuing education programs (Stead et al., 2020).
4 A continuing reward-recognition system that does not mandate climate awareness much less readiness (RAIC, 2020).
5 Competing priorities stemming from the pandemic response in 2020.
6 And numerous other challenges that relate to client readiness for political or other reasons. However, to paraphrase John Lewis, if you see something is wrong, say something, do something. The AIA Code of Ethics notes such (AIA, 2020). **Say something. Do something.**

Recognizing the gap between the conversations that professional associations, educators, practitioners, and clients hold, along with the pulsing need to act on climate, in collaboration with a number of leading climate scientists, a team of advocates hosted an event at the Global Climate Action Summit in California in 2018. The purpose of the event was to encourage the adoption of seven principles that could guide design practice toward better climate integration and offer resources for how to do so (Barnes et al, 2018).

1. ***Assess future climate conditions projected to occur over a project's life span in design and implementation of projects****, including using the best available climate science in understanding and preparing for potential climate impacts such as extreme weather, floods, droughts, wildfire, heatwaves, sea level rise and more intense precipitation, across the anticipated lifetime of our projects*
2. ***Adapt our designs, plans, materials choices and implementation processes to limit climate-related risks and limit carbon emissions***
3. ***Consider how to minimize current and future climate-related risks in site selection***
4. ***Ensure that our environmental assessments****, including impacts on habitat and water supplies, also* ***consider future climate conditions***
5. ***Incorporate adaptive design principles*** *that allow for a range of future conditions*
6. ***Encourage the involvement of all affected communities in planning and design processes***
7. ***Acknowledge and address climate-related social and environmental equity issues*** *that are directly or indirectly impacted by the project*

FIGURE 11.2 Design principles for climate action.

These principles underscore a desperate need for transformational change in design practice. A change that seeks to redirect misguided, unguided, or unguarded investments toward a more climate-ready future, and a call for designers to heed their ethical responsibilities, offer the best possible advice, and reduce the risks to health, safety, and welfare of occupants. "We all live in the same house" (Lewis, 2019). No one in this house gets to opt out of climate change. **#WeCantUnknowThis**

References

American Institute of Architects (2017) *The Standard of Care: Should I Care?* https://www.aia.org/articles/146491-the-standard-of-care-should-i-care. Retrieved August 22, 2020.

American Institute of Architects (2019) *Resilience and Adaptation Online Certificate Program.* https://aiau.aia.org/aia-resilience-and-adaptation-online-certificate-program. Retrieved August 30, 2020.

American Institute of Architects (2019) *Where We Stand: Climate Action.* https://www.aia.org/resources/77541-where-we-stand-climate-change. Retrieved August 21, 2020.

American Institute of Architects (2020) *Code of Ethics.* https://www.aia.org/pages/3296-code-of-ethics-and-professional-conduct. Retrieved August 30, 2020.

American Institute of Architect (January 10, 2020) *Minimizing Risk When Designing for Climate Change: Source of Risk.* https://www.aia.org/articles/6255157-minimizing-risk-when-designing-for-climate:46. Retrieved August 22, 2020.

Barnes, Janice (2016) *Perkins+Will Resilience Lab Center of Excellence Annual Meeting*, Chicago, IL. September 2016.

Barnes, Janice (2016) Working Session Discussion. *Confidential Federal Participant. AIA National Resilience Conference.* Washington, DC (February 2016).

Barnes, Janice, Katherine Jacobs, Anne Waple (2018) *Spurring Professional Activities toward Climate Leadership (SPACL) Global Climate Action Summit.* San Francisco, CA, September 2018.

Barnes, Janice (2019) Personal Communication with Confidential AIA Representative, *Louisiana AIA Regional Convention* (November 2019).

Carney, Mark (2015) *Breaking the Tragedy of the Horizon – Climate Change and Financial Stability.* https://www.bankofengland.co.uk/speech/2015/breaking-the-tragedy-of-the-horizon-climate-change-and-financial-stability. Retrieved August 21, 2020.

Carter, Jacob, Gretchen Goldman, Genna Reed, Peter Hansel, Michael Halpern, Andrew Roseberg (2017) *Sidelining Science Since Day One. How the Trump Administration has Harmed Public Health and Safety in Its First Six Months.*

Cusick, Daniel (2020) Past Racist Redlining Practices Increased Climate Burden on Minority Neighborhoods. *Scientific American.* https://www.scientificamerican.com/article/past-racist-redlining-practices-increased-climate-burden-on-minority-neighborhoods/. Retrieved August 21, 2020.

District Office of Energy and Environment (2016) *Climate Ready DC.* https://doee.dc.gov/climateready. Retrieved August 30, 2020.

Dunlap, R. E. and A. M. McCright (2010) A Widening Gap: Republican and Democratic Views on Climate Change. *Journal of Environment: Science and Policy for Sustainable Development*, Volume 50, Issue 5: 26–35, August 07, 2010.

Eligon, John (2019) Stopped, Tickets, Fined: The Pitfalls of Drive While Black in Ferguson. *New York Times.* https://www.nytimes.com/2019/08/06/us/black-drivers-traffic-stops.html. Retrieved August 21, 2020.

Enterprise Community Partners (2019) Keep Safe: A Gide for Resilient Housing Design in Island Communities. https://www.enterprisecommunity.org/solutions-and-innovation/disaster-recovery-and-rebuilding/keepsafe. Retrieved August 30, 2020

Freitas, Frank and Jing Zhang (November 2019) *Climate Risk – The Science, The Economics, and the Time to Act.* https://www.moodysanalytics.com/-/media/presentation/2019/mas-gs2-climate-risk-the-time-to-act.pdf. Retrieved August 22, 202

Freitas, Frank, Michael Denton and Cris DeRitis (November 5, 2019) *The Risk Management Impact of Climate Change and ESG*. https://www.moodysanalytics.com/-/media/presentation/2019/mas-t3d2-risk-mgt-impact-of-climage-change.pdf. Retrieved August 22, 2020.

Friedersdorf, Conor (2015) Ferguson's Conspiracy Against Black Citizens. *The Atlantic*. March 5. 2015. https://www.theatlantic.com/national/archive/2015/03/ferguson-as-a-criminal-conspiracy-against-its-black-residents-michael-brown-department-of-justice-report/386887/. Retrieved August 21, 2020.

Friedman, Tom (2013) Without Water, Revolution. *New York Times*, May 18, 2013. https://www.nytimes.com/2013/05/19/opinion/sunday/friedman-without-water-revolution.html

G20 Climate Change Initiatives Team (GCIT) (2016) *G20 Climate Initiatives*. Toronto, ON: University of Toronto, Munk School of Global Affairs.

Global Change (2020) *Assess the U.S. Climate*. https://www.globalchange.gov/what-we-do/assessment. Retrieved August 21, 2020.

Hansen, James, A. Lacis Johnson, S. Lebedeff, P. Lee, D. Rind, and G. Russell (1981) Climate Impact of Increasing Atmospheric Carbon Dioxide. *Science*, Volume 213: 957–966.

Hansen, James (1988) *Congressional Testimony of Dr. James Hansen*, June 23, 1988 https://www.sealevel.info/1988_Hansen_Senate_Testimony.html. Retrieved August 22, 2020.

Hardin, Garrett (1968) The Tragedy of the Commons. Science. Lloyd, William Forster (1833). *Two Lectures on the Checks to Population*. Oxford: Oxford University.

Hoffman, Andrew (2015) *How Culture Shapes the Climate Change Debate*. Stanford University Press.

Intergovernmental Panel on Climate Change (2020) https://www.ipcc.ch/. Retrieved August 30, 2020

Knobloch, Dennis (2005) Moving a Community in the Aftermath of the Great 1993 Midwest Flood. Universities Council on Water Resources. *Journal of Contemporary Water Research and Education*, Issue 130: 41–45, March 2005. https://opensiuc.lib.siu.edu/cgi/viewcontent.cgi?article=1070&context=jcwre. Retrieved August 22, 2020.

Lewis, John (2019) Floor Statement of Rep. John Lewis (D-GA) on House Resolution 755, Impeaching the President of the United States for High Crimes and Misdemeanors December 18, 2019 https://www.youtube.com/watch?v=XLyysOX6HXU. Retrieved August 30, 2020

Lloyd, William Forster (1833) *Two Lectures on the Checks to Population*. Oxford: Oxford University.

Lustgarten, Abahm (2020) *The Great Climate Migration*. July 23, 2020. https://www.nytimes.com/interactive/2020/07/23/magazine/climate-migration.html. Retrieved August 21, 2020.

Royal Architectural Institute of Canada (2020) *Designing for the Future*. https://raic.org/raic/designing-future. Retrieved August 22, 2020.

Stamp, Elizabeth (2020) How the Architecture Industry Is Reacting to Climate Change. *Architectural Digest*. https://www.architecturaldigest.com/story/climate-change-design-architecture. Retrieved August 22, 2020.

Stead, Naomi, Philip Oldfield, Chris Knapp (August 10, 2020) *Designing Hope: The Role of Architecture Education in the Climate Crisis*. https://architectureau.com/articles/designing-hope-the-role-of-architecture-education-in-the-climate-crisis/. Retrieved August 22. 2020.

UN Environmental Program (December 11, 2019) *Global Status Report for Buildings and Construction Sector.* https://www.unenvironment.org/resources/publication/2019-global-status-report-buildings-and-construction-sector. Retrieved August 22, 2020.

Urban Land Institute (2016) *Returns on Resilience.* https://uli.org/wp-content/uploads/ULI-Documents/Returns-on-Resilience-The-Business-Case.pdf. Retrieved August 30, 2020.

Wall, Tom (May 18, 2019) 'This is a wake-up call': The Villagers Who Could Be Britain's First Climate Refugees. *The Guardian.* https://www.theguardian.com/environment/2019/may/18/this-is-a-wake-up-call-the-villagers-who-could-be-britains-first-climate-refugees. Retrieved August 22, 2020

Watt, Nick et al. (2018) The 2018 Report of the Lancet Countdown on Health and Climate Change: Shaping the Health of Nations for Centuries to Come. *The Lancet*, Volume 392, Issue 10163: 2479–2514, December 08, 2018.

Watts, Nick et al. (2017) The Lancet Countdown on Health and Climate Change: From 25 years of Inaction to a Global Transformation for Public Health. *The Lancet*, Volume 391, Issue 10120: 581–630, October 30, 2017.

Watts, Nick et al. (2019) The 2019 Report of the Lancet Countdown on Health and Climate Change: Ensuring that the Health of a Child Born Today Is Not Defined by a Changing Climate. *The Lancet*, Volume 394, Issue 10211: 1836–1878, November 16, 2019.

White House Briefing Room (2021, January 27) *FACT SHEET: President Biden Takes Executive Actions to Tackle the Climate Crisis at Home and Abroad, Create Jobs, and Restore Scientific Integrity across Federal Government.* https://www.whitehouse.gov/briefing-room/statements-releases/2021/01/27/fact-sheet-president-biden-takes-executive-actions-to-tackle-the-climate-crisis-at-home-and-abroad-create-jobs-and-restore-scientific-integrity-across-federal-government/. Retrieved February 15, 2021.

World Economic Forum (2020) *The Global Risks Report 2020.* https://www3.weforum.org/docs/WEF_Global_Risk_Report_2020.pdf. Retrieved August 21, 2020.

White House Office of Science and Technology Policy (2013, April 2) *21st Century Grand Challenges.* https://obamawhitehouse.archives.gov/administration/eop/ostp/grand-challenges. Retrieved August 21, 2020.

CONNECTING 12

In the next chapter, environmental psychologist Judith Heerwagen echoes Barnes's global call to action, urging everyone to examine their connection with nature and how it could influence climate change. Heerwagen encourages all of us to step back and evaluate the built environment's role in disconnecting people from outside. While buildings provide shelter and protection from the natural world, they also limit people's contact with the outdoors. The engineering and construction industries have advanced mechanical, electrical, and plumbing systems, transforming how people live in many countries. For example, artificial lighting is available today regardless of the time of day. Heating and cooling systems keep building occupants within a narrow temperature range, and readily accessible water has improved hygiene and made daily life easier.

However, the world is changing. Drastic weather patterns, hotter temperatures, and natural disasters are increasing at an alarming rate, impacting people worldwide. The reality is that many current building approaches that condition interior environments simultaneously contribute to climate change while boosting people's reliance on built space. This deepening codependence not only disconnects people from the natural world but also actively harms it. Heerwagen suggests that fostering a love of nature, known as biophilia, and increasing contact with the earth can ultimately make humans and the planet more resilient. Heerwagen recommends incorporating integral biophilic elements into buildings and enhancing direct interaction with the outdoors to unlock people's willingness to protect the natural environment, which is urgently needed.

DOI: 10.4324/9781003004622-30

12

THE URGENCY OF BIOPHILIA AS AN INTEGRATED APPROACH IN THE FACE OF CLIMATE CHANGE

Judith Heerwagen

Biophilia and Climate Change

Biophilia is not just about living entities in the environment (plants and animals), although the term suggests that. Instead, biophilia includes a full range of elements that support life. These include water, light, fire, refuge, views, plants, animals, and natural materials, all of which support survival and well-being.

To understand our powerful relationship with the natural environment, imagine you went to sleep one night after an evening spent outdoors in your backyard. There you were enjoying the sights and sounds of a garden lush with trees, plants, butterflies, hummingbirds sipping nectar from the flowers, a well-used birdbath, and welcomed shade on a warm summer night.

When you wake up the next day and head back to the garden to enjoy your morning coffee, you are alarmed to see the lush garden and its animal visitors are all gone, replaced by dead grass. How would you feel? After the initial shock, you would likely feel you had lost something of tremendous emotional value that may not be retrievable.

Although this is an imaginary scenario, at the time of writing this essay, across the globe we are facing the consequences of climate change at a rapid pace. For example, currently, forest fires, droughts, floods, and temperatures well into the 100s (~38°C and over) are increasingly common. Nature is under siege, leading to increased negative consequences for the life and health of both humans and other living species that share our planet.

Do we really want a future with a diminished and increasingly hazardous natural world? What would we lose? And, more importantly, what would we gain by implementing policies and practices that prioritize a flourishing natural

DOI: 10.4324/9781003004622-31

FIGURE 12.1 View of a lush garden.

Source: AveCalvar, Envato Elements, Licensed image.

world that provides health and well-being benefits to humans and other living entities, as well as to the health of the planet?

To understand better our deep connection to the natural world, we will begin with a brief discussion of the lifestyle of our hunting and gathering ancestors. This lifestyle started on the savannahs of Africa millions of years ago and continues to influence our response to environments today.

Theory: Origins and Emerging Perspectives on Biophilia

The term "biophilia" was first used by psychoanalyst Eric Fromm. Fromm argued that humanity needed to establish a non-destructive relationship with the natural environment by fostering a love of living beings—which he called "biophilia." Without this love of nature, Fromm argued that humanity would see increased pollution of air, water, soil, and loss of animals (Fromm, 1973).

In his 1984 book, *Biophilia*, E.O. Wilson describes biophilia from an evolutionary perspective:

> To explore and affiliate with life is a deep and complicated process in mental development. To an extent still undervalued in philosophy and religion, our existence depends on this propensity, our spirit is woven from it, hope rises on its currents.

If there is an evolutionary basis for biophilia, as asserted by Wilson, then contact with nature is a basic human need, not a cultural amenity, not an individual preference, but a primary need. Just as we need healthy food and regular exercise, we may need ongoing connections with a flourishing natural world. Wilson also saw biophilia as a natural force that could be called upon to combat worldwide loss of biodiversity. If we love nature enough, we will be willing to save it from destruction.

To understand the deep underpinnings of biophilia and its manifestation in today's cultural and physical landscape, we need to understand our ancestral life as mobile hunting and gathering bands. Built structures are newcomers on the evolutionary scene—a mere 6,000 or so years old. For most of human existence, the natural landscape provided the resources necessary for survival, chief among them water, vegetation, sunlight, animals, building materials, shelter, sky, and fire. The sun provided warmth and light. The big sky provided information about weather and time of day that was critical to wayfinding and safety. Large trees provided shelter from the midday sun and places to sleep at night to avoid terrestrial predators. Flowers and seasonal vegetation provided food, materials, and medicinal treatments. Rivers and watering holes provided the foundation for life itself—drinkable water.

A significant body of research tells us that, as a species, we are powerfully responsive to natural landscapes, forms, sounds, and patterns (Kellert and Wilson, 1993; Kellert, Heerwagen and Mador, 2008; Gillis and Getersleben, 2015). This strong attachment to nature may be a critical factor in our willingness to support new ways of living with and protecting our natural environment as climate change wreaks havoc on the only home we have known for millions of years.

Tidball (2012) argues that the impact of climate change on natural systems is creating an "urgent biophilia" that leads us to increase our contact with nature as a source of resilience in the face of adversity. But as more landscapes are harmed by fire, draught, floods and radical temperature changes, the ability to find solace and joy from contact with natural environments and systems is diminishing. According to Tidball, this situation can be altered if we act now to increase focus on stewardship and better management of ecological systems including increases in urban green space, community gardens, and tree planting.

In contrast to the evolutionary and resilience perspectives on biophilia, Besson (2017) argues that an optimal human habitat is not a collection of fixed elements but rather an environment that provides a beneficial feedback loop based on response to cognitive, emotional, and aesthetic needs. Different environments can hinder or support these needs and thus enhance or decrease a sense of well-being. For instance, Besson notes that many natural habitats—such as wilderness and jungle—can be a source of fear for people who are not adapted to those environments. Although Besson argues that emotional affiliation with natural habitats is more likely linked to the places where people grow up, he also notes that we should expect cross-cultural preference for some aspects of the natural environment. These include prospect and refuge, vegetation, animals, and sunshine that can be components of varied landscapes. Interestingly, these features are considered vital elements of biophilia and biophilic design.

These features suggest the presence of an evolved, universal emotional and cognitive approach to environments—one that continually assesses the opportunities and hazards we might face in a particular place, whether it is a natural or a built environment. We adjust our behavior to assure safety and well-being. This idea clearly supports the fact that humans now inhabit a wide range of environments, from the arctic to the desert and deep forests.

Besson proposes that optimal places are not places of perfection but environments that support a full range of experiences from danger and thrill to reflection and enjoyment. The theory and science of biophilia do not sufficiently address this thought. The biophilia hypothesis addresses, but does not fully explore, the range of emotional and physical experiences that underscore our responses to nature—both positive and negative. For instance, an urban park may be experienced as calming and pleasurable during the day, but frightening at night when darkness hides dangers. Fire has similar contrasts—inviting and enjoyable when it is a campfire or fireplace, but terrifying when raging through the landscape. The advent of controlled fire is considered a central driver of human social and cognitive development because it enabled behavior—especially storytelling—to extend into the evening around the campfire where our ancestors felt safe.

From a behavioral perspective, Berleant (2015) also sees the appeal of nature linked, not to its "naturalness," but to its support for a variety of human behaviors, including the ability to roam, explore, gather information, forage, sit around a campfire, and feel a sense of freedom. In this sense, the ancestral human environment may not be a place, but rather nature itself in its many forms, functions, and behavioral opportunities.

Biophilia, Design, and Climate

Given the evidence for our strong emotional and cultural links to nature and its continuing health, we need to ask how we can more effectively harness this emotional energy to address climate change policy and action. The previously discussed perspectives on the human-nature experience create a framework for thinking about biophilia and design for the health and well-being of both humans and the planet.

These thoughts are expanded by Africa et al. (2019) to explore biophilic design that integrates buildings, site, and occupant needs by creating a "comprehensive habitat" that includes building materials, management of energy and waste flows, and support for on-site biodiversity. Biophilic design is not a separate element. Instead, it runs through these components, serving as an environmental "interstitial tissue" analogous to that of the human body providing "a connective language, practice or ethos that unites disparate disciplines in the built environment more broadly" (Africa et al., 2019).

A key component of this approach is to connect people more effectively to the natural world by creating habitats that integrate the built and natural components to address and enhance the ecological carrying capacity of the site. Biophilic design serves as the integrator by incorporating the contributions of other nature-based design techniques. In addition, it can act as a platform or "interstitial tissue," providing a connective language, practice, or ethos that unites disparate disciplines in the built environment more broadly. Africa et al. (2019) argue that

> Our disconnection from the natural environment that has supported human civilization imperils every living being on the planet. In the Anthropocene, a geological era wherein global environmental conditions are manipulated by human activities, we have unfortunately appointed ourselves as masters of planetary fate.

A central question we need to address is: Can biophilic design be more intentionally incorporated into building design as a fundamental aspect of health and well-being? To be effective, biophilic approaches and strategies need to be integrated into building projects at the start of project planning. Further, the principles and methods of biophilic design need to be more fully understood as an integral component of building and outdoor space design and not just an add-on. At present, many projects use biophilia as decoration rather than seeing it as a key component of an integrative approach that contributes to the building as a habitat for people.

When thinking about biophilia and biophilic design, it is essential also to note that natural environments are not equally attractive or beneficial.

Barren spaces or spaces with dead and dying plants and trees signal habitat depletion and are largely avoided. In contrast, places with rich vegetation, flowers, large trees, water, and meandering pathways that open suddenly to views are sought out as places of relaxation and enjoyment. These features characterize the most beloved urban parks and arboreta across the globe. But even small spots of nature—a flowerpot, flowering tree, or a small garden—can also delight. That is the real story of our connection to nature—it has many faces and many ways to create positive experiences in our homes, offices, backyards, or common spaces. The genetic basis for biophilia does not, of course, dismiss cultural, geographic, or ecotype specificity. Instead, using inspiration from both the local natural environment and vernacular cultural expressions for creating a sense of place is critical to the success of biophilic design.

Nature can play a positive role in our daily lives if we focus on making biophilia benefits available to all citizens of planet Earth, and not just to those who live in places with natural amenities. The COVID-19 pandemic of 2020 showed us how important nature is. Having access to walkable greenspace, backyard gardens, urban forests, lakes, rivers, and other natural elements made a difference to health and well-being in ways that should guide the democratization of biophilic design in the future. It's an amenity that all people should experience in their daily lives. We must also wonder: how can biophilic design help diminish negative impacts on natural habitats and human health brought on by climate change?

We need to remember also that nature is not always beneficial and benign. The natural world is rife with hazards that create fear and anxiety. These "biophobic" experiences include animal fears (especially snakes, rats, and spiders) as well as environmental anxieties (darkness, enclosed spaces, heights, loud noises, storms, unkempt spaces, being in the open without protection). Unfortunately, these hazards are largely neglected in the literature and research on biophilia.

Although biophilic design focuses largely on building-level applications, there is an increasing cross-disciplinary interest in creating larger-scale biophilic habitats and ecosystems that support the health of people and the health of our natural environments that face increased risks from climate change and development pressures. With each year reflecting rapid weather changes and an increase in natural disasters the need for integrated approaches to the environment, climate, and health becomes all the more urgent. The pandemic, fires, floods, drought, and excessive heat experienced across the globe are witness to human-influenced climate change leading to widespread destruction of natural environments and loss of both human and animal lives, as well as the loss of built habitats. These dramatic/devastating events make the need for integration between the natural and built environments ever more critical to human health and to the health of the planet.

References

Africa, J, Heerwagen, J, Loftness, V. and Ryan, C. 2019. Biophilic Design and Climate Change: Performance Parameters for Health. *Frontiers in Built Environment*, on line. https://www.frontiersin.org/journals/built-environment/articles/10.3389/fbuil.2019.00028/full

Berleant, A. 2015. Aesthetic Sensibility. *International Journal of Sensory Environment, Architecture and Urban Space*, Open edition on line. https://journals.openedition.org/ambiances/526

Besson, A. 2017. Building a Paradise? On the Quest for an Optimal Human Habitat. *Contemporary Aesthetics*. 15, 1–12. article 8.

Fromme, E. (1973). *The Anatomy of Human Destructiveness*. New York: Holt, Reinhart, and Winston.

Gillis, K. and B. Gatrsleben, 2015. A Review of the Psychological Literature on the Health and Well Being Benefits of Biophilic Design. *Building*, 5: 948–963.

Kellert, S.R. and Wilson, E.O. 1993. *The Biophilia Hypothesis*, Washington, DC: Island Press.

Kellert, S.R, Heerwagen, J., and Mador, M. 2008. *Biophilic Design: The Theory, Science and Practice of Bringing Buildings to Life*. New York: Wiley.

Tidball, K.G. 2012. Urgent Biophilia: Human-Nature Interactions and Biological Attraction in Disaster Resilience. *Ecology and Society*, 17(2): 5.

Wilson, E.O. 1984. *Biophilia*. Cambridge: Harvard University Press.

Reflecting on Ethics

For all of us, our lives are inseparable from the spaces we inhabit. Even when we immerse our minds in a virtual world, we cannot escape the physical one. As we stated at the beginning of the book, people spend over 90% of their time inside spaces. *Shaping Experiences* taught us that creating spaces is far from a trivial endeavor. Built environments can profoundly impact people, both positively and negatively. Sometimes, spaces can nudge occupants to feel carefree and safe, but spaces can also be limiting, degrading, and harmful. And if buildings are shelter, what happens if they do not protect people in the ways occupants need? Or, what if built environments are destroying the planet in service of making people feel comfortable? And with all these factors at play, it often depends on where you are on the power spectrum as to how the built environment affects you and those you love.

In *Considering Ethics*, you read how physical and digital spaces can affect people's health, sense of belonging, and safety while potentially limiting their access to opportunities and the ability to express their identities. Based on this section and many sources beyond this book, the influence that built environments have on individuals and the planet is becoming increasingly apparent. Consequently, the authors in this section implore you to consider the ethical responsibilities that come with this understanding. Should professionals be held to a higher standard of responsibility than the general public? Is it possible for society to course-correct the harmful impacts of spaces? Remember that if built environments did not have the potential for such detrimental effects, there would be no need to ask these questions.

The authors in this section presented their work and unique journeys, which extend far beyond a mere job. Each one grapples with challenging questions yet still embraces the call to action. Despite the daunting nature of

DOI: 10.4324/9781003004622-32

society's complex systems, these contributors maintain an optimistic outlook and actively strive to make a difference. Their perspectives and approaches beg the question—what can we all do collectively to magnify our individual impact?

In answer to this question, we can change the way we practice. We can refuse to be defined by our titles and the limitations others might place on us. We can elect to go where we are needed most and where our unique perspective can help others evolve. We can give a face and name to people and circumstances that others might dismiss as someone else's problem. We can choose to see the larger system where individual parts influence the whole. Each author urged us to confront harsh realities, even when it means more work, more responsibility, and often discomfort. Being ethical can be a arduous path. It requires courage and can leave you feeling vulnerable.

In the upcoming section on *Crafting Intent*, you will discover how to apply some of the numerous insights gained so far in *People and Spaces.* Intentional practice requires designing collaborative, research-informed processes and approaching projects related to the built environment with resolve and purpose.

PART 4

Crafting Intent

Framing Intent

Creating spaces and built environments well-suited for people is a deliberate and purposeful act that involves thoughtful decision-making and a mindful process. This final section explores the nuanced *how* of designing and researching spaces that adapt, evolve, and resonate with the ever-changing nature of the human experience and the built world, while uncovering ways to plan for the dynamic interplay between people and their surroundings.

Looking back at *People and Spaces*, we have collectively explored how occupants experience spatial settings, including how thoughts, expectations, behaviors, values, and even beliefs impact perceptions of the built world. In doing so, contributors have underscored the true importance of a place—the people who dwell within it. From there, we discussed how everyone has an ethical obligation to ensure that the needs of people are always at the center of every space, paying particular attention to those who may be more vulnerable. Contributors called for reflection on how broader societal systems, when unchecked, can lead to inequality and erode the health and wellbeing of ourselves and our environments. We also examined the roles and the related disciplines whose work involves humans and built environments. Through this, authors have imparted a deeper understanding of how, individually and together, we can leverage our domains to drive decisions toward a sustainable and resilient world.

But what does this look like in research and practice? What methods will ensure that people are at the center of every project? How can occupants be empowered to fully engage, value, and cultivate their relationship with built spaces? Ultimately, how can our surroundings be designed to support success and wellness for ever-evolving individuals in an ever-changing world?

DOI: 10.4324/9781003004622-34

In *Crafting Intent*, you will hear how contributors to this volume tackle such questions. Authors highlight the methods they employ and the benefits and challenges of each. They discuss how surveys, evidence-based design, interdisciplinary collaboration, design thinking, interviews, and unobtrusive measures like sensors can help inform design. You will learn how incorporating historical context and viewpoints from other disciplines can help generate a well-rounded environment where people can thrive. Contributors also explain various types of spaces, emphasizing the importance of and different ways to include clients and occupants in the design process. Further, you will hear about certification systems and their role in determining and driving design goals and outcomes to better serve a building's occupants, community, and planet. Lastly, this section examines how bridging disciplines is the key to advancing the work of shaping the built world.

When creating a space, merely hoping for a favorable result is unlikely to yield one. Therefore, designers, researchers, clients, and others who influence built environments must be purposeful in their actions, realizing that what they do is as important as what they *don't* do. While many design and research processes are imperfect and require constant iteration, crafting intent is critical in creating positive and ethical spatial experiences.

CONNECTING 13

More than ever, experts recognize the significant role of the built environment in climate change. Ironically, shelter from the elements of nature is why constructed spaces originally emerged. These structures have transformed people from nomads to dwellers, leading many to spend most of their lives indoors. As a result, buildings have become climates of their own, operating independently of the outside world. The climatization of interior environments has led to over-conditioning, making many interior spaces uncomfortable and high-energy consumers.

In the following chapter, authors Kit Elsworth, Billie Faircloth, Ryan Welch, and Roderick Bates zero in on the built environment's impact on human comfort, productivity, and energy consumption. As specialists in architecture, technology development, environmental research, and building performance, they present a project developed at architecture firm KieranTimberlake. Utilizing the company's employees and office (an expansive retrofit of an industrial warehouse) as a testbed, they took on the challenge to see how design could reduce energy usage without compromising the thermal comfort (how warm or cool we feel) of their workforce.

Typically, many of the qualities of a building that passively influence its thermal comfort get addressed during the initial design phase. For example, strategies often involve decisions around the structure's orientation to the sun and the size and location of windows. But with a keen eye towards sustainability and reusing an existing structure, the authors took a less conventional approach. Specifically, the team explored the relationship between clothing and architecture and how attire can be instrumental in achieving

DOI: 10.4324/9781003004622-35

thermal comfort. They explain how it is possible to create energy-efficient buildings that rely less on mechanical heating and cooling systems by considering the impact of clothing and organizational culture. By exploring these interconnected factors, the group demonstrates and emphasizes the need for more holistic design approaches to tackle the challenges of climate change.

13

GETTING TO KNOW *CLO*

Kit Elsworth, Billie Faircloth, Ryan Welch and Roderick Bates

> Interaction between animal organism and its environment occurs across one interface – that of the epidermis. But civilization introduces two artificial membranes to modify this relationship – clothing and architecture.
>
> —James Marston Fitch

Introduction

Architectural designers shape a building's massing, orientation, and fenestration; these design decisions govern the heat exchange pathways between human bodies and the environment.[1] But to what degree do architectural designers shape a person's daily choice of clothing? Clothes govern the heat exchange between the body and the spaces it inhabits. What people wear is presumably driven more by fashion, occupation, beliefs, or habits than explicit thermal function. Often, humans turn to clothes as the last resort to stay comfortable in highly conditioned spaces (Put on a sweater!/Take off your jacket!). However, researchers curious about the body-clothing-building relationship have demonstrated that humans can tolerate a wide range of temperatures by using clothing as the primary means of adaptation (Schiavon & Lee, 2013). *If clothing can act as shelter, to what degree might it shape the elements and systems of a building?*

Architectural designers might be reluctant to entertain the notion that clothing design is a legitimate strategy for energy-efficient, low-carbon building design. We might have never strayed into asking this question at our design firm had we not conducted an office-wide experiment at our studio in Philadelphia. Without air-conditioning, we surveyed ourselves across two summers

DOI: 10.4324/9781003004622-36

and collected thousands of responses on how we felt inside our studio. We experienced the interlacing between body, clothing, and building firsthand. As we explored the data to understand how to run our office and meet our energy goals, we discovered another story about our clothes and their unresolved role in the thermal comfort narrative. We found that while most of us were willing to dress down in the summer and layer up in the winter, some preferred a uniform despite large swings in temperature. We posed interesting and awkward questions: *Can designers create more energy-efficient buildings if people use their clothes as an adaptation strategy? To what degree should designers and building inhabitants share accountability for energy consumption? Can people abandon the thermostat and instead put on a sweater when they're cold? Given humanity's need to rapidly address climate change, shouldn't clothes play a more significant role in climate adaptation?*

How Historians Know Clothes

People's relationship to workplace clothing has changed over time. According to Jade Papa, the Curator of the Textile and Costume Design Collection at the Jefferson University Design Center, US workplace apparel over the last century—as captured through books, movies, and photographs—was governed primarily by textile limitations and social conformity. These factors manifested as quite formal, impossibly restrictive, and undoubtedly hotter clothing than people are accustomed to now. However, the clothes, and the culture surrounding them, did integrate several techniques to manage and adapt to hot indoor temperatures. Weave patterns and wool treatments, such as worsting, meant clothes could trap less heat than the heavier winter wardrobe.[2] Seldom seen today, clothes used sacrificial underlayers, collars, and cuffs, to enable the more valuable garments to avoid sweat damage. At the same time, regularly soiled portions could be easily washed or replaced. Workplace clothing also evolved through gender-based expectations for dressing. For instance, after the First World War, returning male veterans began to dress more casually, evolving US social norms by going as far as removing their suit jackets and rolling up their sleeves. Women began to embrace more casual attire as they had grown accustomed to working industrial jobs during the war and realized the benefits of less formal and restrictive clothing. However, in the transition to factory-scale production, manufacturers abandoned the techniques that made earlier garments thermally adaptable. This tradeoff persists today, where simple layering of clothing is our primary means of achieving thermal comfort.

How Researchers Knows *Clo*

Clothing's thermal effects on human comfort and building energy use can be quantified through well-established methods. In 1941, researchers studying

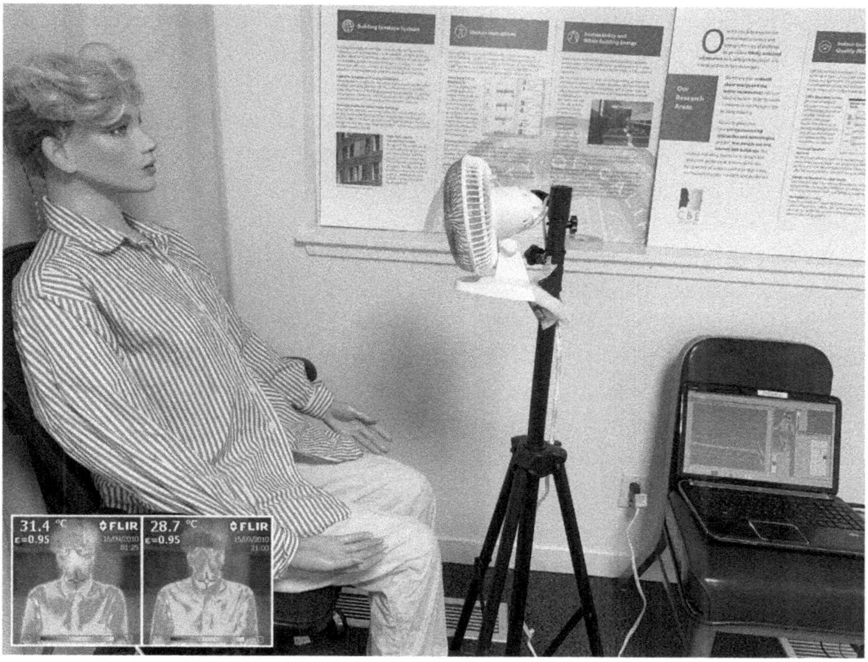

FIGURE 13.1 A thermal mannequin is used to simulate heat loss rate from the body while wearing clothing. The inset infrared photograph shows approximate skin temperature while showing the ability of the pants and long-sleeves to resist heat loss. (Photograph by Hui Zhang).

our bodies' comfort and metabolism found sufficient motivation to coordinate terminology across diverse perspectives, shortening the word "clothing" to "clo" and proposing the *clo* unit (Gagge, 1941).[3] *Clo* is an approximation of the insulation value of clothing. It accounts for the convective, radiant, and evaporative heat loss from human skin to the ambient environment with consideration for clothing materials, layers, and the degree of bodily coverage. The *clo* values for various fabric weights are well documented in industry standards (ISO 9920, ASHRAE 55). Both ISO and ASHRAE standards quantify *clo* values using a thermal mannequin—a human body model rigged with electrical resistance wiring to emulate the heat loss of a person dressed in various outfits. Compared to the historical approach of layering clothing for comfort, the thermal mannequin helps researchers understand the local effects of clothing on the body.

Mechanical engineers have historically approached *clo* without nuance, preferring the static values offered by ASHRAE 55 to our seasonal clothing choices. When designing a heating and cooling system, a mechanical engineer may assume a winter 1.0 *clo* and a summer 0.5 *clo* for all people. Using field studies, researchers have globally disproved the simplified seasonal dichotomy of our clothing choices. By surveying people in naturally ventilated buildings with flexible dress codes, they found participants employed wide-ranging *clo* values to stay comfortable under varied environmental conditions. (Schiavon & Lee, 2013) This work proves that clothing choice plays a critical role in our comfort and provides a much-needed update to static *clo* values. More to the point, it demonstrates that humans can tolerate a wide range of temperatures by using clothing as the primary means of adaptation. However, the industry has yet to embrace these findings. Given the room to flourish, designers could use adaptive clothing practices to challenge the traditional building design approach that favors narrow temperature swings, stable indoor thermal environments, and static *clo* values. Designers can imagine active or passive features that allow for greater temperature swings on the building interior, or they can advocate for clients to adopt protocols to loosen the heating and cooling setpoints. These are building strategies shaped by our clothing choices.

Our First Attempt to Know *Clo*

At KieranTimberlake, we began to ponder our personal clothing choices when, in May 2015, the interior temperatures of the firm's new studio began to climb, and we began to sweat. That January, our firm had completed a deep energy retrofit of Ortlieb's Bottling House. We converted the mid-century industrial building once equipped to bottle and ship beer into a contemporary architecture studio equipped to support a highly collaborative design culture. Then and now, the building is designed for passive cooling, natural lighting, and natural ventilation. It features masonry walls, continuous operable ribbon windows, a high-bay interior space, and a central light monitor running the ridge of a massive gable roof. The firm planned the renovation without central air-conditioning, instead opting to leverage the building's features and expand their performance by distributing dehumidified outdoor air at a low velocity around our ankles. The firm also planned a flexible dress code, acknowledging that relaxing our individual clothing choices might be an equally important strategy during Philadelphia's hot and humid summer season. Finally, with the ambition to operate the building responsibly—to increase its energy efficiency and decrease its operational carbon footprint—we collected data every hour. We measured the ambient temperature and relative humidity throughout the office using approximately 300 integrated sensors. Staff voluntarily completed an anonymized digital survey twice daily, morning and afternoon, to reflect upon their experience. Were they *much too hot, too hot, warm but comfortable, comfortable, cold but comfortable, too cold, or much too cold*? We designed the questionnaire to meet the best practices of thermal comfort survey design, including asking everyone to identify their

FIGURE 13.2 Ortlieb's Bottling House utilized many passive features to maintain working conditions through the 20th century. Thick slabs absorbed heat, and monitor windows helped ventilate hot air. (Courtesy of Ortlieb Brewing Company).

attire in each response. We gathered responses over two summer seasons, amounting to almost 10,000 *clo* values. Analyzing these data helped us see trends between body, clothing, and building operations.

Most staff adopted a flexible dress code to cope with warmer than usual indoor conditions. As temperatures climbed from 70° to 80°F, people kept cool by dressing lighter. Above 80°F, as people hit their limit for acceptable office wear, *clo* remained constant, and thermal discomfort began to increase. Yet most staff remained comfortable up to 83°F, well above a traditional office cooling setpoint.[4]

The Ortlieb's comfort study reflects the firm's design philosophy and its commitment to researching the limits of architecture, even when it requires spontaneous interventions (ice cream for everyone!). Organizations with standardized clothing policies may arrive at different comfort thresholds, but overall, the findings will likely be the same: people can use clothing to maintain comfort at higher indoor temperatures than what the industry assumes

FIGURE 13.3 Kieran Timberlake's renovation harnessed the original architectural features to create a comfortable and energy-efficient studio (Photograph by Michael Moran).

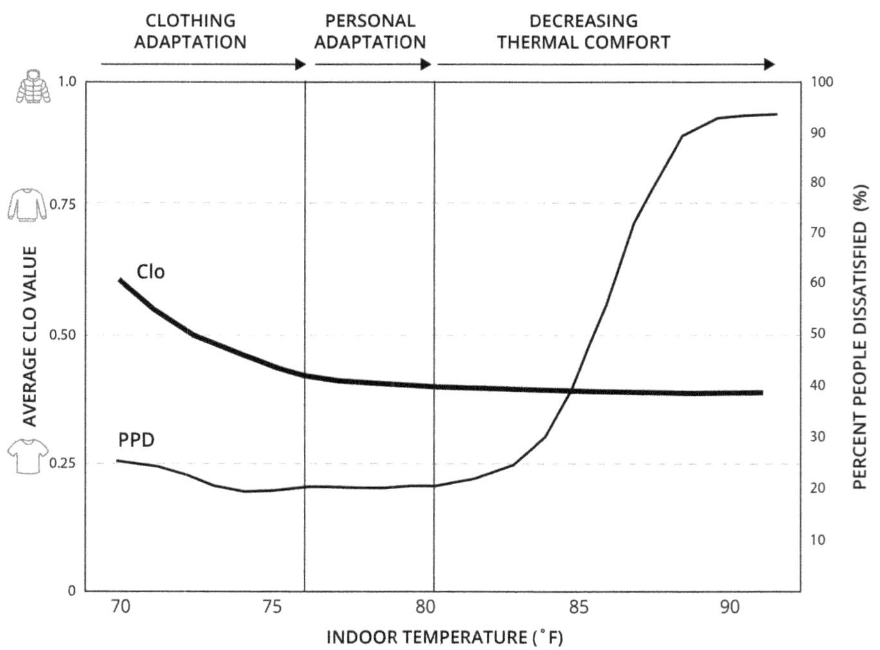

FIGURE 13.4 Between 70° and 80°F, the *clo* value decreases while thermal comfort is steady. Above this temperature, the trends switch—demonstrating the limit of clothing as a thermal comfort adaptive measure.

today. But in order for this to be a viable climate adaptation and energy-saving strategy, designers must also consider how clothing preferences differ seasonally and individually.

Our Second Attempt to Know *Clo*

The degree to which we know and use our clothes for adaptation remains a central curiosity in the firm's attempts to run Ortlieb's Bottling House. The summer-season study confirmed the building's need for air conditioning, but it also affirmed KieranTimberlake's commitment to operate the studio as a mixed-mode building. Now, we switch daily between natural ventilation and air-conditioning, and we broadcast the operating mode to everyone *before* the workday to inform how they dress. Reporting on "how we feel" has become integral to our workflow. Our comfort survey has evolved into a workplace comfort application called Roast. This web-based tool offers building managers the ability to collect a range of thermal, visual, and aural comfort data. It also allows them to collect factors influencing discomfort, such as draftiness, and the actions taken by users to improve their comfort, such as turning on a personal desk fan. Early user feedback revealed that people wanted to report what they were wearing more accurately. In developing Roast, we adopted a library of 40 separate articles of clothing that users can assemble into personalized seasonal outfits. This makes it easier for users to complete the surveys, improving response rates and capturing individual clothing habits.

Our interest was piqued. *How do our adaptation behaviors compare to those in other global field studies? Can designers leverage a refreshed dataset of high-resolution clo values collected across seasons to understand people's clothing preferences better? Can designers describe individual adaptation behavior*? The ASHRAE Global Thermal Comfort Database II provides access to *clo* values from numerous international field studies where people expressed an opinion about how they felt through similar survey methods. We began by comparing the *clo* values in our dataset to four studies within this database, selecting these studies because they were also conducted in mixed-mode and naturally ventilated buildings much like our own. (Hawighorst, Schweiker, & Wagner, 2013) (Honnekeri, Brager, Dhaka, & Mathur, 2014) (Langevin, Gurian, & Wen, 2015) (Stoops, 2000)

When comparing Roast and ASHRAE survey responses in aggregate, we found that our behavior differed from the larger population in two critical ways. On average, we dressed lighter than those surveyed in international field studies; and on average, we exhibited less clothing adaptation in response to temperature change. But what is more striking is how poorly the average statistical trends in both datasets predict *clo* for individual survey responses. We suspected that personal preference played a major role, and we confirmed that our Roast predictions could be improved dramatically by disaggregating survey data into personalized statistical models (Figure 13.5). These models

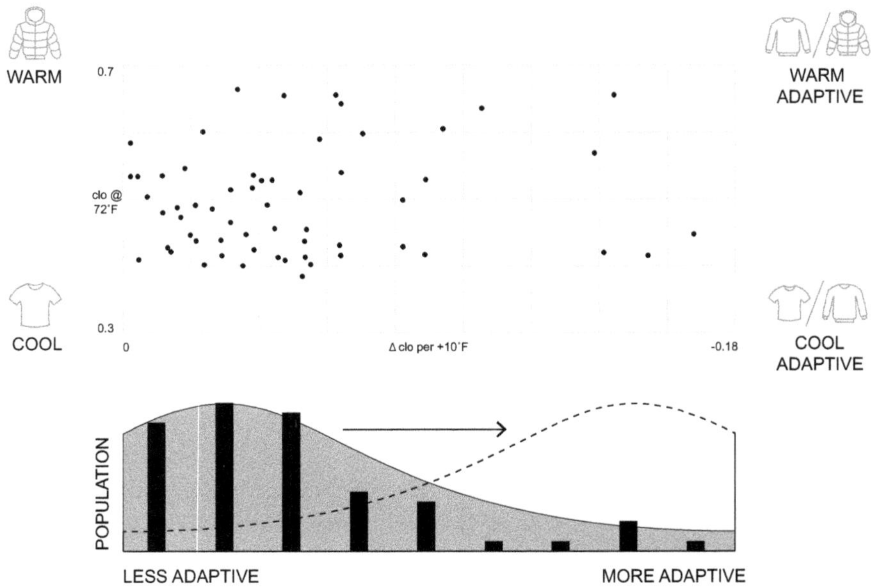

FIGURE 13.5 Individuals have clothing preferences: Each dot represents one individual according to how warm they dress under moderate conditions (y-axis) and how much they adapt clothing insulation in response to temperature changes (x-axis). The histogram below indicates inflexible dressers far outnumber adaptive dressers—a trend that we hope will reverse in due course with a shift toward the dashed line.

do more than offer more accurate forecasts of clothing adaptation. Collectively, they describe wide-ranging clothing-personality profiles that challenge our convention of designing buildings around a single standard. Further, they beg ethical questions about the use of personalized data to inform people's wardrobe choices and shed some of the burdens from building design and operations.

Elevating *Clo*

People have an innate capacity to use clothing for thermal adaptation, so should our climate action plans address what they wear to work? Reframing personal and professional ethics might motivate some to embrace flexible dress codes and improve comfort at broader temperature ranges. We have seen how global events can influence what is worn: federal and local governments across the world adopted mask mandates in response to the COVID-19 global pandemic, and mask wearing became the norm in many workplaces. *If people can mask-up for the pandemic, why can't they dress-down for the climate crisis?*

Can designers resurrect clothing design as an essential intermediary in the body-clothing-building relationship? Materials scientists and clothing designers know *clo* intimately and are researching ways to engineer clothing to tune the thermal exchange between our bodies and their environment (Peng & Cui, 2020). We might think high-performance fabrics are reserved for activewear, but these fabrics are also entering the formalwear market. *If people won't change the way they dress to fight climate change, will textile design do it for us?*

To what degree might clothing shape the elements and systems of a building? Leveraging *clo* as an energy-efficiency strategy in building design is challenging because it engages the knowledge of several disciplines. Architects, engineers, business owners, and clothing designers need to understand and utilize *clo*. But they must also recognize the urgency of crossing disciplinary boundaries to reshape the body-clothing-building relationship.

Notes

1 James Marston Fitch diagrams this effectively in *American Building 2*, Figure 6, Page 17.

2 Worsting is a type of yarn weave made from long strains of wool and woven in a parallel pattern. The product is a smoother, finer wool.

3 One *clo* is defined as "the *amount of clothing* required by a resting person to be indefinitely comfortable at ambient conditions where temperature is 70 °F, relative humidity is less than 50 percent, and wind velocity is 20 feet per second." (Gagge, B. B. (1941). A Practical System of Units for the Description of the Heat Exchange of Man with His Environment. *Science*, vol 94, issue 2445, 428–430).

4 ASHRAE 55 defines acceptable indoor environmental conditions to be a thermal environment that 80% of the occupants find thermally acceptable (ASHRAE, A. S. (n.d.). *ASHRAE 55. Thermal Environment Condition for Human Occupancy*).

References

ASHRAE, A. S. (2023). ASHRAE 55. *Thermal Environment Condition for Human Occupancy.* Peachtree Corners, GA.

Gagge, B. B. (1941). A Practical System of Units for the Description of the Heat Exchange of Man with His Environment. *Science, 7*(94), 2445, 428–430.

Hawighorst, M., Schweiker, M., & Wagner, A. (2013). Thermo-Specific Self-Efficacy (SpecSE) in Relation to Perceived Comfort and Control. *Building and Environment*, 193–206.

Honnekeri, A., Brager, G., Dhaka, S., & Mathur, J. (2014). Comfort and Adaptation in Mixed-Mode Buildings in a Hot-dry Climate. *Windsor Conference.* Windsor.

Hsu, P.-C., Liu, C., Song, A. Y., Zhang, Z., Peng, Y., Xie, J., … & Cui, Y. (2018). A Dual-Mode Textile for Human Body Radiative Heating. *Applied Sciences and Engineering, 3*(11)1–8.

ISO. (2007). ISO 9920:2007: Ergonomics of the thermal environment — Estimation of thermal insulation and water vapor resistance of a clothing ensemble.

Langevin, J., Gurian, P., & Wen, J. (2015). One Year Occupant Behavior/environment Data for Medium U.S. Office. *Jounral of Environmental Psychology, 42*, 94–115.

Peng, Y., & Cui, Y. (2020). Advanced Textiles for Personal Thermal Management and Energy. *Joule*, *4*(4), 724–742.

Schiavon, S., & Lee, K. H. (2013). Dynamic Predictive Clothing Insulation Models Based on Outdoor Air and Indoor Operative Temperatures. *Building and Environment*, *59*, 250–260.

Stoops, J. L. (2000). *The Thermal Environmentand Occupant Perceptions in European Office Buildings*. Doctoral Thesis. Gothenburg, Sweden: Chalmers University of Technology.

CONNECTING 14

Just as built spaces vary widely, so do their design methods. For example, as we just saw, KieranTimberlake took an innovative and novel strategy to increase energy efficiency and thermal comfort by integrating clothing and occupant feedback into their design. In this next chapter, environmental psychologist and health care designer Dak Kopec focuses on a different design approach. He introduces the concept of condition-based design, which promotes self-sufficiency and autonomy for people living with common health conditions.

Kopec demonstrates condition-based design through a case study involving the redesign of a day habilitation center. The project aims to foster life skills for low-income, inner-city young adults affected by varying levels of intellectual disability. He shares his process, which combines evidenced-based design with human-centered design, using a design thinking method. While these design frameworks share some similarities, they draw upon different types of reasoning, including positivist (empirical studies) and post-positivist (empathy and multiple perspectives).

By employing this unique blend of approaches, Kopec nudges designers and researchers alike to push the boundaries of these ways of thinking, encouraging all of us to consider the untapped potential at the intersection of design and science.

DOI: 10.4324/9781003004622-37

14

PERSON AND CONDITION CENTERED DESIGN

Dak Kopec

In today's western society, the number of people affected by a specific health condition has risen to a level that commands the development and design of specialized environments. This assertion is evidenced by the Autism Speaks competition of 2016 to design a transitional housing model for young adults living with Autism. Borrowing from the term Special Care Units (SCU'S), which are defined as designated areas within a healthcare environment for people who share specific health needs (Daly, n.d.), a condition-based design focuses on building types intended for groups of people who share a common health condition. To meet this need, the health care designer should understand common symptoms and behaviors of the subject health condition to meet the requirements of the end-user population.

For the past two decades, the idea of evidence-based design has become part of the design community's lexicon. As the phrase indicates, evidence-based design can generate designs based on verifiable evidence that can repeat from place to place with similar outcomes. The purpose for condition-based designs is to promote self-sufficiency and autonomous living whenever possible. Elmurzaeva and Zhumanova (2020) identify activities such as the acquisition of money and budgeting skills, organization and engagement in meaningful leisure activities, and the use of common household items and services as part of specific programming needs for specialized day and boarding schools.

The Boston based agency, Bay Cove Human Services, LLC (BCHS), is an organization that supports environmental design within the continuum of care. Among the target population, they provide services for people affected by varying levels of an intellectual disability with a low-income background, often supported by a single-provider home. The American Psychiatric Association's

DOI: 10.4324/9781003004622-38

Diagnostic Statistical Manual fifth edition (DSM-V) defines intellectual disabilities as a neurodevelopmental condition present since childhood. Therefore, people affected by an intellectual disability have varying capabilities to perform activities of daily living. Likewise, Burke and Heller (2017) and Emerson (2007), state that the level of income, quality of neighborhoods, and degree of organization within a community serve as factors that can negatively affect one's self-reliance.

Here I discuss a project tracking the redesign of two levels within a four-level day habilitation center that serves low-income inner-city young adults affected by varying levels of an intellectual disability. The end-users that occupy the two subject levels of the building are affected by mild to moderate intellectual impairments, and the remaining two levels not addressed in this project, support end-users with moderate to severe impairments. The project's primary objective was to develop designs that promote life skills for recreation, social etiquette, and employment. Research has demonstrated the value of the environment's effect on learning outcomes (Tanner, 2008). The evidence has shown positive results of designs that complement specific health conditions as an adjunct to agency programs and services (Ryan et al., 2006; Emond-Pelletier and Joussemet, 2017).

Predesign research for this project was based on design thinking methods using both positivist and post-positivist reasoning. Positivist reasoning ascribes a direct cause and effect from a deductive analysis (Pushkala, 2017). Post-positivist reasoning allows for the subjectivity of reality and rejects the one-to-one connection between cause and effect (Pushkala, 2017) because outcomes are based on generalizations (Harvey, 2012). Design thinking as a method of discovery is based on a five-step process that begins with the identification of a problem and ends with the testing of solutions (Jalaluddin, Edros, and Khalil, 2017). A hallmark of design thinking is the production of innovative ideas (Dam and Siang, 2019). The process has been shown to have applications to a diverse array of professions, including nursing education (e.g., Beaird, Geist, and Lewis, 2018), social entrepreneurship (e.g., Chou, 2018), and coaching sports teams (e.g., Leeder, 2018).

When applying the design thinking method, we focused on an end-user population affected by an intellectual disability within a human-centered design, beginning with a positivist's approach. Specifically, from the health condition perspective, we identified and defined generalized symptoms and behaviors common to the subject end-users. While person-centered design focuses on the needs and outcomes of an individual, human-centered design focuses on common needs and outcomes of multiple end-users. Identifying and defining issues of concern was then followed by post-positivist reasoning within a design thinking process. Identified symptoms and behavioral responses were understood through empathy and ideation development using

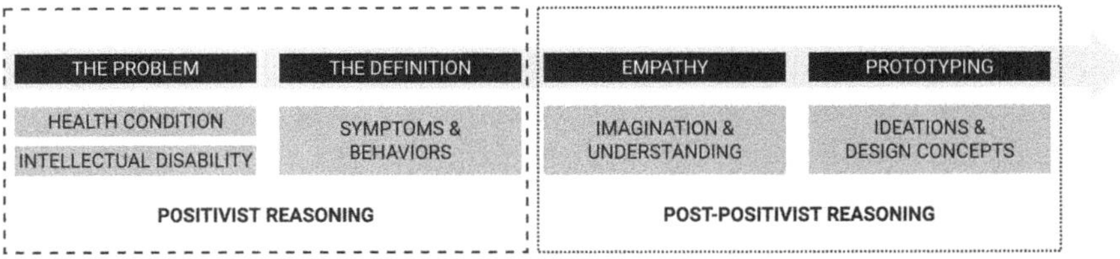

FIGURE 14.1 The design begins with having an understanding of the end-user and their health condition. From this understanding comes empathy, the attempt of the designer to put themselves in the shoes of the end-user. Once the designer is able to empathize with the end-users, they can develop design ideas.

post-positivist reasoning, because the outcome holds no promise to address the issue of concern (see Figure 14.1). This is because data obtained from the positivist's orientation may have been too general, or over-generalized, to have meaning for the specific end-user population. Similarly, faulty data could derive from the researcher's limited skills to empathize. For example, Konrath, O'Brien, and Hsing (2010), found that sympathy for others has declined by 48%, and empathy—people's ability to imagine another's perspective or point of view—declined by 34%, between 1979 and 2009; the greatest decline occurred between 2000 and 2009.

The final step in a design thinking process is based on positivist approaches that assess direct cause and effect. However, the practice of design does not always allow for a post occupancy evaluation, and when it does, the implementation of the design must have been carried out exactly as the designer had intended for the results to have validity.

Intellectual Disabilities

The causes of intellectual disabilities include a traumatic brain injury early in life, exposure to high levels of environmental contaminants while in utero or as an infant, or from a genetic condition. A child who is born with an intellectual disability will require social support throughout their life. The level of support, however, is dependent upon the severity and how the disability manifests. The Centers for Disease Control (2018) identifies poor physical performance, limited learning capabilities, and underdeveloped language acquisition and conveyance as common effects of an intellectual disability. Boat and Wu (2015) expand on these effects to include the conceptualization of ideas, performance abilities within social situations, and the ability to execute practical aspects of daily living.

The use of symbols visa vie pictographs can serve as a design tool for communication. Symbolic representations inform associative meaning and serve as a means of communication of what is known and understood (Galbiati, 2020). From symbolic meaning comes associations which can be polysemic, allowing for multiple meanings depending upon the person's point of reference. For example, Cross (1994) uses the image of a red apple to describe an association with food, cider, or a rainbow. Cider is a common New England beverage in the autumn, and the apple is a common snack. In the Hawaiian Islands, though, the apple is not as common, but the bright red color might be associated with the copious rainbows often seen throughout the islands. Based on regional associations, there is a reciprocal deterministic relationship between the way an environment appears and the subsequent responses; hunger, thirst, or a smile.

People affected by an intellectual disability are often limited in their autonomy and self-determination. Wehmeyer and Bolding (2001) referred to autonomy as a sense of independence and how individuals behave according to personal beliefs, abilities, and values. The person affected by an intellectual disability often has a skewed understanding of beliefs, abilities, and values resulting in inappropriate behaviors. Hartman et al. (2010) discuss the neurobiological relationships between physical and intellectual performance. The National Academies of Sciences, Engineering, and Medicine suggest that people affected by an intellectual disability have a limited capacity to learn abstract concepts (Boat and Wu, 2015). However, early intervention is critical, as the ideas can extend from children to young adults. These ideas build from the formation of long-term memory. Understanding sensory norms from a person's community and neighborhood—and using those norms as foundations for design—can thus serve as an anchor within the acquisition process of new information. Design elements conforming to environmental expectations commonly found within the target population's community (Rafaeli and Vilnai-Yavetz, 2004) should therefore be incorporated into the outcome design.

Activities that promote long-term memory, strategizing, and problem-solving are based on cause and effect. The inclusion of recreational activities has shown positive outcomes related to muscle strength and coordination and the development of social skills (Thompson, Wozencroft, and Parsons, 2017). Problem-solving and musculoskeletal development are skills essential for people affected by an intellectual disability to prevent the onset of a coordination disorder (Wuang and Su, 2009; Vuijk et al., 2010) that can lead to injury or a possible physical disability. The inclusion of interactive items within a design can promote recreational activities that support problem-solving and strategizing while concurrently supporting musculoskeletal coordination and body awareness.

A coordination disorder is a comorbid condition. Comorbidities are conditions that come about because of, or in tandem with a health condition. Another comorbid condition common among those affected by an intellectual disability is Diogenes' syndrome. This syndrome results in self-neglect, domestic squalor, social withdrawal, and hoarding (Williams et al., 1998), resulting from learned or primal behaviors. Diogenes' syndrome is often seen in neglected children such as 'Genie.' In the early 1970s a young girl was discovered isolated in a single room; she had been neglected for several years. Whether her intellectual disability resulted from the neglect, or was present from birth is unknown. However, Genie did not like to bathe or brush her hair and engaged in gathering and hoarding behaviors (Rymer, 1994), symptoms commonly associated with Diogenes' syndrome. The inclusion of diverse clothing options and the ability to incorporate play within the grooming process may overcome hygiene effects common with Diogenes' syndrome.

Diogenes syndrome and self-determination have strong connections to each other and the development of adaptive behaviors that support self-care come from routine. An older study by Horner, Day, and Day (1997), found that core or rote behaviors arise from daily routines. However, for an environment to support routine, it must facilitate trust and evoke positive emotion-based responses (Roessler, 2012). Many employment opportunities are based on routine. For example, janitors might begin cleaning a building by sweeping at one end of a building and finishing at another. Then, they might begin mopping the floor following the same pattern.

Rote behaviors based on routine, along with the completion of school, for young adults with severe disabilities is directly related to having more independence, better self-care, more household responsibilities, and higher parental expectations, which translates to future employment prospects (Carter, Austin, and Trainor, 2011). For these reasons, the designed environment should help facilitate participation within and the completion of routine activities of daily living.

Socialization is vital for the healthy development of interpersonal relations. However, socialization encompasses a spectrum that ranges from casual encounters to intimacy. Gil-Llario et al. (2018) studied adults with various intellectual disabilities and found that 89.4% of 360 participants expressed more dialogue on the topic of sex. Jose and Nair (2017) suggest that poorly thought-out sexual behaviors result from poor judgment and social skills combined with a desire for affection. When groups of young people come together under an agency umbrella, the agency assumes responsibility for the potential of sexual exploration. Young adults affected by an intellectual disability often find themselves in servitude to their hormones. Therefore, schools and human service agencies must use design measures such as limiting concealed spaces, using furnishings that limit multiple occupancy, and facilitating continual surveillance without invading privacy.

Despite having an intellectual disability, these occupants must be afforded the same privacy rights as any other citizen (Ziefle, Rocker, and Holzinger, 2011). Privacy is a concept that falls on a spectrum and within different classifications. Physical privacy is the ability to control being seen, heard, or smelled. Informational privacy is the ability to control what others learn or know about you. Unfortunately, young adults with an intellectual disability are at risk of exploitation from the conveyance of personal information, and they lack the skills to make judgment-based decisions regarding their informational and physical privacy (Khanlou, et. al., 2018).

Process

Our project explored the promotion and development of intellectual, physical, and social skills within the context of the physical environment through a design thinking process. Based on a positivist process, the cause (intellectual disability) served as the problem, and the subsequent behavior served as the definition of the problem. The following two steps of the design thinking process relied on post-positivist reasoning whereby empathy was used to understand specific facilitators of given behaviors, and brainstorming activities guided the formation of intervening prototypes.

Data from scientific journals visa vie a literature review was augmented by a survey of websites that included WebMD, American Psychiatry Association, American Association on Intellectual and Developmental Disabilities, MedLine Plus, National Down Syndrome Society, and the Centers for Disease Control and Prevention. These websites provided probable symptoms and behaviors common among those affected by an intellectual disability. This data was then aggregated using charts where data was clustered according to the subjects of cognition, musculature, and socialization, which were obtained from the literature review.

Each subject was then broken down into specific behaviors or symptoms identified from a survey of websites. Behaviors and symptoms were then analyzed according to the first four steps of a five-step design thinking process. The first step in identifying the problem was to identify the main categories under investigation (cognition, musculature, and socialization). The remaining three columns focused on symptoms and behaviors as definitions of cognition (Table 14.1), musculature (Table 14.2), and socialization (Table 14.3). Finally, the third and fourth columns addressed empathy as related to the definition and then an ideation as a prototype for the definition.

These tables reveal programming needs that informed design ideas to address specific symptoms. However, the relationship between causality and a single design element could be affected or influenced through the comprehensive design approach. Therefore, for a design to address causality, each aspect was assessed in its singularity and within the larger context. The result was the redesign of two levels within a four-level structure. The first floor serves as an employment readiness area where clients learn specific job skills, application completion, interview preparation, and interviewing skills. The second redesigned floor focuses on developing multileveled social and physical skills through everyday activities of daily living.

TABLE 14.1 Cognition

Symptom (Identification)	*Implication (Define)*	*Meaning (Empathy)*	*Ideation (Prototype)*
Limited capacity for adaptation.	Alter behaviors from one environmental expectation to the next.	Macro clues to indicate a transition in social rules.	Use macro stimulation levels based on color, lighting levels, and sound.
Diminished comprehension of a cause-and-effect relationship.	Understand the reaction to an action.	Opportunities to experience different effects from different causes.	Use automatic and reactive elements.
Inability to form conceptualizations.	Use of imagination to link differing ideas to an outcome.	Expression of thought and creativity through different venues.	Encourage writing and drawing wherever possible.
Reduced capacity to form generalizations.	Extension of a set of behaviors within a given space to another.	Micro clues to inform behaviors from one space to another.	Provide multiple spaces based on similar behaviors.
Poor memory formation.	Ability to retain social rules that inform behaviors, and identifiers associated with environmental intelligence.	Different ways to evoke memory.	Use abstract and symbolic features to assist with wayfinding and territoriality.
Reasoning	Projecting sets of outcomes to select the most desired.	The ability to set one's own rules.	Temporal ability to change the purpose of a space for a reason.
Self-Determination	Making choices from a series of options.	Same as above.	Same as above.
Strategizing	Planning a series of actions to achieve an end goal.	Ability to manipulate objects and bring about different outcomes.	Puzzles and games that have a multitude of outcomes.

TABLE 14.2 Musculature

Symptom (Identification)	*Implication (Define)*	*Meaning (Empathy)*	*Ideation (Prototype)*
Poor balance and motor control.	Movement compensation to retain a movement outcome.	Games to practice and still have fun.	Lines, intermittent blocks, and low level-backless seating.
Contracted coordination skills.	Ability to use multiple body parts and sensory detection to achieve a movement goal.	Same as above.	Same as above.
Limited endurance levels.	Ability to use select muscle groups for a period without exhaustion.	Ability to exercise without being bored.	Enhance stairwells to promote greater use, include a circular walking path around a space.
Diminished muscle formation and overall strength.	Ability to lift, jump, and push off some object with a targeted single thrust.	Same as above.	Provide opportunities for a person to jump vertically and horizontally.

TABLE 14.3 Socialization

Symptom (Identification)	*Implication (Define)*	*Meaning (Empathy)*	*Ideation (Prototype)*
Inappropriate selection of conversation topics.	Introducing issues of concern at the wrong time and with the wrong people.	Not addressed through design.	Not addressed through design.
Lack or limited ability to empathize.	Inability to imagine how another might feel.	Ability to watch another and project or discuss feelings.	Introduction of large-scale enclosure to watch and discuss feelings.
Limited vocabulary and sentence formation.	Unable to find the right word to express an idea or concern.	To see and hear common words and phrases to express oneself.	Provide diverse exposure opportunities, and practice different words and phrases.

(*Continued*)

TABLE 14.3 (*Continued*)

Symptom (Identification)	*Implication (Define)*	*Meaning (Empathy)*	*Ideation (Prototype)*
Limited ability to express a thought.	Unable to communicate a feeling.	Similar to above.	Provide diverse opportunities to write or draw a feeling.
Poor judgment skills.	Unable to make good decisions.	Ability to choose an activity and action.	Allow for alternative actions as a means of ranking experience.
Reduced ability to retain social networks.	Inability to make and retain friendships.	Not addressed through design.	Not addressed through design.

Results

Identification, definition, and empathy led to the formation of ideations, which were assembled into a design concept that served as a prototype. The following are select images of the design that resulted from the first four steps of a design thinking process for a population affected by mild to moderate intellectual disabilities. The concepts are based on the design's capacity to address cognition, musculature, and socialization as identified in the three programming charts, developed from the following criteria:

- Use color, light and sound as macro stimulation sources.
- Use automatic and reactive elements.
- Encourage writing and drawing.
- Provide multiple spaces based on behaviors.
- Provide abstract and symbolic features for wayfinding and territoriality.
- Offer the ability to change the purpose of a space.
- Include puzzles and games that have a multitude of outcomes.
- Incorporate lines, intermittent blocks, and low level-backless seating.
- Enhance stairwells to promote greater use and include a circular walking path around a space.
- Provide opportunities for a person to jump vertically and horizontally.
- Introduce a large-scale enclosure to watch and discuss feelings.
- Provide diverse opportunities to be exposed to, and then practice, different words and phrases.
- Allow for alternative actions as a means of ranking experience.

"Floor One: Employment Readiness" (Figure 14.2) demonstrates how these criteria informed the overall design for the employment readiness floor. "Floor Two: Multileveled Social and Physical Skills" (Figure 14.3) demonstrates how these criteria informed the overall design for the multileveled social and physical skills floor.

FIGURE 14.2 The first level was conceived as a multifunctional space, serving as both a functioning café and an office aimed at cultivating essential job skills. Within the café component, individuals are trained in a range of roles, including janitorial duties, busing tables, waiting tables, operating as baristas, and cashier responsibilities. The office segment serves as a platform for imparting managerial skills, encompassing tasks such as inventory, financial record-keeping, and staff scheduling. Additionally, the office serves as a hub for teaching professional etiquette, encompassing aspects like appropriate attire and personal grooming, as well as providing guidance on navigating online applications, conducting virtual interviews, and mastering face-to-face interview techniques. Rendering by Rebecca Vancompernolle.

Floor One: Employment Readiness (Figure 14.2)

- Five different spaces affording opportunities for five different behaviors.
- Mural and painting on the wall are a source of color for stimulation.
- Columns wrapped and covered with blackboard paint encourage writing and drawing.
- Coffee bar and fuse ball table serve as recognizable features indicating behavioral norms.
- Large seating and recreation area can be cleared and reconfigured for different purposes.
- Blackboard paint and fuse ball table allow for games and recreational play.
- Inclusion of diverse seating opportunities for back and hip musculature and coordination.
- Large mural (to the right) signals stairwell location.
- Seating and game area in the center of space facilitate perimeter walking.
- Words and phrases written on columns can be erased and replaced regularly.
- Spatial segmentation allows for ranking of spaces in terms of behavioral expectations.

Floor Two: Multileveled Social and Physical Skills (Figure 14.3)

- Use of colored lines and colorful artwork along with rich sources of natural lighting serve as sources for macro stimulation.
- Music station, classrooms, and bays allow for reactive elements that coincide with behavioral expectations.
- Select walls have been painted with blackboard paint to facilitate impromptu writing and drawing.
- Multiple spaces and the ability for further spatial segmentation with collapsible walls allow for diverse activities and behaviors.
- The use of lines and layout for each bay serves as symbolic features for way-finding and behavioral expectations.
- Collapsible walls for each of the three bays allows them to be open and included in the larger recreational space or closed off for a specific smaller activity.
- Area for computer games or to play corn hole can help develop hand-eye coordination.
- Use of lines to walk on along with intermittent blocks and low level-backless seating assist with enhancing muscle formation and coordination skills.
- Spatial configuration allows for a circular perimeter pathway.
- Conference/classrooms and each bay can be used for larger or smaller group therapy sessions.
- Segmentation of the space allows for ranking of spaces as being private, semi-private, or public.

FIGURE 14.3 The uppermost level was designed as a day activity center catering to high-functioning clients. Within these spaces, ample provisions were made for private consultations between clients and their advocates, as well as designated areas for therapeutic and recreational activities. Moreover, the layout incorporates a variety of versatile spaces conducive to both group engagements and solitary pursuits, offering flexibility to accommodate diverse preferences and needs. Rendering by Rebecca Vancompernolle.

Conclusion

Following a systemized process to arrive at a design proposal helps designers consider options that they may not have thought about. It can provide substantiation to specific design features that a layperson may regard as purely aesthetic. In this project the overarching design objectives pertained to cognitive, musculature, and socialization factors known to affect young adults with an intellectual ability. Each of these objectives was then understood in terms of probable behaviors and symptoms. Using the design thinking process from positivist reasoning followed by a post-positivist analysis, we were able to identify and define the potential problems. We then come to imagine and understand perspectives and reactions that led to the formation of ideations aggregated into a final design approach. Each ideation and subsequent design concept were inspired by an intellectual understanding of the occupant -population. We assert that the design concepts in this project hold equal or greater aesthetic value while concurrently yielding better outcome benefits with fewer unintended consequences.

The use of design thinking methods to develop the interior space for individuals affected by shared sets of symptoms associated with a health condition is likely to be limited in specific outcomes, thereby challenging to replicate. However, the careful attention given to each of the contributing factors of concern should allow for greater consistency. Given that this was an exploratory study, further analysis of the outcomes and relative value will need to be studied further. If these design concepts are proven effective, design thinking as a method for exploratory research could provide a foundation for future interior design.

References

Beaird, G., Geist, M., and Lewis, E. J. (2018). Design thinking: Opportunities for application in nursing education. *Nursing Education Today*, 64: 115–118.

Boat, T. F., and Wu, J. T. Editors (2015). *Mental Disorders and Disabilities among Low-Income Children*. Washington, DC: The National Academies Press.

Burke, M. M., and Heller, T. (2017). Disparities in unmet service needs among adults with intellectual and other developmental disabilities. *Journal of Applied Research in Intellectual Disabilities*, 30: 898–910.

Carter, E. W., Austin, D., and Trainor, A. A. (2011). Predictors of postschool employment outcomes for young adults with severe disabilities. *Journal of Disability Policy Studies*, 23 (1): 50–63.

Centers for Disease Control (last reviewed 2018, April 17). *Facts about Developmental Disabilities*. Retrieved January 7, 2019 from: https://www.cdc.gov/ncbddd/developmentaldisabilities/facts.html.

Chou, D. C. (2018). Applying design thinking method to social entrepreneurship project. *Computer Standards & Interfaces*, 55: 73–79.

Cross, R. T. (1994). Iconicity and associative meaning: What are we looking for? In *Proceedings of the 6th Biennial Conference of the International Society for Augmentative and Alternative Communication*, Hoensbroek: IRV, 126–127.

Daly, B. (n.d.). Special care units for the critically ill: Providing key technology while also meeting emotional/social needs. *Academy of Nursing*. Retrieved May 28, 2021 from: https://www.aannet.org/initiatives/edge-runners/profiles/edge-runners--special-care-units-for-the-critically-ill.

Dam, R., and Siang, T. (23 October, 2019). Stage 3 in the design thinking process: Ideate. *Interaction Design Foundation*. Retrieved November 16, 2019 from: https://www.interaction-design.org/literature/article/stage-3-in-the-design-thinking-process-ideate.

Elmurzaeva, N., and Zhumanova, F. (2020). Organization of the educational process in specialized schools and boarding schools pedagogical problem. *European Journal of Molecular & Clinical Medicine*, 7 (7): 7020–7027.

Emerson, E. (2007). Poverty and people with intellectual disabilities. *Mental Retardation and Developmental Disabilities*, 13: 107–113.

Galbiati, E. (2020). The significance of art therapy. In Colombo, B. (ed.) *Brain and Art*. Nature Switzerland: Springer, 169–182.

Gil-Llario, M. D., Morell-Mengual, V., Ballester-Arnal, R., and Diaz-Rodriguez, I. (2018). The experience of sexuality in adults with intellectual disability. *Journal of Intellectual Disability Research*, 62 (1): 72–80.

Hartman, E., Houwen, S., Scherder, E., and Visscher, C. (2010). On the relationship between motor performance and executive functioning in children with intellectual disabilities. *Journal of Intellectual Disability Research*, 54 (5): 468–477.

Harvey, L. (2012). *Social Research Glossary*. Retrieved from: https://www.qualityresearchinternational.com/socialresearch/positivism.htm.

Horner, R. H., Day, H. M., and Day, J. R. (1997). Using neutralizing routines to reduce problem behaviors. *Journal of Applied Behavior Analysis*, 30 (4): 601–614.

Jalaluddin, J., Edros, S. A., and Khalil, K. (2017). Design thinking as problem-solving approach to create innovation. *Advanced Journal of Technical and Vocational Education*, 1 (4): 33–38.

Khanlou, N., Mantini., A. Khan, A., Degendorfer, K., and Zangeneh, M. (2018). Protection of privacy of information rights among young adults with developmental disabilities. *International Journal of Mental Health and Addiction*, 16 (3): 545–572.

Konrath, S. H., O'Brien, E. H., and Hsing, C. (2010). Changes in dispositional empathy in American college students over time: A meta-analysis. *Personality and Social Psychology Review*, 15 (2): 180–198.

Leeder, T., (2018). Learning to mentor in sports coaching: a design thinking approach. *Sports Education and Society*, 2: 208–211.

Nair, S. A., and Jose, S. (2017). Teacher perspectives on managing Manifest sexual behaviour among individuals with intellectual bisability. *Rajagiri Journal of Social Development*, 9 (2): 85–109.

Pushkala, P. (2017). *Crafting Qualitative Research: Beyond Positivist Traditions*. London: Routledge.

Rafaeli, A., and Vilnai-Yavetz, I. (2004). Instrumentality, aesthetics and symbolism of physical artifacts as triggers of emotion. *Theoretical Issues in Ergonomics Science*, 5 (1): 91–112.

Roessler, K. K. (2012). Healthy architecture! Can environments evoke emotional responses? *Global Journal of Health Sciences*, 4 (4): 83–89.
Rymer, R. (1994). *Genie: A Scientific Tragedy*. New York: Harper Collins.
Tanner, C. K. (2008). Explaining relationships among student outcomes and the school's physical environment. *Journal of Advanced Academics*, 19 (3): 444–471.
Thompson, A. R. A., Wozencroft, A. J., Parsons, M. D. (2017). The impact of therapeutic recreation camps on adults with disabilities. *American Journal of Recreation Therapy*, 16 (2): 21–28.
Vuijk, P. J., Hartman, E., Scherder, E., and Visscher, C. (2010). Motor performance of children with mild intellectual disability and borderline intellectual functioning. *Journal of Intellectual Disability Research*, 54 (11): 955–965.
Wehmeyer, M. L., and Bolding, N. (2001). Enhanced self-determination of adults with intellectual disability as an outcome of moving to community-based work or living environments. *Journal of Intellectual Disability Research*, 45 (5): 371–383.
Williams, H., Clarke, R., Fashola, Y., and Holt, G. (1998). Diogenes' syndrome in patients with intellectual disability: 'A rose by any other name'? *Journal of Intellectual Disability Research*, 42 (4): 316–320.
Wuang, Y-P., and Su, C-Y. (2009). Reliability and responsiveness of the Bruininks–Oseretsky test of motor proficiency-second edition in children with intellectual disability. *Research in Developmental Disabilities*, 30 (5): 847–855.
Ziefle, M., Rocker, C., and Holzinger, A. (2011). Medical technology in smart homes: Exploring the user's perspective on privacy, intimacy and trust. In *2011 35th IEEE Annual Computer Software and Applications Conference Workshops*, Washington, DC.

CONNECTING 15

Regardless of the project type or design method, the connection between the client and the designer is undeniably critical. Next, interior designer Ellen Fisher and client and head of Alexandria County Day School Scott Baytosh highlight the power of this connection as they share their perspectives on a classroom renovation project they worked on together.

As you follow Fisher and Baytosh's accounts, consider where their explanations intersect and how each individually supports the project's aims and ambitions. Baytosh is well attuned to the instructional requirements and needs of students and staff. He understands that there is a correlation between students' classrooms and their learning and wellbeing. As the design consultant, Fisher carefully grounds her work in these goals and uses her knowledge of current research to translate the school's mission and values into its physical spaces. Fisher's research-informed design approach considers the impact of interior spaces and furnishings on social interactions and their effects on children's mental and physical health during their developmental years.

But Fisher goes a step further than is typical in the design process. She did not just work for the client; she worked *with* the teachers. Fisher visited and documented the teacher's spaces. Then, she spent time teaching them basic design principles while training the teachers how to use their newly designed classrooms. Often, much consideration goes into building projects from both clients and designers to shape spaces for the desired outcomes. However, many intentions can go by the wayside as people occupy the spaces. All built environments will continue to adapt and evolve. Still, like institutional knowledge, design intent can be valuable to co-create and pass along after design and construction ends.

DOI: 10.4324/9781003004622-39

15

CREATING OPTIMAL LEARNING ENVIRONMENTS

A Case Study of Alexandria Country Day School's Classroom Renovation

Ellen Fisher and Scott Baytosh

As a certified interior designer and design consultant, I had the privilege of working with Alexandria Country Day School (ACDS) in 2015 under the leadership of the head of school Scott Baytosh. Our goal was to create optimal learning environments for students in grades K-8 through the renovation of existing classrooms. The mission of ACDS is to, "Challenge students intellectually; inspire their confidence, curiosity and creativity; and prepare them to thrive in a diverse and complex world by ensuring that they are independent learners, effective communicators community minded citizens, and balanced individuals." This clear statement of values informed our design process and is evident in the final result. Based on my research and experience, I understood that the best learning environments were those designed and used as tools to learn and teach with; actively supporting and enabling the work of both teachers and students.

Guided by a shared vision, my client (Scott Baytosh) and I embarked on a journey to create a mission-driven, evidence-based solution for the school's renovation. Beginning with Scott, the following provides a glimpse into our individual thought processes and design objectives, and ultimately how these merged into the final design.

Client: Scott Baytosh, Head of School, ACDS

The spaces our students inhabit and the ways in which they engage in them are essential to their learning and wellbeing. When presented with an opportunity to make a substantial improvement to our facilities, this belief guided our efforts and ultimately led us to retain an interior design expert who brought insight into the relationship between spaces and student learning to lead our

DOI: 10.4324/9781003004622-40

FIGURE 15.1 Classroom before renovation. Photograph by Ellen Fisher.

renovation. The result has been crafting spaces that are healthy, flexible, and conducive to multiple learning modalities and varied teaching methods.

Alexandria Country Day School (ACDS) is a Kindergarten through Eighth-Grade, non-sectarian, coed, independent school in Alexandria, Virginia, that serves approximately 212 students. The school is housed in a single brick building that was originally built as a Catholic High School in 1947. In 1992, the building was purchased by ACDS and became the home of its growing student population. In its early days, the school pulled together what furniture it could to provide warm and functional classroom spaces. Teachers helped by adding their own furnishings over time, and when I arrived in 2012, the classrooms were chock full of old-fashioned school desks and chairs, cabinets, shelving units, couches, and rugs. Most teachers had established "teacher desk" areas that were cordoned off spaces for the teachers' private work and materials.

While few teachers still lectured from the front of the room, furnishings were inflexible and hard to rearrange leading to static, traditional room arrangements that did not align with current teaching methods. In the Middle School (grades 5–8) connected desk-and-chair units were packed into small classrooms leaving little room for student or teacher movement.

Despite these limitations, a culture of growth and professional development was strong and teachers were working to embrace innovative and contemporary

FIGURE 15.2 Classroom before renovation. Photograph by Ellen Fisher.

curricula and teaching methods. So, when a large donation created the possibility of renovating all of the school's classroom spaces, school leadership saw a chance to integrate educational philosophy, teaching methodology, and interior design. Since the school would not be rebuilding spaces, but rather upgrading them within the existing structure and improving furnishings and classroom layout options, the school did not follow the traditional approach of contracting with an architectural firm. Instead, we retained an interior designer who understood the relationship between spaces and people and could work with teachers to strengthen their understanding of the relationship between their classroom spaces, their teaching, and student learning.

Over the course of the project, the School developed three essential goals:

1 **Flexibility.** Spaces needed to be flexible in order to adapt to varied instructional requirements and the individual needs of students.

FIGURE 15.3 Classroom before renovation. Photograph by Ellen Fisher.

Effective instruction takes many forms, including introductory lessons by a teacher to the whole group of students, small-group work where students collaborate in learning activities, partner work where students engage one-on-one in discussion, and solo work where students work independently. Moreover, these different modes may all be employed not just during a single school day, but even within a 40-minute instructional period. Classroom spaces need to facilitate this variety by allowing the easy and rapid rearrangement of furnishings. Spaces are also well-served by furnishings that are not overly specific in their design. For example, the classic "kidney bean" shaped table, which can be quite effective for teacher-led, small-group instruction, is only useful for that purpose, which may only constitute a small portion of any given day. In our case, we selected desks that were simple tabletops that could be arranged as single desks or combined into large table surfaces. Likewise, small, lightweight Hokki stools are very easy for even our youngest students to move, so they can be used in class circles discussions, brought to alternative spaces (even outdoors), or simply moved out of the way.

Our most versatile choice was the adjustable sit/stand desk employed in Middle School classrooms. Each unit only takes up 3.6 square feet but provides ample surface area for student work. Because they are on casters, the desks

FIGURE 15.4 Renovated classroom. Photograph by Abe Mousavi and provided courtesy of Alexandria Country Day School.

can be rapidly moved into groups, out to the hall for quiet solo work, or moved to the outer edges of the room to create open spaces for free movement. Accompanying stools are light, easy to move, and stack away easily. Where once teachers needed to work around the furnishings to employ effective teaching techniques, now the furniture is another instructional resource. Students also appreciate the flexible opportunities the tables and stools create. Standing or sitting is left to the student's discretion so they can respond to their physical needs at will without disrupting the class.

2 **Movement.** Spaces needed to facilitate the physical engagement of students and allow for regular movement.

At the time of our renovation, a great deal of attention was being paid to research that pointed to the negative effects of prolonged sitting. Standing

FIGURE 15.5 Renovated classroom. Photograph by Abe Mousavi and provided courtesy of Alexandria Country Day School.

FIGURE 15.6 Renovated classroom. Photograph by Abe Mousavi and provided courtesy of Alexandria Country Day School.

desks were becoming more popular, and we were gaining awareness that asking children to sit still for extended periods was not conducive to concentration, engagement, or physical health. Furthermore, our instructional methods asked students to transition frequently between whole-group instruction, small-group instruction, partner work, and individual study. With this project, we had the opportunity to respond boldly to these concerns in our selection of classroom furniture. Consequently, we employed Hokki stools in our K-4 classrooms and adjustable sit/stand desks in our 5–8 classrooms.

Wobbling Hokki stools, by VS, provide a stable seat while allowing for continuous movement. They are also extremely lightweight, so they can be moved about the room easily. For most of our students, we have found that the ability to move dissipates excess energy, strengthens focus, and responds to the physical needs of children. Occasionally, students find the wobbling over-stimulating or have motor coordination issues that make managing the stool difficult. In these cases, the stool can simply be flipped over creating a non-wobbling option, further demonstrating the flexibility of this resource.

Adjustable sit/stand desks by Ergotron were employed in every middle school classroom other than the science lab and have transformed our classroom spaces. Students have reported that they appreciate the opportunity to shift between sitting and standing and have related that doing so can help with focus. Sometimes students need to be reminded to stand, and teachers may employ this technique when they see student focus or energy flagging. The VS stools that are paired with the desks encourage strong posture and the development of core strength. The desk/stool combinations also facilitate easy movement between large and small-group instruction, partner or group work, and individual study. Virtually no time is lost in these transitions.

Teachers were also equipped with adjustable, movable sit/stand desks and large teacher desks were removed, moving teachers more into the action of the room and capturing more space for instruction.

3 **Focus and engagement.** Spaces needed to mitigate visual and aural distraction, allow for the clear display of instructional material, bring focus to student work, and allow students to engage actively in their learning.

Cluttered and visually "noisy" spaces were distracting and inefficient. Students were not always able to quickly find learning resources or see visual instructional reminders, and students prone to distraction were disadvantaged by these environments. Consequently, we sought ways to set up classroom spaces that diminished visual distraction, allowed for the prominent display of instructional material such as anchor charts, and allowed student work to take center stage.

Each classroom was stripped down and emptied, woodwork was restored, and rooms were painted a bright, neutral white. Neutral, dark carpeting

FIGURE 15.7 Classroom before renovation. Photograph by Ellen Fisher.

FIGURE 15.8 Photography by Meredith Kirchner and provided courtesy of Alexandria Country Day School.

was installed in all classrooms utilizing carpet squares to enable easy damage repair. Carpeting mitigated noise and warmed up classrooms that had previously been tiled. Whiteboards were expanded to make more surfaces instructionally valuable, and Forbo tack board was installed in place of limited bulletin boards to allow for more attractive and functional displays of student work and instructional material.

Consistent and appropriate classroom furniture was acquired to allow for the efficient storage and display of materials making rooms more organized and more accessible for independent student engagement.

In addition, our interior designer met with every teacher to teach them about basic design principles and to help them arrange the rooms in ways that matched their styles but also met the needs of students and followed good design practices.

Interior Designer and Consultant: Dr. Ellen Fisher, FASID, FIDEC

The collaboration with Alexandria Country Day School presented an opportunity to implement key Environment and Behavior strategies to create flexible, adaptable, and supportive learning spaces within existing classrooms. ACDS follows a student-centered learning appraoch, which emphasizes the individuality of each learner, promotes self-directed and independent learning, and empowers each student to become an independent learner. Therefore, each classroom had to be designed in a way to support individual, small group, and large group learning. The spaces had to provide environmental cues such as anchor charts that recapped past lessons, allowing students to find answers or guidance without approaching the teacher. In fact, teachers became guides to learning, and had no desks, special furniture, or space separate from the children's spaces within the classrooms.

The key design strategies I employed to create student-centered learning spaces were to:

- A increase daylight and lighting control
- B improve acoustics
- C improve indoor air quality
- D reduce visual clutter and increase visual organization
- E support independent and individualized learning; increase flexible and adaptable furniture groupings to support collaboration, movement, and choice
- F involve the teachers in the design of the classrooms; train the teachers in the design fundamentals underlying the design, so that going forward, they would be making changes to the learning environments based on research

Here, I provide more detailed information about each of these strategies. Although these were implemented at ACDS, they are evidence-based and may be applicable to the design of other learning environments.

Strategies

A Increase daylight and lighting control

There is substantial research on the significant impact of daylight on test scores for elementary school children (Heschong & Mahone, 1999). Heschong's study found that when controlling for all other factors, students with the most daylighting in their classrooms progressed up to 20% faster in math tests and up to 26% faster in reading tests over one year compared to those students with the least daylight in their classrooms. Similar results were found in classrooms with skylights, and even more benefit was gained from rooms with operable windows.

Therefore, all the ACDS classroom windows were outfitted with mesh roller blinds, operable using a manual chain. The color selected was black, which allowed for maximum view through the shade to the outside as well as the most control over glare from the sun at various times of the day. This decision was important because the school building was sited so that half the classrooms on the double-loaded corridor faced east, and the morning sun was blinding. The new shades precluded teachers from taping student work or anchor charts to the windows, thereby also reducing visual clutter.

B Improve acoustics

Many studies have shown that learning is impeded in classrooms with poor acoustics, including external noise. Flexer (2004) found that poor acoustics impede brain function and growth, affect listening and the development of literacy skills, and overall have a negative impact on learning.

The ACDS building was at least 75 years old with interior plaster and masonry walls, and existing VCT tile in the classrooms. In the renovation, all classrooms received Interface carpet tiles that provided many benefits, including mitigating noise. Also, a FORBO tack surface was installed floor-to-ceiling on at least two walls of every room.

C Improve indoor air quality

Indoor air quality (IAQ) has been found to be a significant factor in student absenteeism and health, both of which affect learning. Teachers' health and productivity are also negatively impacted by poor IAQ. An article commissioned by the Environmental Protection Agency (EPA, 2022) suggests that environmental factors are linked to students' ability to perform, and that indoor air quality is a necessary component of an optimal learning environment. A related EPA Quick Reference Guide (https://www.epa.gov/sites/default/files/2014-08/documents/student_performance_findings.pdf) reinforces the recommended interventions for schools, including the design of better physical conditions, improved maintenance, and ongoing awareness of the need for proper ventilation and air filtration.

The design strategy to improve the indoor air quality in ACDS classrooms was implemented by specifying Interface carpet tiles, window shades, and Benjamin Moore Aura paint on walls and trim, all of which met very high sustainability standards, reducing off-gassing both at initial installation and over time.

D Reduce visual clutter and increase visual organization

I met individually and in small groups with the classroom teachers, and gave them a brief lesson on the design principle of alignment and the design concept of a "datum," as tools that could be applied to consistently control the location, size, and groupings of notes, charts, and student work on display within each room

E Support independent and individualized learning; increase flexible and adaptable furniture groupings to support collaboration, movement, and choice

With the active contributions of the client, furniture was selected from a range of early childhood furnishings companies, school outfitters, and designer sources to be lightweight, easily moved by children, stable and safe, and flexible within a limited physical footprint. The Ergotron sit-stand desk was an essential element in providing movable and adjustable surfaces that could accommodate students of wildly varied heights and size, along with its ability to be grouped or used individually. Furniture such as shelving, bookcases, and storage units from Childcraft was used, because it could be arranged to create nooks and more private study and work spaces, allowing for rooms-within-rooms.

F Involve the teachers in the design of the classrooms; train the teachers in the design fundamentals underlying the design

I worked with each teacher individually to assist in setting up the classrooms to support the teacher's style and approach as much as possible. This was also used as a teaching moment for the teacher – I aimed to instill within each teacher a sense of agency in themselves as designers of the physical classroom environment, with research and design principles to refer to, and why this was important to their teaching and to the growth of their students as learners.

Conclusion

This project was initiated with a gift to a school in honor of both the donor and recipient's shared recognition of the value of beautiful and functional learning spaces that supported a values-based education. The values included respect for students, their individual learning needs, their physical and mental growth, and for those who teach. By collaborating closely as a team—designer, school administration, and teachers—we were able to create research-informed environments that embodied these values and created settings that allowed students to maximize their potential and self-efficacy. Students were able to clearly and non-verbally understand that the renovated classrooms were places in which they would be respected and nurtured in mind and body.

References

U.S. Environmental Protection Agency. (2022). *How does indoor air quality impact student health and academic performance?* Retrieved August 10, 2022, from https://www.epa.gov/iaq-schools/how-does-indoor-air-quality-impact-student-health-and-academic-performance

U.S. Environmental Protection Agency. (2014). *Student performance and indoor air quality: Findings from the School Health Policies and Practices Study.* Retrieved August 10, 2022, from https://www.epa.gov/sites/default/files/2014-08/documents/student_performance_findings.pdf

Flexer, C. (2004). The Impact of Classroom Acoustics: Listening, Learning, and Literacy. *Seminars in Hearing*, 25: 131–140. 10.1055/s-2004-828664.

Heschong, L., Heshong, & Mahone Group. (1999). *Daylighting in Schools: An Investigation int the Relationship Between Daylighting and Human Performance.* https://www.h-m-g.com/downloads/Daylighting/schoolc.pdf. Accessed 8/10/2022.

CONNECTING 16

Most of us spend so much of our lives indoors that we feel the emotional impact of interior spaces on us and are vulnerable to how they shape our behaviors. For better or worse, many daily experiences are merely the incidental byproducts of maneuvering through the built world. The *exception* is when people encounter planned environments tailored to their specific needs and desires, elevating their experience.

The layout of a space and its arrangement of furniture and objects contribute to its experiential qualities, setting the stage for human behavior. For example, a rectangular classroom with fixed seats facing a podium at the front will successfully serve a teacher who plans to deliver lectures. However, suppose another teacher intends to use the classroom to facilitate activities in small collaborative groups. In that case, the same space will likely lead to frustration and a less-than-optimal experience for the teacher and students. We all strive to live and work in harmonious behavior settings where our environment aligns with our goals, yet on many occasions, we confront spaces that hinder our objectives (Glass, 2018).

Designing for people in real-world environments involves much more than planning a typical physical layout based on the assumption of how occupants will use a space. The task is complex and requires embracing uncertainty and unpredictability. Designers must define as many unknowns and constraints as possible while also taking a systems approach. In the following case study, Diana Siebenaler, an interior designer specializing in experiential design, presents a university health clinic envisioned through the lens of experience to support the holistic needs of patients and caregivers. Siebenaler offers

DOI: 10.4324/9781003004622-41

invaluable insights and a glimpse into designing at the intersection of services and spaces as she reflects on lessons learned when concepts become a reality.

Reference

Glass, T. (2018). *Prompt: Socially Engaging Objects and Environments*. Birkhäuser.

16

DESIGNING A VALUE-BASED (HEALTH) CARE EXPERIENCE

Diana Siebenaler

Historically healthcare in the United States has largely been based on what is referred to as a fee-for-service system. Payment happens at each healthcare event; a visit to the doctor's office, blood work, diagnostics, seeing a specialist, and each interaction has an associated code and payment. This system encourages both healthcare providers and patients to seek episodic care that is more reactive in nature. The incentives in the fee-for-service system do not encourage or reward preventive care; instead, they make complex procedures and diagnoses more financially viable.

Rising costs and an unhealthy population have created the need for an evolution in the healthcare system. There has been a recognition that the fee-for-service model may not be delivering the most desirable outcomes. Similarly, there has been an acknowledgment that keeping people healthy, via a more proactive approach to care, might be better for the humans in the system and a way to reduce costs.

Value-Based Care

Value-based care is part of that evolution and one of the models being tested across the United States today. So, what does value-based care mean?

The basic premise of value-based care is that healthcare providers are given a dollar amount per patient to deliver their care which is based on quality rather than quantity. The amount per patient varies based on how healthy or sick the patient is, but the goal with this type of payment is that doctors are now incentivized to keep their patients healthier. The healthier they are and the less they need to use healthcare services, the greater the potential to make money as a provider. This is also sometimes called risk-based payment models

DOI: 10.4324/9781003004622-42

or bundled services and is more than a passing trend or fad. Value-based care has been heralded as one of the solutions to our rising healthcare costs since it caps costs per patient—even being mandated by government initiatives to incrementally take hold in the United States, causing significant systemic pressure within the healthcare industry. The benefit of this approach is that clinicians are incentivized to perform proactive care and keep patients healthy and out of the hospital—the healthier the patient, the greater the opportunity for creating a positive margin on health care expenditures.

The Opportunity

The University of Texas at Austin was one of the first organizations in the United States to explore a value-based care model and specifically design physical spaces to support the new ways care can be delivered. I had the opportunity to partner with the Dell Medical School's Design Institute for Health[1] and Page architecture on the design of these new value-based clinics.[2] The process which involved several months of design charrettes, mockups, and user work sessions to help walk providers (the people and entities providing care) and future patients through the space and explore new ways of working.

Value-based care inherently requires different clinical interactions on the back end. Because the goal is to reduce the cost of care and proactively prevent acute illness, provider teams are more inclined to work collaboratively and interdepartmentally to address patient concerns and whole-person health. For example, instead of each patient seeing multiple specialists and extended care team members (nutrition, physical therapy, social work, etc.) who would charge them individually, they would instead be seen by a team of cross-functional providers who would work collaboratively to address the patient's concerns. One way this works is that an entire cross-functional team may meet at the beginning of the day to do a "huddle." In this daily huddle, the team goes over every patient coming in that day and discusses their case as a team. So when the patient is roomed for their appointment, the care team has already reviewed the patient's available history and potential needs for their visit that day. An appropriate mix of providers would then come and see that patient during their visit to address their medical concerns and any social, mental, and behavioral factors that could affect their recovery outcomes over time. In this approach, the team is more likely to know that a patient is struggling to pay their rent or may have difficulty following recommended prescription drug therapies due to cost. Therefore, addressing social determinants of health and root causes (such as economic stability or food access) is also an important part of the value-based model to allow patients the greatest chance of success. Dell Medical School recognized those inherent human needs of patients and designed their value-based care model to include physical therapy, nutrition, brain health, and social work to support the needs of patients more holistically.

The Design Process

Human-centered design is based on understanding the humans being served through the lens of empathy. Through patient and provider interviews, working groups, and observations, the Design Institute and I discovered a desire for both sets of constituents to share information, educate each other, and be involved in shared co-decision making regarding the patient's care plan.

During the Discovery Phase, we were curious to learn:

- What existing behaviors/processes/workflows we needed to support?
- What new behaviors/processes/workflows did we need to design for?
- How did patients and providers feel in their current spaces or going through their current health experiences? What challenges or frustrations did they have, and when had they had an experience that exceeded their expectations?
- What unmet needs existed with patients or providers?

We heard over and over again the need to make a sterile and clinical space feel more comforting to help reduce anxiety. Patients shared their desire for comprehensive care that was better coordinated to minimize their time away from work and other commitments. They shared their frustrations with the current fee-for-service model. In those circumstances, they felt rushed by their providers, who had only allocated 15 minutes or less to address their concerns. They didn't feel there was any proactive discussion around health goals or a forum outside of the clinical sphere to address other areas impacting their health (such as food, housing, and finances). Many had to manage a complex network of referrals and struggled to keep up with the many moving pieces of scheduling appointments and understanding testing and diagnostics. For most patients, their current experience with the healthcare system had been disappointing, frustrating, and confusing, and had left them with a lack of trust in the system.

After discovery, it is common for designers to collectively review what they have learned and agree upon the design challenge that is before them. They then construct the challenge as one or more "How Might We" (HMW) questions. This technique of problem-framing, often associated with Design Thinking, helps set the stage for the design team to move into coming up with creative ideas. Here were our HMW questions: *How might we build trust with patients in an environment that better meets their needs and makes them feel comfortable? How might we design environments for providers that allow them to deliver collaborative patient care that builds trust?*

At the beginning of the Ideation Phase, we mapped out a series of new value-based experience interactions (Figure 16.1) that the patient would have at each moment along their journey with us. Everything from the moment they booked an appointment to arriving at the parking garage, and finally to checking out at the end of their visit. Who would they interact with? For how

FIGURE 16.1 The Experience Blueprint describes the value-based care experience at each moment of the patient journey. For each stage, the blueprint captures the needs and goals of patients, providers, and the enterprise. This tool became important for both design decisions and training of staff.

Source: Design Institute, 2019.

long? What technology, environment, and processes did they need to support their interactions? What information would be exchanged? What equipment or tools might be needed? What role would each person play? What happened during the transitions between experiences? How would the next provider know the patient was ready?

In a value-based model, patients spend more time with their providers, as well as ideally meet more than one cross-functional provider on a single visit. At this point, more HMWs followed: *How might we create a space that supports these longer visits? For example, how might we design an un-intimidating exam room that serves as a place to have in-depth conversations with providers, in addition to having it function as an exam room?* From these, we established our design goals to guide us through the design process.

Summary of design goals to support new behaviors:

- Create an effortless patient check-in and arrival experience to reduce patient anxiety.
- Support value-based care by creating collaborative spaces for providers where they can connect in real time to discuss patient needs.
- Develop exam rooms for both physical exams and in-depth conversations with patient and provider to encourage shared-design making between patient and provider.
- Integrate flexibility into the design so that the space could be modified beyond day two as the needs of patients and providers evolved.

Designed Experiences and Lessons Learned

Because architectural design and construction is a lengthy, multi-year process, the building shell and floor plate were already set prior to the full formation of the UTHA clinics or the Design Institute for Health. This reality required us to work within those existing parameters and the building shell. The Design Institute prototyped and developed experience design protocols to inform and dovetail with the new clinical spaces being constructed. The build-out of the physical spaces and implementation of the experience design provided us with a significant opportunity to test our designs, allowing us to evaluate and assess successes and areas for improvement. This section outlines how the design team planned to accommodate some of the predetermined interactions and scenarios of a patient's visit to the clinic and the resulting outcomes. They are organized here into three experiences: the arrival and check-in experience, the provider experience, and the exam room experience. In the spirit of reflective practice, I am sharing some of the team's design intentions and the lessons we learned along the way.

1 The Arrival and Check-In Experience

The original intent of the design was to have a seamless and technologically integrated care system that would allow patients to effortlessly and intuitively navigate the parking structure, entry lobby, elevator bay, and clinical hallways. The goal was to have patient-enabled GPS devices (similar to a cellphone's "find my friend" feature) that would allow patients to easily find their room once they had arrived at the building (through a series of step by step instructions and navigation) and eliminate the need for waiting. Patients would have filled out the necessary paperwork prior to arrival via their phone or at-home computer. The layers of coordination needed to make this a reality were much more logistically challenging than anticipated. First and foremost, we discovered patients would enter the building via multiple entry points. One arrival pathway is from the street level if coming via public transit, medical transport, or rideshare. This pathway is, in some ways, the easiest to navigate as building security can greet patients and direct them to the appropriate floor. Ideally, in this scenario, whoever the patient has spoken with to book their appointment can also provide specific directions about what floor and clinic they need to be going to.

Lessons Learned:

In reality, patient arrival and pre-arrival directions were inconsistent and variable. In hindsight designing communication that went to all referring providers and patients with clear maps, directions, and navigation, as well as a number to call if you were lost would have been very helpful. Similarly, offering printed and digital instructions with directions available in multiple languages and including maps and pictures (to accommodate varying degrees of literacy and language abilities) to make the arrival process more intuitive would have been helpful for many of our patients.

The other arrival scenario involves patients driving themselves or being driven by a family member or friend to their appointment. In this scenario, patients receive clear directions on how to find the building and parking structure. The ideal situation assumes patients with mobility challenges will be dropped off on the 2nd floor in an arrival zone (or will park on the floor closest to their clinic if they are driving themselves). Then their family or friend will park and meet them at their appointment on the appropriate floor.

Lessons Learned:

In actuality, we encountered a myriad of different challenges with this scenario. First, this plan required staffing in the arrival zone to help navigate patients to the appropriate floor. This was a cost-prohibitive solution to operate, and providing a self-navigated or digital kiosk solution also proved to be difficult. Additionally, patients who were being dropped at the arrival zone generally couldn't make their way, without assistance, to the specific clinician they were there to see. Their loved ones had to leave their vehicles in a loading zone, take them up to their appointment and return to their vehicle to park which created stress for both the patient and their caretaker.

Could we revist the design process, we would have spent much more time practicing and reviewing the entry sequence in different scenarios to understand how patients would learn about the clinics in the first place. This process would have allowed us to pay more attention to each component of the entry journey, the communication being shared, and the key members who were sharing the information. Then, we would have noticed the knowledge gaps and how much we were relying on the patient to "figure things out" upon arrival. We (the design team) made some critical assumptions about what technology would be available and how easy it would be to get patients to their specific clinic location that we weren't able to deliver on as we had intended.

Additionally, with the large number of clinic specialties and providers, we would have incorporated an interactive wayfinding map or directory that could detail where you were and allow you to search for the provider/specialty you needed. This was also the first time some of our patients had experienced a parking fee to attend an appointment which was a shock for many. We could have appropriately set expectations more proactively before their visit. As you may have noted, the arrival experience, particularly transportation and parking, did not align with our original design intent.

Luckily, if our patients could get past some of the initial hurdles, their experience upon arriving to a clinical floor often made up for the navigation woes. Upon arrival, patients are greeted by a care concierge who welcomes the patient, checks them in, and reviews any outstanding paperwork. This team is expertly trained in customer service best practices. They do a beautiful job of anticipating patient needs, helping them review or translate paperwork and assisting them in finding their provider. The arrival concourse (Figures 16.2 and 16.3) was designed by Page to have attractive backlit imagery on both sides, providing the illusion of natural light and creating subtle wayfinding for each floor with different Texas landscape images (clouds, trees, grasses, etc.). This part of the experience also incorporates thoughtful furnishings for a variety of postures, ample areas to charge personal devices, and carpeting which reduces sound transfer in the space. The concourse sets the tone that this was not just an ordinary clinic—it conveys a message to the patients that we value their experience. The space is intended to reduce anxiety and leave patients and loved ones feeling confident in the care they are about to receive.

Lessons Learned:

Although the original intent of the space was not to have any waiting areas, the lack of technology access for some of our patients and the extensive communication and coordination needed prior to appointments to fill out the appropriate paperwork in advance made the concourse the de facto waiting space. The good news is that it felt welcoming and comfortable and

FIGURES 16.2 The concourse is the first thing patients see upon entering the clinics. This is a strictly "front-of-house" space for patients and family only and is designed to be quiet and calming. Alcoves along the concourse accommodate different group sizes and interactions.

Source: Design Institute, 2019.

FIGURE 16.3 At the end of the concourse, windows overlook the cityscape and additional spaces are provided for focused work, or for larger families.

allowed ample space between different groups so that each person retained a certain level of privacy. The bad news is that it resulted in patients still being called awkwardly back to their exam room. Better technology integration would have helped, and ideally, we would have been able to deploy patient text messages with directions and rooming instructions. Even with improved technologies, we still would have encountered patients with varying degrees of literacy or a lack of access to technology. There was an underlying need for detailed logistics coordination if you intend to create seamless handoffs and reduce wait times as much as possible. We also know from patient feedback that the paperwork they are asked to fill out is daunting and hard to understand. We recognize the need to make this paperwork more inclusive and accessible. However, we discovered the language and requirements to meet regulatory and compliance standards for paperwork like this are by nature exclusionary and often less accessible.

All in all, the entry and arrival experiences still have many opportunities for transformation. Lessons can be learned from the hospitality industry about how we would like our patients to feel at each stage in the journey. It is important to note that the success of the entry space is incredibly dependent on the dedicated and thoughtful concierge team that is the first person-to-person contact for our patients. This team plays an instrumental role in setting the tone for the experience and creating patient expectations.

2 The Provider Experience

In the provider space, we knew there was the need for a team-based work environment (Figure 16.4). The open work station design of each Integrated Practice Unit helps to increase collaboration and reduce hierarchy among providers. The physical proximity and large digital and analog boards for tracking daily patient progress allows the providers to connect seamlessly to discuss patient needs (Figures 16.5 and 16.6). One bonus is that teaching and learning behaviors became second nature in such an open environment. Team members can feel more comfortable raising concerns or asking questions knowing that they were collectively responsible for the care of the patient. It is important to note that it isn't just the non-hierarchical physical space at play, but the combination of the space with the organizational culture and a growth mindset that helps support behaviors of openness and vulnerability.

Lessons Learned:

The Multi-purpose Meeting Room in each unit proved useful for morning huddles but sat empty for portions of the day since it wasn't visually connected to the work station space. In hindsight, it would have been helpful

FIGURE 16.4 The back-of-house (work stations) is designed to encourage care team members to intersect and overlap. More informal contact leads to better communication and coordination, and the design of the space enables this. Physicians, nurses, researchers, and the rest of the staff all share the same working space.

Source: Design Institute, 2019.

to have that space closer to the workspace and potentially with clear glass or windows that looked into the workspace to make it more inviting. Given the limited square footage it would have been great to leverage this space more consistently throughout the day while providing the visual connectivity to the work station space so that if someone needed something they could easily motion to each other as a signal.

A new care model requires new ways of working. Some providers were on board with the new open work station collaboration model and others were taken aback by their lack of private offices and space to hang their diplomas. Additionally, providers were used to having private spaces for dictation, charting, making calls, and note-taking. The new space design was a dramatic behavior shift for some providers and required an openness to a new workflow and model. In an effort to bring providers along in the process many efforts were put in place to model new behaviors and lead by example as well as showcase the benefits of the new model as part of the change management plan.

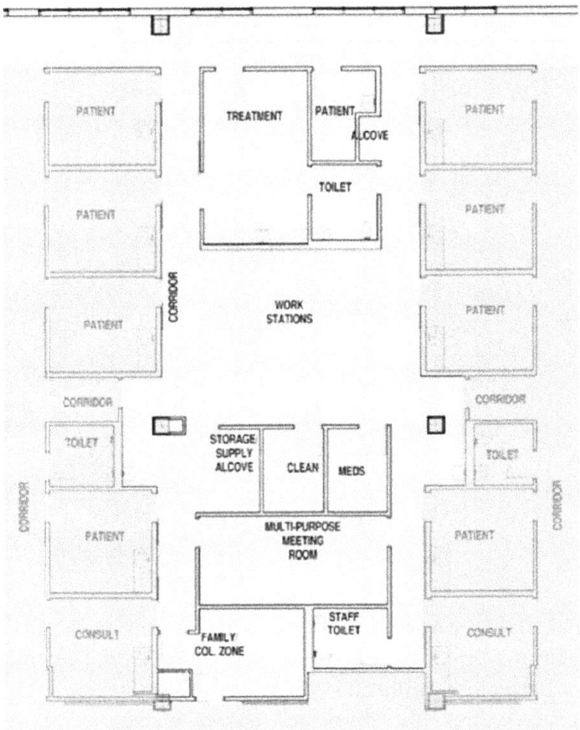

FIGURE 16.5 The layout for each Integrated Practice Unit is identical, regardless of specialty. The clinic is separated into "front-of-house" (gray) and "back-of-house" (white) zones. The "front-of-house" is for patient flow and the "back-of-house" is for care team members.

Source: Design Institute, 2019.

Unfortunately, the shared spaces at the end of each floor (similar to Figure 16.3 but intended for staff only) that were designed for provider interaction between units are not used as frequently as originally intended. This is likely due in part to the lack of consistent programming in the space as well as the end of hallway location. In hindsight having a more centrally located gathering space may have been more effective.

3 The Exam Room Experience

Since 80% of the time a patient is in the exam room, they are in conversations with their providers (only 20% of the time is generally needed for the physical portion of the exam), we designed the space intentionally to democratize the interaction. We started by trying to emulate a living room environment in the exam room (Figure 16.7). Patients have the option to sit on a two

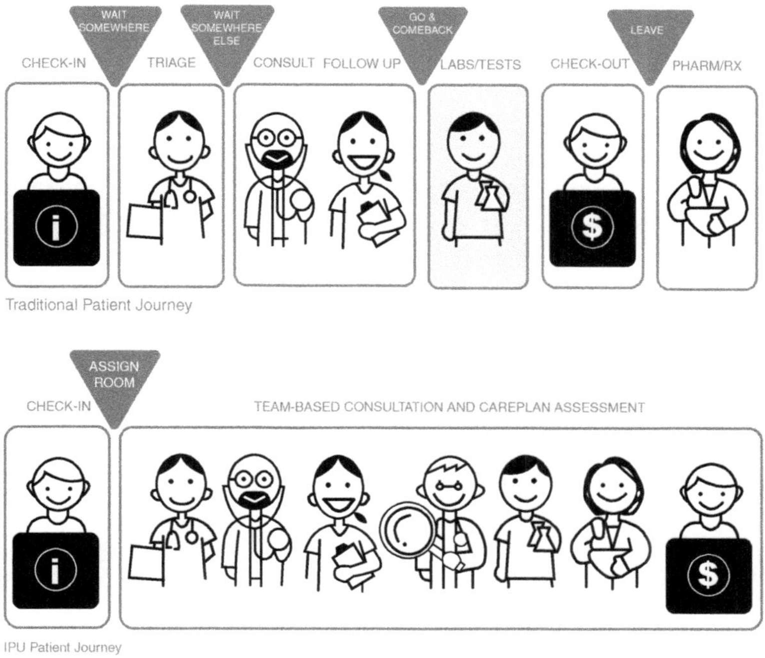

FIGURES 16.6 Patients waiting in a clinic are akin to materials being held in staging in a factory production line. They are paused, then moved, only when the next stage of the production line is ready to process them. A traditional clinic prioritizes the factory—an integrated practice unit returns focus to the patient.

Source: Design Institute, 2019.

seater sofa or an exam table that looks more like a recliner. The provider(s) are intentionally meant to enter the exam room and sit on a chair or stool at the same eye level as the patient. Additionally, we placed the sink at the entry door, in such a position, that providers can wash their hands upon entering the room while greeting the patient and maintaining eye contact. This subtle detail aims to demonstrate transparency and build trust between patient and provider regarding infection control and safety. A TV-style monitor in the room can be used to show the patient information or display educational videos or tele-consults. The monitor is meant to be an homage to a TV one might find in their own home, while also being a place to view relevant information. Lastly, signage encourages the patient to adjust the lights, thermostat, lock the door, or place their belongings in a locker. The goal of all of these design elements was to give patients more control and autonomy, reduce their anxiety, and give them a familiar room typology (i.e., a living room) to increase their comfort level.

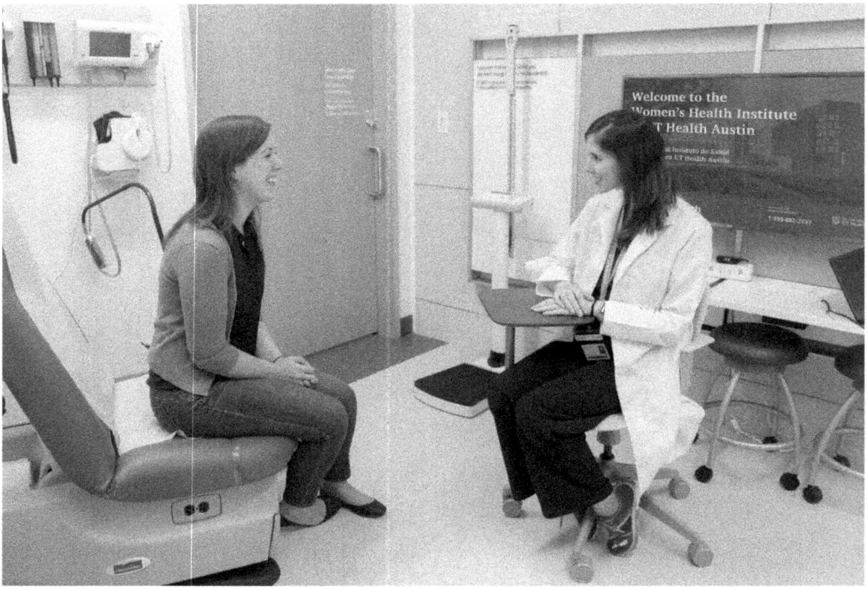

FIGURES 16.7 The care rooms are designed to be owned by the patients for the duration of their stay and to equalize the power balance between care team members and patients.

Source: Design Institute, 2019.

Lessons Learned:

We learned that mocking up a detailed exam room would have been helpful prior to the build out. We did build and mock-up several exam rooms but none with the detailed wall/ceiling/door conditions that would exist in the final design. The sound attenuation between rooms ended up being a significant distraction. The sliding doors created a noticeable sound transfer between rooms, so additional sound masking is needed to prevent nearby rooms from overhearing private patient conversations. Similarly, our original designs had further integrated sound, temperature, and lighting technologies that became cost prohibitive during construction. Although we made great strides to have the exam room feel less clinical and more home-like, the fluorescent lighting, large supply carts, and clinical-looking chair/exam bed still felt formal to our patients.

Additional Observations:

One of the units was designed with modular walls with the intention of being adjusted as we learned more about the needs of the patients and care teams over time. Unfortunately, at the time of writing this, the modular walls have yet to be moved. A lack of ongoing budget for these modifications and the growing clinical demands made it difficult to honor the commitment to adjust the space over time.

Reflections and Recommendations

We made progress in how we supported the emotional needs of our patients and providers in the space. We often receive feedback on how soothing the concourse is and how "nice" the space feels. However, as mentioned earlier, there is still a significant opportunity to improve the experience further. So, what would we do differently or recommend to others?

- Closely examine technology integration/accessibility/cost and build more mockups to test for interoperability and ease of use of technology with patients and providers at both the building and individual level.
- Account for the extensive time required to document the information exchanges needed throughout the experience, as well as detail how information will be input into the electronic medical record or other software throughout the patient journey.
- Create alternative journeys for different user types and allow for greater customization in the experience. Plan for various caregiver scenarios, as well as varying literacy and technology needs.
- Thoroughly review the entry sequence and the needed infrastructure and support needed for success.
- Expand the set of design possibilities to make the experience more intuitive and comfortable for patients. Explore additional ways to reduce the clinical feel of the exam room and adjust the lighting and sound in the rooms in particular.
- Incorporate more wayfinding and signage earlier on in the arrival sequence. The floor-by-floor back-lit imagery was great, but patients needed more detailed directory type of information.

The physical and experience design of modern-day healthcare settings is increasingly complex. Therefore, taking advantage of every opportunity to reflect and improve is imperative. By sharing this information, we hope others can learn from our challenges and continue to elevate what we expect from our healthcare journeys.

Note: Since architectural design is such a lengthy, multi-year process, the building shell and floor plate were already set in stone prior to even the full formation of the UTHA clinics or the Design Institute for Health. This reality required us to work within those existing parameters and the building shell and didn't leave much room for redesign outside of the interior build-out. If we were to approach this process again, we would love to be involved much sooner in the design of the building shell and have greater involvement in bringing the human-centered design conversations we had with providers and patients to the early architectural design concepts. We recognize this increases complexity, but we feel we would have been able to deliver an even more thoughtful experience had we been able to collaborate sooner in the process. In particular, the patient entry sequence into the building and the integration of technology would have been one of the first things we would have explored.

Notes

1 The Design Institute for Health closed in August 2022. To read more: https://dellmed.utexas.edu/about/mission-and-vision/history/about-the-design-institute-for-health

2 At the time of this clinic conceptualization, I was an employee of Steelcase Health, working in collaboration with the Design Institute for Health. We were tasked to work within the existing floor plate by Page architecture to enhance the design of the space and the experience. The key Design Institute for Health designers were José Colucci, Stacey Chang, Beto Lopez, and Lucas Artusi.

CONNECTING 17

Building certification programs can help drive and improve outcomes by providing a framework and strategies for designing and maintaining sustainable, healthy spaces for people. This next chapter introduces two such programs: LEED (Leadership in Energy and Environmental Design) and WELL (WELL Building Standard). LEED is a comprehensive and widely recognized green building certification program. It examines sustainability criteria, including energy efficiency, water conservation, materials selection, indoor environmental quality, and responsible site development. These factors are critical to consider during a project's planning and construction phases. Conversely, WELL places focus on the wellbeing and health of the people who live and work in buildings. This certification program goes beyond traditional sustainability standards by addressing aspects such as air, water, nourishment, light, fitness, and comfort to enhance the health and productivity of occupants. While it is possible to integrate the elements of WELL into a project's design and construction phases, the standard's emphasis on occupants makes it particularly relevant for ongoing building operations.

Occupant feedback is relied upon to help benchmark building success through pre- and post-occupancy evaluations (often as surveys and observations). Historically, these measures are done immediately before and after a space's construction—and are usually required for building certification programs. More recently, though, the field has begun questioning the frequency and depth of conducting these measures (Graham et al., 2021). To this end, the authors of the following chapter—researchers and interior designers Susan Sung Eun Chung and So-Yeon Yoon, along with researcher and public health advocate Whitney Austin Gray—argue that longitudinal research on occupant

DOI: 10.4324/9781003004622-43

experience is critical to yield data on how a space performs for people and how their needs evolve.

Employing a model similar to KieranTimberlake, the American Society of Interior Designers (ASID) also used its headquarters as a testing ground. Through this case study, Chung, Yoon, and Austin Gray demonstrate the power of more involved and frequent measurement, focusing on occupant satisfaction, health, and wellbeing. The team's work contributes to the advancing conversation around measuring impact and sets a precedent for ASID's 25,000 members and beyond.

Reference

Graham, L.T., Parkinson, T., Schiavon, S. (2021). Lessons learned from 20 years of CBE's occupant surveys. *Buildings & Cities, 2*(1), 166-184, http://doi.org/10.5334/bc.76

17

DESIGN R[E]VOLUTION

Rethinking People and the Built Environment

Susan Sung Eun Chung, Whitney Austin Gray and So-Yeon Yoon

The industrial and technological revolution not only impacts how we work, but its continuous disruptive nature challenges us to rethink how we engage physical space (along with its virtual capabilities) to create positive user experience. Increasingly, an argument is being made that certain knowledge-based work can be done anywhere. At the same time is the increasing awareness that not all spaces are created equal, and having flexibility in work location does not necessarily trump having a healthy space to work. Physical space plays a significant role in our lives as we spend approximately 90% of our time indoors, and it can impact our collaboration, performance, and overall health and wellbeing from day to day. With changes in work progressing faster than ever, people and organizations are demanding data and evidence to make informed decisions. Longitudinal research on occupant experience can achieve these increasing organizational demands by providing critical data on how the space is performing for users, and how users' needs have evolved in the space. It goes beyond assuming that one survey during move-in will deliver information needed over the life of the building. It also allows organizations to prolong the usability of their physical workplaces and to empower employees in becoming active players in the environment. The evolution of the workplace is not merely about flexibility but rather a function of time and the input of data at multiple points through continuous environmental design research.

ASID HQ Case Study: A Comprehensive Design Research Undertaking

Interior design has employed post-occupancy evaluations for years to gather building performance and occupant satisfaction data, but it requires more

DOI: 10.4324/9781003004622-44

effective strategies to result in meaningful outcomes (Li, Froese & Brager, 2018). The American Society of Interior Designers (ASID) embarked on a journey to confirm that design impacts the human experience through continuous research of their headquarters (HQ) office in Washington, D.C. This opportunity came when the ASID National Board of Directors decided in 2012 to sell the 20,000 square foot three-story single occupant building which was last renovated in 1998 with high partition cubicles, private offices, and formal meeting spaces (Figure 17.1). The decision led to finding a more appropriate place to lease that fit organizational goals (in size, location, design, etc.). With the opportunity to start from scratch, ASID temporarily moved into approximately 2,500 square foot space in a co-working office, renting a floor with six shared office spaces for ASID employee use, and sharing meeting rooms and common areas with other companies in a four-story mixed-use building. The two years spent in the co-working facility became an ideal situation to gather user data. To this end, ASID commissioned an interdisciplinary project team, led by Perkins and Will's Washington D.C. office, to translate evidence-based design principles and pre-occupancy research to design a workplace of the future that functions as a living laboratory that seeks continuous improvement over the years. Understanding the importance of engaging with various

FIGURE 17.1 American Society of Interior Designers (ASID) Previous Headquarters Office (1998–2014).

experts, ASID collaborated with multiple research institutions to gather pre-/post-occupancy data to measure desired outcomes, validate goals set for the office, and test multiple research tools and methodologies.

ASID HQ Case Study: Goal Setting for a WELL Certified Space

As workplace design has evolved to meet the changing needs of work, agility is critical (Sargent, Nurse & Lacey, 2017). As such, ASID requested the office to be a workplace of the future that could evolve based on user needs over time, not only when it was originally designed. ASID turned to existing resources such as the Leadership in Energy and Environmental Design (LEED) standards for seeking environmental sustainability and the WELL Building Standard for human sustainability through occupant health and wellbeing to guide the design.

The WELL Building Standard ("WELL") is a performance-based system for measuring, certifying, and monitoring organizational and design strategies on human health and wellbeing over time. WELL combines best practices in building design, construction, and management with evidence-based research on environmental health, behavioral factors, health outcomes, and demographic risk factors. Building scientists, behavioral scientists, health care practitioners, and public health professionals helped to develop the standard's ten core concepts that support and advance human wellbeing: air, water, light, sound, thermal comfort, movement, nourishment, materials, mind, and community. Third-party verification holds organizations accountable through onsite performance testing, reporting, monitoring, and recertification, positioning the certification as a symbol of trust that the building has achieved its mark on wellbeing.

As a pre-condition for certification, projects are required to conduct post-occupancy surveys and submit results annually through the WELL digital platform. Projects are encouraged to work with pre-approved survey providers and are awarded additional points toward certification level if they utilize a pre- and post-occupancy survey, conduct qualitative research (i.e., focus groups, interviews, observation), and achieve enhanced survey functions (i.e., tracking physical and mental health outcomes, creative thinking, and engagement). To encourage projects to evolve over time, WELL awards points for projects that create and implement a plan that addresses the results of the post-occupancy evaluation and provides strategies for unmet satisfaction thresholds.

Understanding the relationship between people and the built environment and recognizing the power of research, ASID and the design project team collected end-user and environmental data to implement evidence-based design. A comprehensive research project was designed by ASID and research collaborators to conduct multiple studies (Figure 17.2) that collected measures from:

- an organizational-level survey to understand key performance indicators from physical space attributes related to innovation strategies and performance,

- individual-level surveys to understand environmental, wellbeing, and job satisfaction, perceptions of workspace and support, work behaviors, health, and performance,
- focus groups by work units to gather team-level qualitative data on how they interact and collaborate,
- interviews with leadership to document organizational background, goals, and culture,
- room reservation data analysis to quantify space usage,
- behavior mapping to qualify space usage and behaviors,
- a socio-metric badge study to examine employees' connectedness, collaboration, and creativity, and
- indoor environment metrics to document physical space conditions.

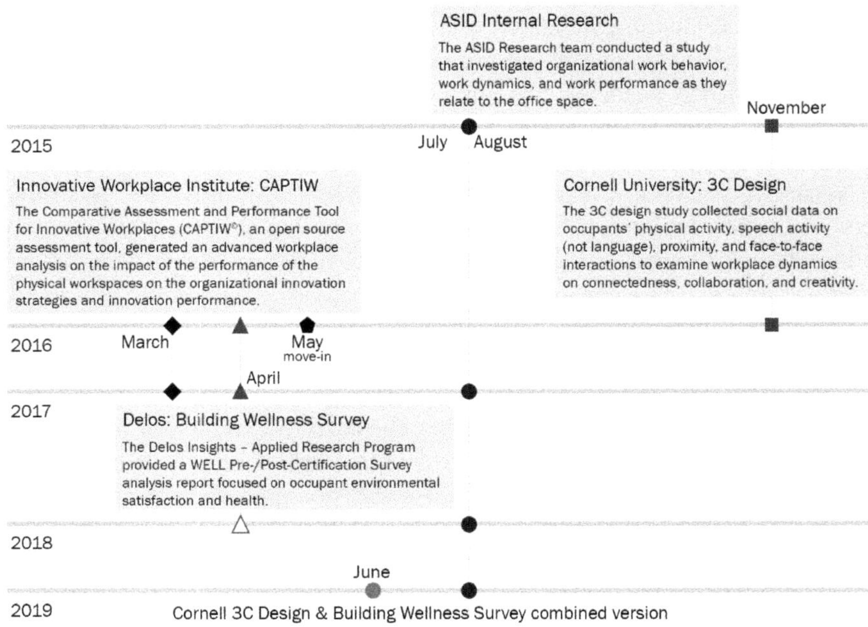

FIGURE 17.2 Description and timeline of ASID HQ Office design and research.

These pre-occupancy data helped ASID to make informed design decisions, further understand team processes and dynamics, and communicate the importance of a WELL Certified office on employee health, wellbeing, and performance.

During the transition between the temporary co-working space to the new HQ, ASID updated employees regularly on the design, construction progress and timeline, and expectations in the new office. With design often done in the background, it was important to bring ongoing awareness of the design process to employees through seminars delivered by respective experts on topics including: (1) how the built environment impacts human sustainability, (2) understanding the benefits of circadian lighting in the office and at home, and (3) learning how to adjust workstations properly for better ergonomics and user experience. The purpose of these seminars evolved around the people in the space—establishing a connection between people and place, enhancing awareness of this relationship, and enabling interactions among the two to continue for further improvement.

ASID HQ Case Study: Outcomes Exceeding Goals

ASID moved into the new HQ office May 2016, leasing an 8,500 square foot space for ten years on a multi-tenant floor of a LEED Gold certified building (Figure 17.3; Figure 17.4). The HQ office is the world's first double platinum space, achieving this certification level through LEED and WELL. All of the pre-occupancy research studies were repeated one year later to collect post-occupancy results, and some on an annual/biennial basis thereafter.

The first-year post-occupancy results (American Society of Interior Designers [ASID], 2017) were astounding: it was shown that collaboration increased 9%, productivity, calculated from absenteeism and presenteeism scores,

FIGURE 17.3 ASID WELL Certified Headquarters Office (2016) entrance (Photo Credit: Eric Laignel).

FIGURE 17.4 ASID WELL Certified Headquarters Office (2016) main space (Photo Credit: Eric Laignel).

increased 19%, and environmental and wellbeing satisfaction significantly increased on all measures (Figure 17.5). The direct causational relationship is difficult to determine; however, along with these improved performance measures, the indoor environmental quality improved as seen in the objective measures: lighting levels and quality increased from most individual workspaces having access to natural daylight and all areas equipped with circadian lighting fixtures that adjusted during sunrise/sunset, acoustical conditions enhanced with decibel levels more than halved from what was measured in the co-working space, and indoor air quality improved with carbon dioxide (CO_2) levels dropping down 58% (Figure 17.6). The follow-up study in 2019 (ASID, 2021) exceeded expectations and validated the 2017 research highlights proving the initial results were not merely due to the "newness" of the design: ASID HQ maintains a healthy environment based on the indoor environmental quality measures and reports stable high levels of employee satisfaction and wellbeing, similar to other WELL certified spaces (Ildiri et al., 2022).

ASID HQ exemplifies a place where occupants actively benefit from the built environment's full potential through interaction with their surroundings and research participation. For example, ASID asked for feedback on the office use by annotating the office floor plan drawn on a whiteboard in a common

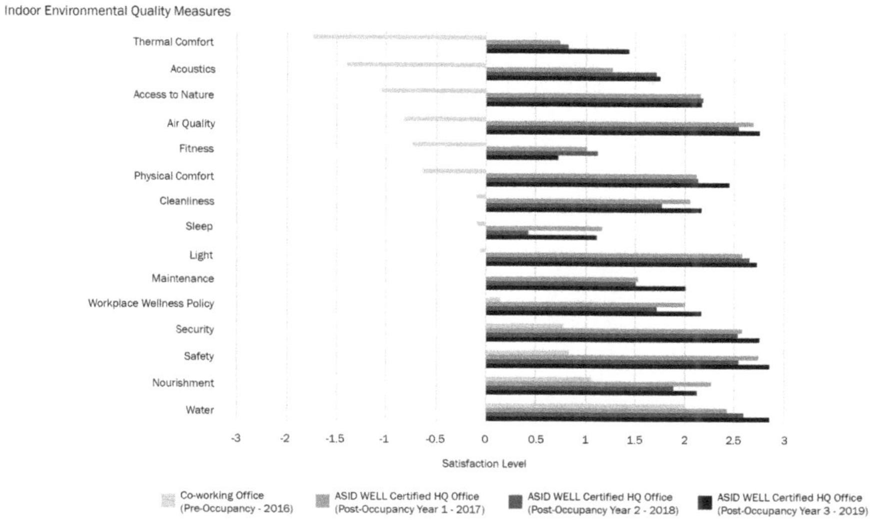

FIGURE 17.5 Pre-post/occupancy comparison of indoor environmental quality measures (2016–2019).

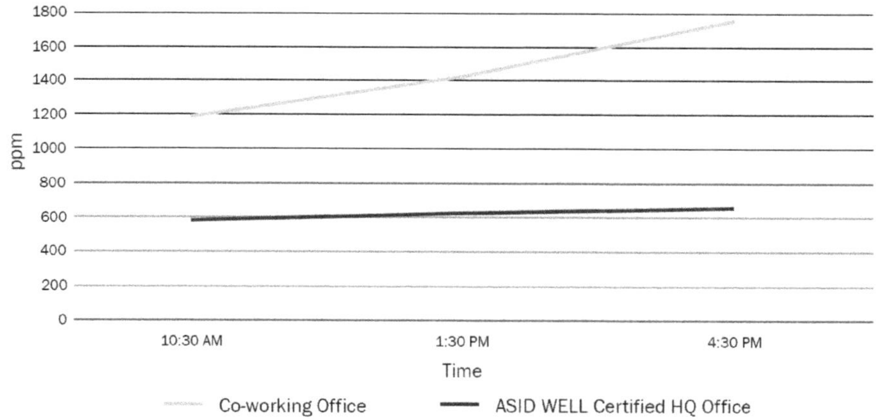

FIGURE 17.6 Pre-/Post-occupancy comparison of CO_2 level changes over time.

area (Figure 17.7). High place attachment scores suggest that employees take ownership of the workplace amid unassigned seating by creating their own space for the day. The efforts to keep ASID employees informed and aware of the ASID HQ health and wellbeing benefits continue through annual presentations on research findings and other topical learning circles. An internal team evaluates critical research findings to identify areas of improvement in the office and conducts brief research studies to explore application. If deemed

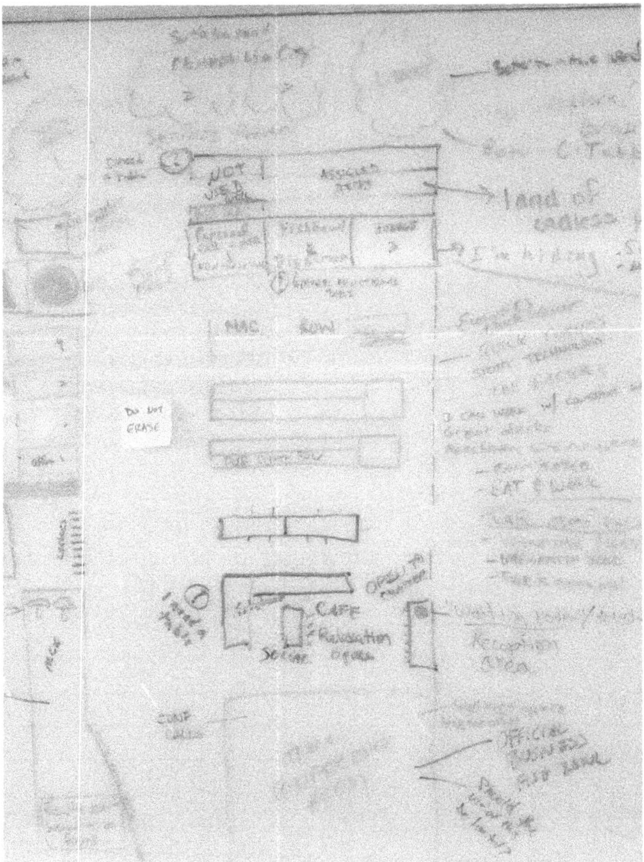

FIGURE 17.7 ASID HQ feedback board.

necessary and beneficial for the employees, the internal team will implement minor changes in the office (e.g., change room function, adjust room capacity, etc.) that do not impact its health and wellbeing and sustainability features. Outcomes are measured from the changes to examine whether improvements led to positive impact and document the evolution of the workplace.

The Power of Continuous Post-Occupancy Research: [R]evolutionizing the Office

Data allows buildings to 'talk,' making the 'invisible' building elements 'visible' to users. Continuous post-occupancy data documents how people are interacting with the space based on evolving work purpose, and it brings a transparency to whether the space is working for the users over many years. Through the process in achieving WELL Certification at the Platinum level,

ASID HQ performance-based measures were taken at multiple points in time from the people and the place and then shared with occupants. In this way, the place 'interacts' with people by making objective environmental data and subjective survey data accessible to users. Further triangulation of data helps decision makers determine if the space is working for occupants and make necessary changes. For example, ASID HQ employees communicated average satisfaction in acoustics via survey during post-occupancy (although a significant improvement from pre-occupancy) and had pinpointed the issue and location during focus groups. Acoustical quality measurements confirmed the need for additional privacy which led to installing sound masking equipment in these rooms. Employee satisfaction in acoustics increased the following year and sustained the year after.

Project data, especially from constructive pre-/post-occupancy research, provides clients with a better understanding of how the design supports desired outcomes, while also allowing other designers and prospective clients to better understand the value of design and identify potential benefits and opportunities for future projects. Simple post-occupancy evaluations that walk through the finished space to check for design discrepancies or other issues are limiting and do not plan for human-centered outcomes. Continuous post-occupancy research or ongoing workplace surveys, on the other hand, enable clients to sustain benefits, manage the built environment effectively, maximize the use of their physical spaces, and take ownership of how to evolve the space optimally for all occupants (Zimmerman & Martin, 2001). The continuous post-occupancy research method exhibits the organization's value for their employees by engaging them in the space, which in turn, increases perceived organizational support. The follow-up from research not only empowers employees to take more control over their workplace to transform it into an environment that enhances their experience but also confirms the organization's commitment toward their people.

The value of continuous research can increase when the researcher is an active part of the research, co-creating the community's desired outcomes occupying the space. This supports the researcher's need to integrate themselves with project owners to better translate findings into practice, as compared to previous practices that may have excluded the researcher or placed them as omniscient to the process. This requires adjusting expectations, timelines, and contractual obligations; shifting the client to focus on investment metrics that track performance over time, instead of tracking at only one point in time. Effective change management is critical to ensure that the intent of the design features is understood and tested and therefore, having a dedicated person to manage these efforts will reap benefits. With focus on sustainability from multiple facets including environmental, human, and financial terms, this is an opportune time to revolutionize space and evolve from occupants' changing needs through data collected in continuous post-occupancy research (Figure 17.8).

FIGURE 17.8 ASID WELL Certified Headquarters Office (2016) collaboration space (Photo Credit: Eric Laignel).

Acknowledgments

The ASID HQ case study research was funded by the ASID Foundation. Susan Sung Eun Chung was affiliated with ASID at the time of this work and is currently affiliated with HKS, Inc.

References

American Society of Interior Designers (2017). *ASID HQ Office Research: Pre-/Post-Occupancy Analysis 2017*. https://www.asid.org/lib24watch/files/download/5715

American Society of Interior Designers (2021). *ASID HQ Office Research: Longitudinal Occupancy Analysis* 2015–2021. [Manuscript in preparation].

Ildiri, N., Bazille, H., Lou, Y., Hinkelman, K., Gray, W. A., & Zuo, W. (2022). Impact of WELL certification on occupant satisfaction and perceived health, well-being, and productivity: A multi-office pre-versus post-occupancy evaluation. *Building and Environment*, 224, 109539.

Li, P., Froese, T., & Brager, G. (2018). Post-occupancy evaluation: State-of-the-art analysis and state-of-the-practice review. *Building and Environment*, 133, 187–202. https://doi.org/10.1016/j.buildenv.2018.02.024

Sargent, K., Nurse, B., & Lacey, A. (2017). Moving beyond open plan spaces. *Work Design Magazine*, https://www.workdesign.com/2017/09/moving-beyond-open-plan-spaces/

Zimmerman, A., & Martin, M. (2001). Post-occupancy evaluation: Benefits and barriers. *Building Research & Information*, 29(2), 168–174. https://doi.org/10.1080/09613210010016857

CONNECTING 18

It has become evident throughout this book that there are many avenues through which professionals and disciplines are making strides to understand the relationship between people and built space. Some of the ways these efforts overlap or deviate—sometimes leaving gaps in our understanding—have also become apparent. And yet, this volume hardly scratches the surface of all the incredible work happening in this area. People in fields related to the person-place dynamic must explore how and where their knowledge and experiences intersect to better comprehend what is known or still unknown. But how do these professionals move beyond knowledge gathering and toward integrated practice and research?

Much of how individuals practice and conduct research around the built environment and human behavior becomes cemented during higher education. However, the academy, steeped in traditional and established methods, often abides by disciplinary boundaries rather than supporting people doing work that happens at the edges, requiring interdisciplinary collaboration.

In the next chapter, we interview Richard Corsi, environmental engineer and dean of the College of Engineering at the University of California, Davis. Corsi describes an early career experience that led him to see the value of interdisciplinary collaboration. He also shares his first-hand struggles of seeking funding for work that does not fit neatly into one area. Through Corsi's experiences, we learn about the culture of academia that often discourages collaboration and puts up barriers that everyone, from students to faculty and administration, must overcome. But we also learn what Corsi is doing as a dean to make a shift that does not dissuade going deep in one's area while encouraging connections across disciplines—precisely what is needed to take on some of the world's most pressing challenges related to people and the built environment.

DOI: 10.4324/9781003004622-45

18

WHEN SPARKS FLY

The Challenges and Rewards of Working across Disciplines

An interview with Richard Corsi
By Tamie Glass and Lindsay T. Graham

Regardless of scale, to truly design for healthy and productive person-place relationships we must collaborate regardless of discipline. But often, this is easier said than done. It requires humility, openness, and curiosity, and few working in this realm embody these values more than engineer, Richard Corsi. As one of the most influential experts in the world on indoor air quality (IAQ), Corsi is no stranger to the advantages of collaborating across disciplines. In addition to his vast and impactful research acumen, Corsi has also devoted significant attention and effort to not only teaching engineers, but inspiring students across disciplines to work towards the common goal of interdisciplinary work in the indoor sciences. We asked Corsi to help shed light on the challenges and rewards of interdisciplinary efforts, and what it's like searching for the spark of innovation outside of silos and trenches.

In a few words, please describe what you do and what is your area of research?

I'm the Dean of the College of Engineering at the University of California, Davis. As a researcher, I investigate the quality of air inside buildings, looking at sources of pollutants from both indoor and outdoor environments. I focus on understanding what happens to these pollutants and finding ways to control and mitigate their impact on our health. The average American lives to be 79 years old and spends 70 of those years inside of buildings leading to a lifetime of exposure through our skin and the air we breathe. Because of the nature of my work, I engage with people from across the building sciences.

Universities seem like the ideal place for synergy around solving some of the world's greatest challenges. From your perspective as someone who does

DOI: 10.4324/9781003004622-46

interdisciplinary work and serves a dean, how does a process like this unfold at the university level?

We know that tackling some of the greatest challenges of our time is not a solo task, but academia has been slow to adopt interdisciplinary ways of working. It's crazy that collaboration doesn't happen more on university campuses, but there seem to be a lot of one-off interactions where a faculty member connects with another faculty member. But they must actually come together of their own volition to do the work, as opposed to being driven by a more systemic attitude at universities that this is something we should all be doing.

The big problem is that most universities don't reward faculty for working across disciplines, and instead, put up barriers. So, for example, if a professor is going up for promotion, there's often no sentiment of, "That's great that you're working with others outside of your college!" And depending on how credit and funding are distributed across units, there can even be a lack of financial incentive to work together. This structure results in a culture of competitiveness among faculty rather than interdisciplinary collaboration.

Can you speak more to these barriers that get in the way of faculty collaboration and interdisciplinary research at universities?

Universities have been part of the problem, particularly around promotion and tenure. For example, suppose you're an early-career faculty member working with faculty from five different areas. In that case, you must *justify* it by explaining *why* to your tenure and promotion committee. These committees often critique faculty for collaborating with others instead of developing their own unique research program. So, from the start in academia, you're taught it's a bad thing to work with other people, and when you drill that in the first five years of a young scholar's journey, it stays with them. That initial condition sets the stage for things going in the wrong direction. Sadly, it can happen even before that, when attempting to enter academia. You might not get the tenure-track job because you don't look the part if you come from more of an interdisciplinary perspective. There's a systemic change that needs to take place.

We are advocates for academic research and professional practice being more integrated. Do you see this happening, and why or why not?

This is another area of frustration for me. Academics tend not to want to work with practitioners. So, it's not just about working across disciplines within the university; it's also taking research ideas and working with the practitioner community to translate them into practice. I feel like a lot gets left on the table in the engineering profession. So many of my colleagues do incredible research, and then they write papers. Then, unfortunately, they move on to something else instead of saying, "Wow, this has a lot of potential, and I want to see this get into people's homes or workplaces and create a positive change somehow."

That sheds light on the researcher's perspective. How about practitioners? Are they invested in academic research?

In my experience, most practitioners don't want to listen to academics. However, some do—and they tend to be the more progressive. They are hungry to connect with scholars and are interested in research that may change the way they practice in the future. But the resistance from the side of faculty is usually time and money, and an overall lack of incentive. Also, doing practical research in some professional disciplines is looked down upon. So, it gets ingrained into scholars early on that even though they may want to pursue certain avenues, they shouldn't because they are not going to benefit other than personally in their soul!

Given all these roadblocks, what made you decide you want to work with others outside of your discipline?

It takes having an experience where everyone comes together to get it. For me, this experience was during my first year as an assistant professor. One of my graduate students wanted to research an area that I was only 25% qualified to advise on. She was interested in the degradation of certain chemicals in sewers. I didn't know anything about microbiology or environmental biology, so we needed to find a way to grow a biofilm in a sewer that would be safe to access in such hazardous conditions. So, we got a couple of professors involved from the Department of Environmental Biology, and this is how it started for me. We would have meetings with them where we were learning how biofilms worked, and I was like, "Wow, this is cool!" They didn't know the engineering part of constructing something, but they were good at saying: "So, these are the things you have to make sure to take into account," which I would have never known. Looking back, I'm sure we were a funny sight on the side of the road with fishing poles hovering over maintenance holes, but it was a great learning experience!

Let's fast forward to more recently in your career. Tell us how you became involved in the National Science Foundation's Integrative Graduate Education and Research Traineeship program (IGERT)?

In the early 2000s, there was just so little money anywhere for indoor air quality research. When you go to the National Science Foundation (NSF) with a proposal, they look at it and say indoor air quality, that's all about health, you should go to the National Institutes of Health (NIH). Then you go to NIH and send them a proposal, and they say, well, you're an engineer, we don't fund engineers. So, you can fall through the cracks when seeking funding for research that crosses disciplines. At some point during this back and forth, I came across IGERT.

The IGERT program hosted by the NSF was specifically for collaborative interdisciplinary research that helps students become future leaders in science and engineering. It was about exploration and new things, so I thought there was an opening there. But we wrote a proposal one year, and it didn't get funded. So, we wrote a proposal for a second year and got better scores, but still didn't get funded. And finally, we got it the third time. So, there has to be persistence. And when I look at where many of the students from the program are now, they are really shaping the field.

Now that you are a dean, what are you doing to change the culture?

I'm working on changing things within my college—I feel like that's a place to start. So, we are developing a strategic vision, and through this, we know what areas we want to pursue at the college level. We will prioritize new faculty positions where multiple department chairs come together and want to build up an area within this strategic vision, for example, the future of mobility. This process will establish internal faculty clusters across departments, and that's just trying to break down the silos in my college. Nonetheless, that's what it takes at the university level!

As a dean, part of my job is to figure out ways of chipping away at silos. I am pushing to get the departments to work together on significant challenges, but it's tough in universities, even universities with a history of collaboration across disciplines. It's surprising how thick the silos have gotten in academia. I think it's fair to say that no matter what university you're at, there are silos that are too thick, and there are too many of them. We can't reach our full potential until we break those silos down—really, I believe that. For me, it's personal because I've worked with so many people, in so many different disciplines during my career, and I've learned so much from them that I can't imagine that other people wouldn't stand to learn a lot from other people, too.

You've mentioned the need for faculty incentives and overall systemic change. How are you setting up new structures for this?

We're starting Next Level—a program that asks faculty to come together across departments and colleges to propose a big idea around our four major challenges (such as artificial intelligence). Groups of faculty then come before college leadership and give five-minute pitches—like the show Shark Tank—but they must include at least two, and preferably more, departments or colleges. It should be an idea that's five to seven years out with what they want to accomplish, along with an 18-month plan to get it going with low-hanging fruit that we can start funding now. So, in this program, faculty are incentivized to find collaborators outside their area and will receive funding for doing so.

For everyone reading this interview, what do you think it takes to be an excellent interdisciplinary researcher or person working in this domain? We've heard you say persistence. What else?

That's a great question. I believe it takes somebody whose needle is far to the right on Openness to Experience (referring to the Big Five personality traits; John et al., 2008). Essentially, someone who is receptive to new ideas and learning from others in different disciplines. Scholars need to have that *one* experience, as I did early in my faculty career standing on the side of the road, that works out well to realize the value of learning from others.

What's needed in the classroom for students to come together from different disciplines?

Flexibility is essential. Lindsay, you'll remember that you took my graduate course as a psychology major without having all the prerequisites in physics and chemistry. Still, we arranged it so that you had different assignments and goals in the class. But I don't know that many professors would be as flexible, especially in fields like engineering, where they tend to be hard-nosed about following the rules. You learned so much in that class, and it didn't matter that you struggled with partial differential equations. It wasn't necessary because that wouldn't be a part of your psychology career. The most important aspect for you was understanding that, for example, low VOC (volatile organic compound) paints might still contain chemicals in them that are bad for you. You could then apply this understanding to individuals' decisions to design a certain ambiance in their spaces. Things like that were the main takeaways, and, to be honest, those are the most important takeaways for everybody in the class!

It helps to have some form of investment on everybody's end, both faculty and students. Hopefully, academia eventually grows into being more supportive of interdisciplinary work because that's the direction we will be faced with in the future.

How about advice for scholars?

Universities are full of brilliant scholars digging deep intellectual trenches. My advice for these scholars is to keep digging in your trenches, but don't be afraid to connect to someone else's who is working in a completely different area. Nothing may come of it, and it may be uncomfortable when you don't see the connections. However, it can be an explosion of positive ideas and innovation when they do appear.

You can take this metaphor further by saying that you can keep digging in that intellectual trench, but eventually, it gets harder and harder and harder until you hit bedrock. It can get more challenging to land on the next innovative thing when you're that deep in a trench. Admittedly, that's not always the case—some people dig deep intellectual trenches and then hit gold and receive a Nobel Prize one day. But for most, that's not the norm.

Is there a time when interdisciplinary work isn't the answer?

Indeed, I think there's a lot of research where a faculty member and their students do some excellent work digging in an intellectual trench. However, we don't do enough trench connecting, so we're somewhat one-dimensional in academia. Occasionally, somebody gets out of their trench and talks to somebody deep in thought in their own trench, and they do something together. But there's not enough meaningful deep intellectual trench connecting—there are some areas where there's just enough overlap that sparks can really fly!

What advice might you have for people going into interdisciplinary work, specifically in the built environment?

To make real change, you will have to work with others who have knowledge that you don't have. The built environment is so complex that it requires researchers with diverse backgrounds ranging from engineering to human behavior.

Human behaviors are so important within the built environment. A few years ago, I gave the closing plenary at a large international indoor air conference in Hong Kong. My presentation was all about interdisciplinary connections. I began by asking, "How many people in the audience study human behavior?" And not one raised their hand. Everybody's looking around, and there are chemists and microbiologists and engineers, but nobody who understands human beings.

We need to make sure that our community working on built environments welcomes those who study human behavior to push our work to another level. Half of the problems and half of the solutions are related to people. All the things we talked about in our sessions that week at the conference were related to what people do inside buildings, especially in their own homes. We decide whether or not to turn on the exhaust fan when we're cooking. We determine if we're going to purchase scented candles. We choose how frequently we're going to clean and how often we're going to change the filter in our HVAC system. These human decisions made inside our buildings affect indoor air quality—and human and environmental health—in a big way.

We couldn't agree more with Corsi about the impact of human behavior and the need for interdisciplinary research and practice—especially in fields and areas of practice that touch upon people and the built environment. We need individuals who possess the openness, flexibility, and perseverance to do this work—even when the direct incentives aren't there, and the connections aren't clear. So, emphatically, YES, systemic change is needed. But for that to happen, we all have to do our part. And the responsibility falls on every one of us, regardless of whether you are in academia or industry, a researcher or practitioner, an instructor or student. So, keep digging, but also begin connecting—and always be on the lookout for the opportunities where much-needed innovation occurs. It just might surprise you what can happen when sparks fly.

Reference

John, O. P., Naumann, L. P., & Soto, C. J. (2008). Paradigm shift to the integrative Big-Five trait taxonomy: History, measurement, and conceptual issues. In O. P. John, R. W. Robins, & L. A. Pervin (Eds.), *Handbook of Personality: Theory and Research* (pp. 114–158). Guilford Press.

Reflecting on Intent

Prioritizing the wellbeing of people and the planet when creating built environments takes resolve and commitment from all parties involved. Every step of the process—from the clients who initiate the work, to the designers who plan and execute the project, to the contractors who construct it, to the researchers who provide insights, and finally, the occupants who use it—necessitates intentional action.

Ultimately, the authors in this section presented an important revelation. When creating environments that genuinely support people, designing the process is as important as designing the space. Typical design and research approaches are not guaranteed to succeed because every space, every client, and every set of occupants is unique. Professionals may begin with a framework or set of tools, but inevitably, they must be additive and agile in implementing various methods within each project. Moreover, what is best for people is not always inherently addressed in every process. While certification systems and building codes, for example, can help guide towards higher and more uniform standards for everyone, no space can be one-size-fits-all because no person fits within a one-size-fits-all framework.

Hindsight is always 20/20, making understanding, evaluating, and critiquing after the fact easier. Although no approach or framework is perfect, each one helps move toward greater cohesion in making all built environments better for all people. It is important to note that designing and studying built spaces are dynamic practices, and a "one-and-done" mindset does not work. All design and research processes, as well as the resulting spaces, are iterative, and even after an environment is constructed, it continues to evolve along with its occupants and the world around it. Within these efforts, it is imperative to remember no one person or discipline holds all the answers.

DOI: 10.4324/9781003004622-47

Professionals must continue reaching across fields and blending their lines of inquiry to make progress.

With this constant evolution, we all must ask ourselves—what are the obligations of everyone involved? When can a project be considered finished? Who is responsible for shepherding it through its lifespan? What voices need to be included, and who might be missing from the table? We must acknowledge that no space, project, or process will ever be flawless. Still, instead of striving for the ideal, we must each focus on creating adaptable spaces and responsive strategies to accommodate the reality that change is the only given.

PART 5
Reflecting Forward

Reflecting Forward

Forging Common Ground

Embarking on writing this book, we began curious and inspired to expand our perspectives on the relationship between people and spaces through the impassioned points-of-view of 27 contributors. Now, as we stand at the threshold of the post-pandemic era, the world is markedly different from a few years ago when the two of us began this project. From here, the outlook reveals the emergence of the next big wave of technological advancement through the rise of generative artificial intelligence, escalating environmental concerns and extreme weather events, an increasingly divisive global political scene, and a revitalized focus on health and wellbeing. Nevertheless, we move ahead firmly believing that the insights garnered from our contributors still hold profound relevance in this rapidly evolving world.

In reflection, how can we all leverage this knowledge to bring people together and forge common ground for advancing the design and science of creating healthier, more inclusive, and sustainable spaces in the future? What implications and risks should we be aware of when charting a course forward? And what universal truths will endure, regardless of when this book is read?

Charting our Course: Assessing Implications and Risks

At its core, this book is a manifesto advocating for a more holistic and mindful understanding of the interactions between people and spaces. The lessons within these chapters transcend this collection, offering guidance to anyone in a position to enhance the person-place connection. A critical takeaway from our contributors is that as inhabitants of spaces, most of us find ourselves in

DOI: 10.4324/9781003004622-49

moments of influence throughout our professional and personal lives whether we realize it or not. Perhaps you are a designer facing an ethical dilemma on a project and determining whose voice to listen to, a researcher with scientific findings that could be more impactful if disseminated beyond academia, or someone deciding where to live. So, what are the broader implications of our individual and collective actions—or inaction—and what is at stake?

How can we all advance and adapt our practices and mindsets to meet today's demands for sustainability, inclusivity, and innovation? Rising to the challenge will reinforce the initial intent of built environments: to protect and support us, individually and as a society. Reflecting on this book's chapters, three primary needs crystalized, each central to developing sustainable environments that prioritize health and inclusivity. Below, we explain each need and share a call to action for each player to progress this work further. In this section, we ask you to consider how you can (1) foster collaborative and integrative design and research, (2) diversify perspectives and methods, and (3) build for sustainability and resilience.

1. Foster Collaborative and Integrative Design and Research

The crux of the first need lies in the synergy that emerges when combining diverse disciplines from across academia and practice. This cross-pollination of ideas from design and science results in more complete and holistic solutions for the built environment. However, there is still a gap between practical design and scholarly scientific research. This disconnect contributes to the general sense that design practitioners find academic research too narrow or theoretical, while academics critique practicing designers for prioritizing style over empirical evidence. This dichotomy, though accurate in many situations, is not insurmountable.

For designers collaborating with researchers: Close collaboration with researchers is one promising way to bridge this divide. This might include design firms hiring in-house researchers, forming alliances with academic institutions, or embracing evidence-based design principles. A prime example is the implementation of the American Society of Interior Designers (ASID) headquarters, as explained by Chung, Austin Gray, and Yoon (see Chapter 17). This case study illustrated effective strategies such as observing a co-working space to assess programmatic needs ahead of the design process, integrating researchers directly into the design team, and utilizing post-occupancy evaluations to test and advance the highest benchmarks and standards. When designers collaborate in this manner, it elevates a design's quality while anchoring it in verifiable data to best support the occupant.

For researchers collaborating with designers: Researchers should be encouraged to translate their findings into practical, applied, and *actionable* insights.

Making research more accessible to designers can aid practitioners in their efforts to improve workplaces, clinical settings, schools, homes, and more. As Corsi highlighted, many researchers produce significant work that holds transformative potential for real-world environments when applied beyond the confines of academic publishing (see Chapter 18). This intersection of research and practical application is where innovations in built environments are borne, reshaping our living and working spaces in profound and meaningful ways. We are not declaring researchers must become experts in design themselves. We are, however, saying that intentional collaboration with practitioners in the field can help scale findings to catalyze evidence-based change—which ultimately is one of the primary goals of scientific pursuit—to better the world and our understanding of it.

How individuals benefit from collaboration: Engaging in collaborative endeavors can prompt introspection about one's professional identity and how everyone uniquely contributes to the collective pursuit of impactful solutions. Setting aside fear and preconceived notions about other disciplines and ways of working can be challenging, but ego-driven work can dilute its impact. Collaboration can create a nexus that brings together individual or disciplinary contributions in novel, often groundbreaking, ways benefiting the collective just as deeply as the individual contributors. Collaborative, integrative design and research broaden the scope of achievable goals while embracing a more inclusive and dynamic professional landscape. Unfortunately, as explained by Weatherspoon, titles, predispositions, and grasping for status and power often get in the way of what is important (see Chapter 8). She confronts ego-related issues directly by reflecting on her experiences and training as an interior designer and how they shape others' perceptions of her and her work.

It is not easy to see beyond your goals, needs, and perspectives—especially when you believe your livelihood, promotion, perceived identity, and the value of your work are at stake. Many of us enter our professions to build further meaning and understanding of our world and the world around us. Engaging in mindful, reflective practices aimed at seeing the bigger picture and tapping back into that deeper purpose for our work can help open ourselves up to others and cultivate an appreciation for difference. When we embrace collaboration from this more generous place, we allow ourselves to experience the fullness—and often fun—that interdisciplinary collaboration can provide.

Call to action: To foster collaborative and integrative design and research, we encourage design practitioners and scientific researchers to create platforms and forums for regular interaction, such as exchanging insights, and co-developing frameworks and solutions. Common engagements include collaborative labs, think tanks, and symposia. Collective efforts of this nature should be supported and incentivized by academia and industry alike. For example, funding opportunities for projects that require a blend of pioneering research and practical application can act as springboards for this much-needed and necessary work. The goal is to balance individual strengths with shared objectives, propelling all our fields forward to improve built environments for people. With more and more synergistic work, silos within research and design communities will lower, giving rise to innovations that are only possible through cross-disciplinary collaboration.

2. Diversify Perspectives and Methods

Bringing experts from different areas and disciplines together is not enough. It is also critical to explore and commit to new ways of doing the work. Many contributors to this volume stressed the importance of effective communication when integrating diverse perspectives and methodologies to improve the planning, design, implementation, and ongoing study of human-centered built spaces. Clear, objective, and inclusive dialogue goes hand in hand with incorporating and valuing multiple viewpoints and varied approaches and methods, including your own.

Valuing diverse perspectives: Bridging the divide between researchers, practitioners, academics, and professionals is essential. However, expanding the knowledge circle further is vital by engaging those who may fall outside of typical design and research collaborations, such as industry professionals, policymakers, clients, community members, and building occupants. For example, Fisher's renovation project embodied the notion of designing *with* not *for* people. Not only did she design classrooms in conjunction with teachers, but she also educated them about design fundamentals. Through this approach, she empowered the teachers to utilize and adapt their classrooms more effectively (see Chapter 15). Similarly, Siebenaler explained how design charrettes, mock-ups, and user work sessions were instrumental in learning from and acclimating care providers and future patients to their new clinic environment (see Chapter 16). Also noteworthy is how Aye and Greater Good Studio go as wide as possible to incorporate different perspectives, from funders and policymakers to community members, into their firm's process. He noted how this inclusivity, which may shed light on uncomfortable truths for the client, is needed to reach comprehensive outcomes representing everyone involved, not just those with power (see Chapter 7). Collaboration should build connections inside the field. Yet, it should also democratize these efforts outside the field by considering and incorporating diverse perspectives throughout a project's processes as often as possible.

Valuing diverse methodologies: In the same way that including diverse points of view must be a priority, centering diverse methods and processes should become fundamental to how we work toward shaping the built environment. Promoting a culture of mutual respect and valuing multiple methods for their unique contributions is necessary to tackle the complex challenges inherent in the relationship between people and spaces. By integrating different methods, we can gain a more well-rounded view of the inquiries and practices under investigation and develop a deeper understanding of what we are exploring. Additionally, merging various viewpoints allows us to learn from standard methods in one field and leverage them in another. For example, in his work, Kopec highlights the contrast between design thinking and the scientific method (see Chapter 14). Design thinking's focus on empathy and prototyping differs from the scientific method's emphasis on hypothesis and replication. Yet, combined, you can utilize the benefits of both to shine even brighter. Just like collaborating with others from different disciplines offers depth in tackling the complexities of the person-place relationship, using methods and tools developed or commonplace in one discipline and applying them in another can help advance our understanding of the built world.

Unifying language: When introducing multiple perspectives, theories, and methods into collaborative, integrated research and design projects, individuals often face communication barriers akin to travelers navigating different dialects in a foreign land. One way of improving discourse is to clarify the terminology across fields. For instance, Rodriguez noted the varied definitions of "universal design," which she explained can obscure and detract from the principal concept: to create products, environments, and experiences that are accessible and usable by the widest range of people possible (see Chapter 9). Similarly, Cranz and Rushton argue for a more objective interpretation of "taste" in the built environment, moving beyond subjective and exclusive notions of good and bad taste for an approachable, teachable formula (see Chapter 1).

Many of us put forth similar efforts across disciplines or have unraveled complexities important to adjacent fields, but the work goes unnoticed because of differing terminology. Recognizing and addressing linguistic nuances is crucial for effective collaboration and advancing the mutual goal of creating supportive built spaces. Certainly, it is essential to articulate overlaps and differences in communication and theories during direct collaborations. However, generally broadening the ways of sharing findings and practices is paramount. As we discussed above, weaving different points of view together—whether through formal forums like professional conferences and panels or casual networking and curious explorations—will consciously and actively break down silos, which is the only way to make headway toward unifying language.

Call to action: By embracing diverse methods and perspectives and intentionally addressing definitional clarity, those of us engaged in shaping spatial experiences for people can deploy multifaceted strategies to enhance the built environment. We encourage leaders to implement training and educational programs to improve communication and collaboration skills, focusing on fostering cross-disciplinary understanding and connection. If you are exploring where to study or have the means to support educational efforts, pursue academic programs that offer interdisciplinary learning opportunities and include multiple methods and stakeholders. Finally, we encourage all designers and researchers to seek and incorporate a wide range of viewpoints into their planning and design process through workshops and forums with many different audiences. Improving discourse, including varying perspectives, and promoting methodological diversity, will lead to more inclusive outcomes, enhancing the quality of research and design in the built environment.

3. Build for Sustainability and Resilience

A final need we want to raise emphasizes designing and planning built environments that do not deplete the world's natural resources and that can be supported and maintained over time. There is a dire need for buildings that can adapt and withstand worsening environmental challenges, fast-advancing technology, and evolving social needs. As different fields work toward effective collaborations across a wide range of stakeholders with a vested interest in improving spaces for people, their approaches must be grounded in creating built environments that are simultaneously contextual and holistic, local and global. To ensure the long-term viability of the constructed world, we must consider three primary needs: planetary and human health, technology integration, and societal inclusion.

Planetary and human health: Today's buildings and interiors are increasingly designed and built with sustainability and resilience in mind, employing strategies that address both environmental challenges and occupant wellbeing. Historically, experts and policymakers have addressed these two areas of concern independently, but there is growing acknowledgment of their interconnectedness. Specifically, many of us now recognize that what is good for the natural environment is also good for people.

One of the critical aspects of sustainability is energy efficiency. KieranTimberlake's office demonstrates how an architecture firm considers energy usage through the design and operation of its workplace. The building integrates passive cooling, natural ventilation, and daylighting strategies (see Chapter 13). Such measures reduce reliance on artificial systems, optimize comfort, and minimize resource consumption. This type of climate-responsive design is crucial in adapting buildings to their specific locales. However, Corsi's interview reminded us, while the way buildings are constructed matters substantially, human behavior also plays a significant role in the sustainability and resilience of built environments (see Chapter 18). To this point, KieranTimberlake's research and design process also addressed their workplace culture, calculating how their employees' behavior, through their selection of attire, impacts the building's energy needs. These daily behaviors were considered and integrated into the overall way in which the building functions, illustrating the importance of aligning design with occupant behavior.

The ASID headquarters presented by Chung, Austin Gray, and Yoon also embodies this ethos (see Chapter 17). The association's workplace achieved the highest standards of two well-recognized certification programs—LEED (Leadership in Energy and Environmental Design) and the WELL Building Standard. The first program underscores a building or interior's environmental sustainability, while the latter prioritizes occupant health and considers the influence of human behavior. Working to achieve dual certification demonstrates ASID's dedication to environmental stewardship and human health and wellbeing. Each program symbolizes a commitment to people and the environment, and the actions required to achieve these certifications ensure that the building positively impacts both. For instance, one strategy employed at the headquarters is circadian lighting, which helps keep our bodies aligned with the world's natural rhythms, enhancing energy efficiency *and* occupant wellness.

Overall, buildings are increasingly being fortified against extreme weather events and incorporating biodiversity features like bird-friendly designs and native plant gardens, as noted by Heerwagen (see Chapter 12). These natural elements support local ecosystems and bolster the mental health of occupants. Collectively, these strategies make buildings more environmentally friendly, additionally resilient to evolving climate conditions, and better for human health and wellbeing. Beyond the level of single projects, Barnes strongly advocated that the architectural design industry has an ethical responsibility to reduce carbon footprints to address climate change. She explained that architects must continue lessening the impact of their work, while also centering these efforts more systemically within their profession (see Chapter 11). We believe this obligation extends to all professions related to the built environment.

Technology integration: Built environments now frequently incorporate innovative technology that improves efficiency, sustainability, and user experience. With these developments, smart buildings have emerged equipped with automation systems and sensors. These advancements, like lighting and climate controls, optimize resource usage and seamlessly blend with sustainable design strategies. The KieranTimberlake and ASID offices both showcased this level of tech integration. For example, KieranTimberlake's 300 sensors monitor ambient interior conditions and enhance thermal comfort and energy efficiency. The ASID headquarters similarly uses indoor environment metrics to fine-tune a variety of environmental factors within its spaces.

The precise management and customization of built environments using data analytics and artificial intelligence also extend into the experiential realm. Scolere explained how buildings are becoming platforms that facilitate data interactions between building systems and occupants (see Chapter 6). This connectivity enables spaces to offer enhanced, shareable, and augmented experiences. Euscher further highlighted how these tools can optimize utility and enrich user experiences. He emphasized the importance of employing a systems perspective when working with interactive technologies to create adaptable spaces responsive to occupant needs and preferences (see Chapter 10).

Technology is changing how built environments are studied, designed, operated, and experienced while ultimately holding the potential to improve the person-place dynamic. These advancements are affording a deeper connection between people and spaces, allowing for more resilient, sustainable, and whole experiences. By bolstering these relationships, technology blurs the lines between humans and their environments. This fast-paced and ever-evolving integration of smart devices and systems make it essential to consider where boundaries are necessary. It also encourages all of us to be forward-thinking. Just as we imagine long-term environmental resilience, we must also future-forecast potential pitfalls and opportunities as new building technologies take shape.

Societal inclusion: Buildings and interior spaces continue to evolve to meet diverse physical and social needs. Contributors shared multiple examples, from accommodating bodily diversity to not allowing socioeconomic differences stand in the way, each advocating for physically functional and aesthetically pleasing spaces that support complex social dynamics. In service of this, Rodriguez encouraged the adoption of a strengths-based model when designing built environments rather than a deficit-based one. She argued that inclusive design is not only a business imperative, but, more importantly, a matter of social justice (see Chapter 9). Weatherspoon reinforced this idea by highlighting that well-designed spaces should be accessible to all communities. This includes focusing inclusivity efforts on a wide-range of individuals to foster more vibrant neighborhoods (see Chapter 8). She explained that by ending design-induced oppression and anchoring built environments in dignity, empathy, and equity it is possible to make just and beautiful spaces for everyone. Whether producing spaces that promote equity across society or bolstering a community in need, societal inclusion envisions a world where everyone is valued, differences are celebrated, and all individuals can contribute to and benefit from a thriving economic, social, and cultural life.

Call to Action: To build for sustainability and resilience, all of us must champion practices and policies that mandate adaptability in the built environment, regardless of whether we are in leadership, an individual practitioner or researcher, or an engaged citizen. Advocacy must be strategic and begin with investments in research and development of materials, technologies, and design strategies that respond to changing conditions to support the planet's and people's health. We must focus these efforts on a project-by-project and systemic basis in our respective professions. Embracing smart building technologies is crucial for many reasons, including optimizing resource utilization and enhancing user experiences. Adopting flexible, inclusive design principles is essential to accommodate a broad spectrum of users and promote social justice, dignity, and equity. Each of these endeavors fuels the creation of more resilient, supportive, and responsive constructed spaces. Engaging in these initiatives ensures that built environments reflect and support the values and needs of people and communities without losing sight of global concerns and conditions.

Neglecting these Needs

What happens if there is not a widespread commitment to fostering collaborative and integrative design and research, diversifying perspectives and methods, and building for sustainability and resilience? The consequences go beyond professional impact—they influence our livelihood. You can hear the conviction and urgency in the voices represented in this book. Many contributors emphasized that the world's defenses against climate change weakens without progress, with dire consequences for society and our planet. Persisting with designs that disregard our communities' diverse needs will exacerbate inequality and exclusion issues while leaving the economic and innovative potential untapped. Yet, stagnation in design and research practices and failure to communicate with one another across disciplines could mean missing out on vital opportunities. Ultimately, when we ignore creating spaces that delight and cultivate connection to ourselves, others, and the world, we risk diminishing a complete human experience.

Identifying Universal Truths

When engaging with the chapters in this book, a set of universal truths becomes evident. These truths are underlying tenets that will orient anyone looking to advance the significant work ahead of improving built environments for people. As fundamental principles, they transcend personal differences and cultural, temporal, and geographical boundaries. The universal truths are unchanging realities that connect with the innate human experience—rooted in a deep understanding of psychology, design, and the intrinsic relationship between people and place. Finally, embracing these universal truths is foundational for creating spaces that fulfill basic functional needs, promote wellbeing, encourage positive social interaction, and nurture the human spirit.

Space holds a timeless significance. Spaces are a fundamental aspect of human existence, and as such, environments play a vital role in human evolution. From the earliest settlements to today's contemporary buildings, built spaces ensure two of our most basic needs—safety and security. We breathe life into spaces, and they serve as registers revealing traces of our preferences, behaviors, and relationships with ourselves and others. As Cranz, Rushton, and Chung highlighted, people's environments symbolize their values, beliefs, and identities (see Chapters 1 and 4, respectively). Additionally, built environments have long been central to economic activities, learning, and societal advancement. Spaces often signify something well beyond their brick-and-mortar qualities. For example, according to Negami and Ellard, the awe-inspiring grandeur of palaces, government buildings, and temples communicates authority and spirituality (see Chapter 2). Similarly, Nute offered an overview of political assemblies and peace conferences, demonstrating how spaces and the arrangement of furnishings within them have represented power and ideology across time (see Chapter 5). Spaces shape human evolution, embody cultural values, and facilitate social progress, leaving a lasting impression on civilizations and playing an ever-present role in our lives.

We always exist in physical spaces. In an era marked by rapid technological advancement, the constancy of our physical environments stands in stark contrast. Even though technology often dominates how we interact with people, objects, and places today, it does not override the reality of our bodies being present in a place. Marsh, Meagher, and Burt helped bring light to this truth by explaining how we interpret and perceive the built environments we encounter. Their chapter highlighted how perception affects human behavior, calling for designing action-scaled spaces and legible affordances (see Chapter 3). Siebenaler also conveyed this necessity as she discussed the navigation through spaces and the resulting wayfinding challenges people often experience in complex environments such as healthcare settings. While there are numerous activities we can now manage remotely, such as a doctor's visit via telehealth, there are still tasks that require—and events when we prefer—being in person. Instead of replacing physical experiences, designers, researchers, and developers may merge digital information with physical architecture to form connected, platformed buildings, as described by Scolere (see Chapter 6), or use generative design systems to create built environments with predictable behavioral outcomes, as presented by Euscher (see Chapter 10). While exploration into virtual, augmented, and mixed realities continues to evolve, our essence as humans remains deeply embedded in the tangible world. Undeniably, the future will bring many advances; regardless, we should always keep sight of our existence in physical spaces.

Spaces afford lived experiences. Just as mice in labs benefit significantly from enriched environments (i.e., generous-sized enclosures with elements that stimulate them physically, cognitively, and socially), so do humans (HKS, Inc. & hume.space, 2021). Spaces can positively influence our mental and physical wellbeing through their organization, aesthetic elements, ergonomic features, access to natural light and ventilation, comfortable furnishings, and other qualities that may stimulate a variety of activities and social interactions.

Physical environments can improve mood, increase productivity, reduce stress, and promote psychological and physiological health. For example, Fisher and Baytosh shared how the renovation of existing classrooms took these qualities into account (see Chapter 15). As designer and client, they intentionally created classrooms optimized to augment teaching and learning. Additionally, technology can enhance experiences, as Scolere illustrated by sharing examples such as art exhibitions and in-store shopping interactions where visitors can unlock delightful images or advanced features for practical purposes (see Chapter 6). Then, there is the awe-inspiring feeling of a grand space described by Negami and Ellard or the tranquility of a harmoniously designed garden noted by Heerwagen (see Chapters 2 and 12, respectively). Both examples tap deep into human nature and show us how our surroundings can move us emotionally and aesthetically. However, just as settings can enhance our lives positively, neglecting their potential can have the opposite effect, resulting in spaces that undermine or harm us. Understanding and respecting the power of physical space is crucial in creating functional, enriching, and meaningful environments. Places that holistically support us and help shape affirming lived experiences while mitigating potential pitfalls are an evergreen need and something everyone deserves.

Spaces are not neutral, and their influence is wide-reaching. The places where our lived experiences play out are dynamic and multi-faceted and may have a full range of simultaneous impacts, both positive and negative. Externally, built environments may influence the surrounding community and the planet, as discussed by Barnes and Heerwagen (see Chapters 11 and 12, respectively). Conversely, Chung articulated how we are internally affected as occupants of a space. Using Chung's example, a thoughtfully designed office may enable us to do our day-to-day tasks but appropriately disrupt us when we need to do more innovative, creative work. Spaces possess the ability to empower or inhibit, to assist or harm. Chung further explained how our interaction with and perception of our surroundings can be reactive or proactive, raising the question: Do we control our environments, or do they control us (see Chapter 4)? Be aware that even if spaces appear as inconsequential backdrops, they are not impartial. Our built environments are manifestations of the forces that shape them, from designers, occupants, and policymakers to systemic and environmental factors. These constructed spaces reflect societal values and collective stories, encompassing perspectives like those of the non-disabled majority, as Rodriguez highlighted through the design of Olympic venues (see Chapter 9). Or, as Weatherspoon shed light upon, they reflect the reinforcement of inequities, as explained through her experiences designing affordable housing (see Chapter 8). Recognizing the non-neutrality of the built world allows us to understand more deeply how places shape our daily lives and interactions. Every space, consciously or unconsciously, communicates messages, embodies specific values, and influences behaviors and emotions.

Collaboration is not optional. Creating healthy, sustainable, and resilient spaces is everyone's responsibility; as Barnes aptly stated, you can't unknow the impact of built environments once you are made aware of it. A single discipline or field cannot achieve this critical task. This obligation rests on more than just the shoulders of the design and construction industry. Similarly, success will not be ensured by a rating system or guaranteed by environmental and social science research. Stated simply, professionals focused on people cannot ignore the environment, and those focused on spaces cannot ignore people. And we should not assume that a standard, one-size-fits-all design process or research method will be sufficient. Not only should we collaborate with others employing varying methods and perspectives, but we must also collaborate with emergent technology. It is not humanly possible to process, let alone leverage, the immense amount of information and data related to people and the built environment. Artificial intelligence holds promise to enhance our capabilities for better, more informed human-centered outcomes. As Euscher explained, augmented intelligence will amplify our cognitive strengths, expanding our thinking for greater creativity, higher-order problem-solving, advanced research, and more (see Chapter 10). But even powerful tools like AI require new considerations and cannot be implemented in a silo. As discussed previously, collaboration can be challenging for many reasons, but given what we must accomplish to best serve people and built environments, it is no longer nice to have but rather a must-have.

Interdisciplinary approaches are imperative. There's a reason we, the authors—a designer and a psychologist—had to go across campus to find one another to educate ourselves about the intersection of psychology and interior environments. While shared interests may unite many of us, the structure of our disciplines and the systems we exist within often keep us apart. The evolution of disciplines and their manifestation at academic institutions have served us well in many ways. Disciplines have allowed for the in-depth study and development of specific knowledge and methods, advancing long-standing professions and spawning new ones. Steeped in institutional history, digging disciplinary trenches, as Corsi described it, can get in our way when addressing our future's complex challenges. He explained how we must promote connecting those trenches (see Chapter 18). These divides can be even more pronounced between academia and industry, often reinforced by structures and incentives that keep them separate. It might help to think about disciplines this way. Martha Boles states in her book *Universal Patterns*, "This world is of a single piece; yet, we invent nets to trap it for our inspection. Then we mistake our nets for the reality of the piece." She explains, "It's not the nets that are at fault but rather our misunderstanding of their function as nets. They do catch the fishes, but never the sea, and it is the sea that we ultimately desire" (Boles and Newman, 1990). And when aiming to understand the person-place relationship, we ultimately need the sea. This final universal truth does not discourage the development of deep expertise. Instead, this truth emphasizes the necessity of exploring intersections across disciplines related to people and built environments.

Final Remarks

Often perceived by many as merely a means to an end, the constructed world encapsulates deeply engrained values, intentions, societal norms, and cultural narratives. The contributors' accounts offered us a glimpse into this reality, from examining how a seemingly simple choice of a *chair* can reflect socio-economic biases (see Chapter 8) to how *room* layouts can express political power dynamics (see Chapter 5). We also saw how a *building* can act as a digital platform for information dissemination (see Chapter 6) and the effects of universal design on *city* planning and government policy (see Chapter 9). Finally, there was a plea highlighting how *society* and the *planet* suffer from the consequences of decisions related to the built environment (see Chapters 11 and 12). At all scales, from furnishings to cities, spaces mirror and shape the lives of people—both those who bring them into existence and those who inhabit them.

Spaces impact our lives, often more profoundly than we realize. Understanding their power requires navigating a complex terrain where multiple fields and disciplines intersect, from neuroscience, psychology, and sociology to interior design, architecture, and more (see Figure 0.3). *People and Spaces* is a concerted effort to explore these diverse perspectives calling attention to the dynamic and multifaceted relationship between humans and their surroundings. As a designer and a psychologist, we provided broad strokes while encouraging a more comprehensive and inclusive discourse. Everyone's voice matters—your insights and actions will advance our collective understanding. We all have the potential to structure our world with empathy and innovation as it continues to evolve. Our journey does not end here. Let's work together to create a future where our built environments enhance the quality of everyone's lived experiences while honoring the delicate balance of our planet.

References

Boles, M., and Newman, R. (1990). *Universal Patterns: The Golden Relationship of Art, Math, and Nature*. Bradford, MA: Pythagorean Press.

HKS, Inc., & hume.space. (2021). Enriched environments for brain health that foster creativity, promote positivity, and reduce stress: A neurogenesis hypothesis. HKS, Inc. https://www.hksinc.com/wp-content/uploads/2021/06/HKS_Neurogenesis Hypothesis_Report.pdf

INDEX

Note: **Bold** page numbers refer to tables; *italic* page numbers refer to figures and page numbers followed by "n" denote endnotes.

Aalto, Alvar and Aino 7–8; Alvar Aalto 41
accessibility 137–148
action-scaled spaces, design of 55, *56*; *see also* affordances
aesthetic integration, in taste and design 20–21; color 20; pattern 20; shape and size 20–21; symmetry/asymmetry designs 21; texture 20; theoretical model 19
affordable housing 129, 131, 283–284; community responsibility 132; factors to consider in 131; income distribution and 132; NIMBYism 132; profit-driven *vs.* bottom-line design 133; *see also* public housing
affordances 49, 55, 61n2, 64, 284; detection 56–58, *57*, *58*; inviting action 58–60, *59*; lived experiences 282–283; sensory 65; theory of 67
Africa, J. 183
After Taste: Expanded Practice in Interior Design (Kleinman, Merwood-Salisbury, and Weinthal) 18
Agrest, D. 144
Alexander, C. 41
Alexandria Country Day School (ACDS) (case study) 221–233
American Institute of Architects (AIA) 167, 169, *169*, 173; Code of Ethics 170
American Psychiatric Association's Diagnostic Statistical Manual fifth edition (DSM-V), intellectual disabilities definition 207
American Society of Interior Designers (ASID) headquarters (case study) *68*, 252–263, 276, 281; Foundation grant-funded project 109n5; Outcome of Design program 72
Americans with Disabilities Act (ADA) 144
Americans with Disabilities Act Accessibility Guidelines (ADAAG) 144
Appleton, J. 40–41
Archer Park project *132*
architecture: awe-inspiring design 42–45; emotional impact 40; monumental 43, 45–46
architectural design 156; procedural *53*; programming 163; rules-based 151–152
Architectural Graphic Standards 151, *153*
ARTECHOUSE seasonal exhibition, In Peak Bloom 92, *93–95*, 102
Artificial Intelligence (AI) 97, 109n7, 120, 164, 281, 286
ASHRAE Global Thermal Comfort Database II 201

ASID *see* American Society of Interior Designers (ASID)
attention-restoration theory 41
augmented intelligence 164, 286
augmented reality (AR) experience 92; IKEA Place app 102–104, *103*; technology 101–104, *104*, *105*
Austin Gray, W. 251, 253–263, 276, 281
Autodesk's research studio (The Living) 161
awe: built environment 43–45, *44*; implications 45–46; threat-based awe 42–43
Aye, G. 119–127, 278

Bacon, F. 89n3
Barnes, J. 166–177, 281, 285–287
Barocas, S. 107
Barry, C. *77*
Bates, R. 193, 195–204, 280
Bay Cove Human Services, LLC (BCHS) 206
Baytosh, S. 221–233, 278, 285
Berleant, A. 182
Besson, A. 182
big data 150–165
Big Five personality traits 268
biometric: measures 40; sensors 93, 108
Biophilia (Wilson) 181
biophilia and climate change 178–184; approaches and strategies 183; behavioral perspective 182; building-level applications 184; democratization 184; design elements 183–184; habitats 182–184; nature-based design techniques 183–184; origins and emerging perspectives 180–182; urgent 181
Black Lives Matter *54*
Boat, T. F. 208
body-clothing-building relationship *see* thermal comfort
Bolding, N. 209
Boles, M. 286
Bouleuterion, Athenian assembly chamber design 78, *79*
Bourdieu, P. 18
Boyz n the Hood (movie) 135
Burke, E. 42
Burke, M. M. 42, 207
Burt, C. J. 49, 51–63, 284
Bush, G. W. 168

California Building, in San Diego 27, *29*
Capitol Vista project *135*
Carney, M. 172
Caudill Rowlett Scott 155
Center for Universal Design 139
Centers for Disease Control (2018) 208
Central Library, Seattle 59
Central Park, New York 28–30
Chapin, F. S. 18
Chung, S. E. 64–73, 251, 253–263, 276, 281, 284, 285
Churchill, W. 76–78
City Beautiful movement 31
classroom design (and renovation) 221–233; client and designer perspectives 222–233; essential goals 224–230; flexible classroom furniture 224–227, 232; focus and engagement 228–230; movement in classrooms 226–228; student-centered learning approach 230–232
climate change 167; adaptation strategies 171, 173; biophilia and 178–184; and design ethics 170; design principles for 174; and health 168; integration 173; liability risk 172; physical risk 172; risk of 172; transition risk 172
clothing of occupants 195–203; energy efficiency 195, 196, 198, 202; flexible dress codes 198, 202; thermal comfort 195–197, 200; workplace 196
cognition 211, **212–213**; cognitive processes 68; spatial 64, 65
collaboration 70; academic and practitioner 267; challenges 266; cross-disciplinary 277–278; designers and researchers 276–277; fostering 276–278; funding 277–278; interdisciplinary *see* interdisciplinary collaboration
condition-based design 205–220
condition-centered design *see* condition-based design
connected places 95–96, 108
Conspicuous Consumption (Veblen) 18
contextual integrity 107
Corsi, R. 3, 264–270, 277, 280, 286
Corsi Code 3, 4, *4*
COVID-19 pandemic 4, 184
Cranz, G. 17–37, 279, 284
Cross, R. T. 209

data-driven in built spaces: access control systems 156; automated systems 156; computer-generated imagery 160; design 150–165; for desired outcomes

149–164; people analytics 160, 161, 164; personalized space 161; predictive analytics models 160, 161; rules-based architecture 151–152; software developments 152
Day, H. M. 102, *104*, 210
Day, J. R. 210
Design Equity® services 129–136
Design Institute for Health (Dell Medical School) 236–250
Design Materials Library, Colorado State University 98
design thinking process 205, 207, *208*, 211, 214, 218, 238, 279
Dewitte, S. 43, 44
Diogenes' syndrome 210
disability 138–148; *see also* accessibility; intellectual disability
dislocation effect 71, *72*
Disney MagicBand, personalized environment integration 97
Dissanayake, E. 21, 35n1
Dodge, M. 95
Dovey, K. 80, 88n1

ecological perspective 51, 53–54
Ellard, C. 37, 39–48, 284, 285
Elmurzaeva, N. 206
Elsworth, K. 193, 195–204, 280
Emerson, E. 207
emotions: emotion regulation 38; environmental factors influencing emotion 40–41; impact on interior spaces design 129–130, 234; mixed-valence 42; physiological responses 40; spaces and 37, 40–43; *see also* awe
empathy: in design 130–132, 134–136
Enterprise Community Partners 173
environmental determinism 70
environmental information: passive *vs.* active view 69, *69*; reactive and proactive approaches in 69–70, *70*
Environmental Protection Agency (EPA) 3, 231; Quick Reference Guide 232
equity: in interior design 130–132, 135, 136
Ethical Standard 6.5 Climate Change 171
Euscher, D. 149–165, 282, 284, 286
evidence-based design 8, 205, 206, 222, 231, 254–255; *see also* research-informed design
Experience Blueprint *239*; *see also* experience design
experience design, the practice of 240, 249; *see also* Experience Blueprint

Faircloth, B. 193, 195–204, 280
Fast Company (2018) 99
Ferguson, G. 171
Financial Stability Board (FSB) 168
Fisher, E. 221–233, 278, 285
Fitch, J. M. 195
Flexer, C. 231
Focke, J. W. 155, *159*
Fromm, E. 180
furnishings: arrangement of 234; flexible and adaptable classroom furniture 222–233; seating arrangement in political assemblies 74–90; visualizing with augmented reality technology 102

Gans, H. 18
Gehry, F. 57
Geneva peace conference (1954) 83–85, *86*
Gibson, J. J. 51, 55, 60n1, 61n2
Gilbreth, F. 150, 151
Gilbreth, L. 150
Gil-Llario, M. D. 210
Girard St. Apartments project *131*
Giridharadas, A.: *Winners Take All: The Elite Charade of Changing the World* 125
Glass, T. 16, 50, 120–127, 265–270
Global Climate Action Summit 174
Global Risks Report 170
Global Status Report for Buildings and Construction (2024) 5
Göbekli Tepe *39*, 39–40, 43
Gordon, A. M. 42, 43
Graham, L. T. 38, 120–127, 251, 265–270
Greater Good Studio (Aye) 120, 278

Haidt, J. 42
Hall, E. T. *56*
Hansen, J. 167
Hartman, E. 209
health care 205, 206, 236–250; architectural design 249–250; design process 238–240; exam room experience 246–249
Heerwagen, J. 178–185, 281, 285, 287
Heft, H. 58
Heller, T. 207
Heschong, L. 231
Hitler, A. 45

HKS, Inc. 65, *66*
Horner, R. H. 210
House of Commons: in St. Stephens Chapel 80, *82*
Hsing, C. 208
human-centered design 205, 207, 238, 250, 261, 286
hybrid spaces 94, 108

identity: brand 22; professional 129–130, 277; social class 17
IKEA Place app 102–104, *103*
inclusive design: accessibility 144, *145*, 146; business case for 146–148; Lima 2019 Parapan American Games 146, *147*; social justice through 138–148; universal design and 138–141
Indacochea, P. 146
indoor air quality (IAQ) 231–232, 265
inequality 10, 128, 130–133
informational privacy 210
Integrative Graduate Education and Research Traineeship program (IGERT) 267
intellectual disability 206, 208–201; Diogenes' syndrome 209–210; symbolic representations 208
interdisciplinary collaboration 192, 264, 265; academia barriers 266; innovation 269; in research 267
Intergovernmental Panel on Climate Change (IPCC) 173

Jefferson University Design Center 196
Jose, S. 210
Joye, Y. 43–45

Kaplan, S. 41
Keltner, D. 42
KieranTimberlake 193, 195–204, 280–281
Kirchner, M. 229
Kitchin, R. 95
Konrath, S. H. 208
Kopec, D. 205–220, 279
Kyoto protocol 168

Lamarque, P. 35n4
The Lancet 167, 168
Lane Tech High School in Chicago 65, *66*
Lawrence Berkeley National Laboratory 3
Leadership in Energy and Environmental Design (LEED) 251, 255, 257
Le Corbusier 26, *28*, 41; Modulor Man *139*
Levy, K. 107
Lima 2019 Parapan American Games 146, *147*
The Living (Autodesk) 161
living laboratory 195–204, 253–263
locative media 94
Lustgarten, A. 170

Madden, S. 99
Malinin, L. 102
Marsh, K. L. 49, 51–63, 284
McKay, G. 25
Meagher, B. R. 49, 51–63, 284
Mendez, C. 99
Michelangelo 138
minority populations 128, 130, 131, 134
mixed-valence emotion 42; *see also* emotions
Modulor Man, Le Corbusier *139*
motion capture technology 150
Municipal Climate Action Plans 173
Museum of Us, San Diego 27, *29*
Muybridge, E. 150

Nair, S. A. 210
National Academies of Sciences, Engineering, and Medicine 209
National Climate Assessment (NCA) 171, 173
National Human Activity Pattern Survey (NHAPS) 3–4, *4*
National Institutes of Health (NIH) 267
National Paralympic Association 147
National Parks Service 168
National Science Foundation (NSF) 267
Negami, H. 37, 39–48, 284, 285
Nike App Scan 97, *98*
Nike's House of Innovation 99, *100*
Nissenbaum, H. 107
Novarini, D. 99
Nute, K. 74, 76–89, 284, 287

O'Brien, E. H. 208
object placement *see* aesthetic integration; symbolic objects
Olmsted, F. L. 28
Ortlieb's Bottling House 198–199, *199*, 201
Osmond, H. 54

Page architecture 237
Papa, J. 196
Paralympic Athletes in Lima 147
2019 Parapan American Games 146, *147*
Parc de La Villette, Paris 30, *31*
Paris, arrondissements of *32*
Paris Climate Accord 169
peace conferences: Geneva peace conference (1954) 83–85, *86*; Paris Peace Conference (1919) 82–83, *84*, *87*; Vietnam Peace Conference (1968) 85–86, *87*
Pena, W. M. 155, *159*
people-space interactions framework *9*, 9–10
perception 51–73; ambient attributes 67–68; cognitive processes 68; design perspective 53–54; ecological perspective 51, 53; proactive *vs.* reactive approach 69–70, 285; psychosocial processes 68; sensory processes 68; spaces affect 51–60; spatial attributes 67
Perkins & Will Minneapolis Office *72*
personal space *56*
Philadelphia Art Museum *54*
place attachment 41, 259
Planned Unit Developments (PUDs) 33
platform technologies 90–108, 284; augmented experiences 101–104, *104*, *105*; data, privacy, and context 105–107; data-sensing technologies 108; digital information and physical space 94–96; Disney MagicBand, personalized environment integration 97; enhanced experiences 96–99; inclusive technologies and access 107–108; shareable experiences 99–101; trade-offs 105–108; types 96
Pnyx, Athenian assembly 80, *81*
political relations (in environments) 74–88; bifurcated Curia Julia, Bouleuterion, Athenian assembly chamber 78, *79*; House of Commons 76–78, *77*, *78*, 80–82, *82*; international conferences, seating arrangement 82–88
positivist reasoning *see* reasoning
post-Darwinian 51
post-occupancy evaluations (POEs) 102–104, 156; Alexandria Country Day School (ACDS) 254, 255, 257, *259*, 260–262
post-positivist reasoning *see* reasoning
Potsdam conference (1945) 83, *85*
power asymmetry: disrupting 121; graphic 121, *121*
pre and post occupancy evaluation 195–204, 208, 238, 251–263, 276
pre-Darwinian theory 52
privacy: classifications 210–211; data 149, 161–162 *see also* data and platformed places
problem-framing technique 238
Problem Seeking method 155, *159*
prospect-refuge theory 40
PSA Taste Model 19, 23, 24; advantages 33–35; cultural application of 34; *see also* taste, in spatial design
public housing 26, *26*; *see also* affordable housing

reasoning: positivist 205, 207, 216; post-positivist 205, 207, 211, 218
refractive surveillance 107
remote meetings/virtual meetings effects 88
research-informed design 221, 233; *see also* evidence-based design
Resilience Training Certification 173
Reversible Destiny Lofts *53*
Rodriguez, I. 137–148, 279, 282, 285, 287
Roosevelt, F. D. 168
Roosevelt, T. 168
rules-based architecture 151–152; grasshopper script flow diagram *156*; kitchen work triangle 151, *152*
Rushton, C. 17–37, 279, 284

Schmidt, K. 40
Scolere, L. 90, 92–111, 281, 284, 285, 287
Scott-Brown, D. 22
Seaside, Florida 33, *33*
seating arrangements for international conferences 82–88; Democratic Republic of Vietnam 83; final agreed table *85*; Geneva peace conference (1954) 83–85, *86*; on human behavior 89n3; Paris Peace Conference (1919) 82–83, *84*, *87*; Potsdam conference (1945) 83, *85*; remote meetings/virtual meetings effects 89; Vietnam Peace Conference (1968) 85–86, *87*

self-determination 70, 209, 210
self-expression 17
Sensory Well-being Hub (HKS, Inc.) *66*
Shand, P. M. 8
Siebenaler, D. 234, 236–250, 278, 284
Slayter Plaza at Denison University *58*
social justice: equity 129–138; through inclusive design 138–148; universal design 138–141
socioecological approach 55; *see also* affordances
sociopetal and sociofugal 54–55, *58*
Speer, A. 45
Standard of Care 171
Steelcase Health 250n2
SteelMaster Steel Storage Building 26, *27*
symbolism 35n2; objects 19–21, 23; urban planning 31–33; utility and expression 20
Systems Theory 155

Task Force on Climate-Related Financial Disclosures (TCFD) 168
taste, in spatial design 17–35; aesthetic integration 20–21; pragmatic objects 19–21, 24; profiles 23, 34; at scales of built environment 23–33; symbolic objects 19–21, 24; teaching 22–23; theoretical model 19–21; *see also* PSA Taste Model
Taylor, F. W. 150, 151, 159, 164n1
Ten Books on Architecture (Vitruvius) 151
thermal comfort 193–204
threat-based awe 42–43; *see also* awe
Tidball, K. G. 181, 182
Tragedy of the Horizon 172
Tschumi, B. 30, *31*

United Nations Convention on the Rights of Persons with Disabilities (2010) 143
United States White House Office of Science and Technology Policy (2013) 167
Unity Health Care Brentwood Waiting Room 66–67, *67*
universal design 138–148, 279
Universal Patterns (Boles) 286
universal truths 283–287
Urban Land Institute 173
U.S. Climate Resilience Toolkit 173
US Department of Housing and Urban Development (HUD) 132
US Department of Labor 141
U.S. Environmental Protection Agency (EPA) 3
U.S. Global Change Research Program (USGCRP) 171, 172

value-based (health) care 236–237
Veblen, T. 18
Venturi, R. 22
Verpooten, J. 43, 45
Vietnam Peace Conference (1968) 85–86, *87*
Villa Gálvez, L. 147
Villa Savoye 27, *28*
Vinci, L. da *155*
virtual reality (VR) 40; immersive virtual tours and 98–99
virtual spaces 97–99
Vitruvian Man *155*
Vitruvius 151; *Ten Books on Architecture* 151
VOC (volatile organic compound) 269

Weatherspoon, K. 128–137, 277, 282, 285, 287
Wehmeyer, M. L. 209
Welch, R. 193, 195–204, 280
WELL Building Standard (WELL) 102, 251, 255; ASID HQ office 253–263
Wikivoyage-style map, downtown Calgary *32*
Wilson, E. O. 181; *Biophilia* 181
Winners Take All: The Elite Charade of Changing the World (Giridharadas) 125
Withagen, R. 60
World Economic Forum (WEF) 170
Wright, F. L. 22, 41
Wu, J. T. 208

Yoon, S. 251, 253–263, 276, 281

Zhumanova, F. 206

For Product Safety Concerns and Information please contact our EU representative GPSR@taylorandfrancis.com
Taylor & Francis Verlag GmbH, Kaufingerstraße 24, 80331 München, Germany

www.ingramcontent.com/pod-product-compliance
Ingram Content Group UK Ltd.
Pitfield, Milton Keynes, MK11 3LW, UK
UKHW021724240926
475702UK00030BA/2682
9780367436162